Moon Sisters,
Krishna Mothers,
Rajneesh Lovers

Women and Gender in North American Religions

Amanda Porterfield and Mary Farrell Bednarowski,

Series Editors

Syracuse University Press is pleased to announce a new series, *Women and Gender in North American Religions*, introduced by *Moon Sisters, Krishna Mothers, Rajneesh Lovers* by Susan Jean Palmer.

Religion has been and continues to be a significant factor in the lives of women within a variety of cultures in North America. Although men have played a dominant role in defining and writing theology, women have played crucial roles as models of piety and interpreters of belief and, in some cases, as founders of new religions.

The purpose of this series is to examine the importance and diversity of women in North American religious history. Books will explore religion as a vehicle of conformity and a force for change; they will investigate how religion can both encourage and stifle personal expression and social initiative. The series will be of interest to scholars in religious studies, history, social science, and theology. Its editors are Amanda Porterfield, Department of Religion, Syracuse University, and Mary Farrell Bednarowski, Theological Seminary of the Twin Cities.

Susan Jean Palmer

Moon Sisters, Krishna Mothers, Rajneesh Lovers

Women's Roles in New Religions

Syracuse University Press

First Edition 1994
94 95 96 97 98 99   6 5 4 3 2 1

The paper used in this publication meets the minimum requirements of
American National Standard for Information Sciences—Permanence of
Paper for Printed Library Materials, ANSI z39.48-1984. ∞ ™

LIBRARY OF CONGRESS CATALOGING-IN-PUBLICATION DATA

Palmer, Susan J.
    Moon sisters, Krishna mothers, Rajneesh lovers : women's roles
in new religions / Susan Jean Palmer.
        p.   cm. — (Women and gender in North American religions)
    Includes bibliographical references and index.
    ISBN 0-8156-0297-9
        1. Women and religion—North America—History—20th
century.   2. Cults—North America—History—20th century.
3. Sex—Religious aspects—History—20th century.   4. Sex role—
Religious aspects—History—20th century.   5. North America—
Religion.   I. Title.
    II. Series.
    BL 2520.P36   1994
    291'.046'082—dc20   94-17364

Manufactured in the United States of America

To Jean, Laida, and my other Mormon foremothers
and to the delightful women who related their adventures in
unconventional spirituality.

Susan Jean Palmer is descended from Mormon pioneers who left the lace-making factories of the British midlands to follow the first two Prophets to Nauvoo, Illinois, and then on to Salt Lake City. Her great-great-grandmothers moved to Alberta, when Utah joined the United States in 1890, to protect their husbands from antipolygamy persecution. She has been researching new religious movements for twenty years and is co-editor of *The Rajneesh Papers* with Arvind Sharma. Her articles have appeared in *Sociological Analysis, Journal for the Scientific Study of Religion, Syzygy,* and in five anthologies, including *New Islamic Movements in the West,* and *From the Ashes: Making Sense of Waco.* She teaches in the religion departments of Dawson College and Concordia University in Montreal, Quebec.

Contents

Illustrations

Tables

Introduction

Throughout the history of heresy in North America women have participated enthusiastically in the "sexual experiments" developing in millenarian and communal movements. Today, fewer than six years before the year 2000, women continue to join similar groups (currently branded as "cults") that often require them to wear veils, live in polygamy, and renounce motherhood or monogamy. One naturally wonders why these women have chosen to live in these emotionally intense communities on the margins of American religious life, and what they learn by embarking on these spiritual adventures. This book is a result of my efforts, as a great-granddaughter of Mormon polygamists, to understand the motives and experiences of contemporary women who drift into (and out of) new religious movements.

I have chosen seven contemporary groups: the International Society for Krishna Consciousness, the Unification Church, the Rajneesh Movement, the Institute of Applied Metaphysics, the Messianic Community, the Raelian Movement, and the Institute for the Development of the Harmonious Human Being. These groups offer the widest possible range in the sexual "lifestyles" they have elaborated for their women, and they espouse conflicting notions of sexual identity.

While moving through—and sometimes into—these small, self-contained worlds, I have repeatedly asked the two questions central to this investigation. The first would be addressed from the vantage point of an outsider looking in: What use are women and men to each other on the spiritual path? Are they viewed as impediments to the other's progress, codependents mutually assisting in the climb toward salvation, or are they equal but independent companions? Next, I would try to "stand in the shoes" of the woman I was interviewing, by asking her which social/sexual problems she sought to resolve by moving into a religious commune and what she hoped to leave behind. In other words, I invited their critiques of secular gender roles to discover what they perceived as the primary emotional malaises or sexual disorders in our society that drove them to seek out the radically alternative, spiritually based models of "ordered love" (Kern 1981) found in intentional communities.

In this way, I have tried to present my informants' understandings of their own experiences, and to resist the temptation to trivialize, satirize, or "reductionize" new religious patterns of sexuality that often seem to strike outsiders (the media, Christian fundamentalists, and anticultists at any rate) as weird and psychologically unhealthy. I have relied, therefore, on a phenomenological analysis of the perceptions of my informants in these movements, rather than on personality profiles or on a quantitative analysis of their social backgrounds. What women say about their experiences in these groups will be taken seriously as part of the process of trying to understand what meaning these new roles and models of sexual identity hold for female participants. This approach self-consciously repudiates the tendency among anticultists to condemn the extreme and often deviant patterns of sexuality found in "cults" as "brainwashing" or to attempt to explain them as "social control."

At the same time, I have tried to arrange these testimonies and ethnographical sketches to demonstrate how aptly they reflect and how deliberately they reconstruct (and sometimes even parody) patterns of gender in the "mainstream." The roles and values these women have adopted, and their rationales for adopting them, I would argue, are meaningful for secular women seeking to understand their own ongoing processes of self-reconstruction in late twentieth-century America.

Historians who have studied women's participation in ecstatic or millenarian movements in Europe have tended to interpret feminine conversion to marginal religions as part of their quest for new, occult, and unconventional avenues to authority, which have been—and still are—denied to women in the mainstream churches. It appears that women are the most likely to enter trances, speak in tongues, or exhibit signs of possession. I. M. Lewis in *Ecstatic Religion* (1971) offers an interesting explanation for woman's cross-cultural susceptibility to spirit possession. He suggests that, denied other access to power, they will resort to oblique strategies of aggression available through trance. While in this state, they are granted the license to express pent-up criticisms of male hegemony, to be assertive, and to make demands on their audiences. A similar argument was adopted by Lawrence Moore (1977) in his study of famous female mediums in the nineteenth-century spiritualist movement. He points out that these ladylike and frequently ailing Victorians, by choosing the role of medium, which required the "womanly" qualities of sensitivity and passivity, were able to travel, perform on stage, express antinomian messages, and subdue rowdy male audiences. Norman Cohn (1970, 160–176) emphasizes the prominence of women in the heretical Free Spirit movement of the thirteenth and fourteenth centuries in Europe, and even refers to it as a "widespread women's movement" attractive to unmarried women and widows in the upper strata of society. He posits his version of the "social change hypothesis" to account for this.

Although these theories require some modification before they can be applied to women in marginal religions in our postfeminist age, they lay the groundwork for my central thesis: Women's conversion to unconventional religions can be interpreted as a response to "rolelessness" resulting from dramatic upheavals in the structure of society. My chapter on Rajneesh women, for example, whose community shares some affinities with what we know about the Free Spirit, argues that "role overload" rather than "rolelessness" makes the child-rejecting life as "lover" and "leader" so appealing to one class of modern woman, but Norman Cohn's insights into the deprivation of intimacy and the insecure family status of Renaissance women could also apply to our "free spirited" Rajneesh women.

This study of Krishna Conscious "mothers" and Unificationist "sisters" suggests that they are responding to the devaluation of traditional women's roles, and to the confusion surrounding issues of gender, rather than rebelling against the narrowness and rigidity of family life that drove their forebears to join ecstatic cults, millenarian movements, and utopian communes. Nevertheless, throughout the different eras, women seem to be seeking a sense of order and meaning—and that missing magical or religious dimension—in secular family relationships.

Before embarking on this exploration of women's roles in new religions, I think it is appropriate to reveal the roots of my fascination with this topic. Because it is difficult (and perhaps impossible) to maintain a rigorously objective stance when analyzing material so controversial and explosive as "heretical" groups and their "sexual experiments," it is only fair to caution the reader about the singular cultural prejudices and experiential bias of the analyst, a strategy that Max Weber himself recommended.

My interest in alternative sexuality within religious minorities was perhaps initially aroused during a conversation with my Mormon great-grandmother. I was five at the time, and she was intent on showing me photographs of my ancestors who had immigrated to Salt Lake City from the British midlands, but after 1890 were forced to cross the border into Alberta to avoid the antipolygamy persecution that broke out after Utah joined the Union. As we turned the pages of the heavy buffalo-hide album, a yellow photograph fell to the floor. "Don't touch that!" she warned me. "That's Grandpa Hudson and it's the only negative we have left of him." I looked at the transparent wedding portrait with deep curiosity, for I had been taught in my nightly prayers to bless my forebearers, who were waiting to welcome me into heaven. Now, at last, I could see what they really looked like "up there" in the celestial sphere. As I examined the negative image, the body's lights and shadows in reverse, I figured this must be what my Sunday school teacher meant by the flesh becoming "translated." Somehow, I had absorbed the message that I was beholden to these prairie procreators, whose weddings for "time and eternity" promised my survival beyond the grave.

My great-grandmother slowly bent over and retrieved the photograph with palsied fingers. She squinted at the shaking ghostly image of her father, who had remained in Utah with his second wife; her mother had taken the train north to Alberta. Great-great-grandma Hudson had been forced to disembark prematurely with her eleven children, because of an impassible blizzard, and had found shelter with a kind farming family until she could build a log cabin in the spring and start her homestead. "Twenty-two copies were made of this picture," great-grandma revealed, "one for each of his children. Eleven he had by each wife. Never forget," she admonished with bitter reverence, "never forget to pray for your Great-great-grandpa Hudson. He lived by the Word of Wisdom."

My parents soon moved to Europe and our family slowly drifted away from the Mormon faith, but as an intensely shy teenager, I attended Fireside—evening meetings for Latter-day Saint youth. The "sister" in whose home these were held volunteered to counsel our group of squirming teens on how to approach the mysteries of dating. We were hunched around the fireplace when she entered the room and announced, "Now I am going to show you a parable." She opened her fist and unwrapped a Kleenex. Nestled in her palm were two pieces of gum; one was white and pristine, the other gray and amorphous. "This is you, girls," she explained. "If you were a boy, which Chicklet would you choose to marry? One is white, sweet, untouched, and the other has lost all its shape and its sugar, and is fit for nothing except to be stuck underneath a restaurant table!"

Years later, living in a hippie commune in California, I would occasionally relate this story, to the amusement of my friends, but secretly I sometimes worried about the eschatological consequences of premarital love. Yet, even in this household of post-psychedelic meditators and artists, I noticed powerful taboos governing sexual behavior. The inmates observed a kind of ritual nudity and rejected the concept of marriage, but most of them had taken private vows of celibacy to enhance their spiritual life. One boy had been expelled for coming on to the girls.

The two love affairs that did take place during my year in the commune were far from casual. They had been prefigured

in dreams (I was told) and sparked by revelations of unresolved
entanglements from previous lifetimes received while in meditation practice. But the determination to uncover divine inspiration in the heart of romantic love is not necessarily confined
to Mormons, troubadours, Harlequin romance novels, and
hippie meditators; it can also be seen operating in new religions.

When I began in 1974 to research new religious movements,
under the direction of Prof. Fred Bird at Concordia University,
I observed among the youthful participants an apparent need
to regulate or explain their sexuality in ways consonant with
their new mystical orientation. Interviewing spiritual seekers in
their late teens or early twenties, who often described themselves as broken or disillusioned by love, I received the impression that for many of them, new religions provided an
honorable time out from their dilemmas. A yoga center might
afford a friendly, celibate space in which to lick emotional
wounds; a workshop in est or Arica might be experienced as a
therapeutic, disciplined environment in which new rules of etiquette in relating to the opposite sex were learned, or higher
standards of authenticity by which to measure past failures in
love were taught. At the Sivanada Yoga Ashram I met the
sorrowful Lakshmi, battling the "karma" of her recent abortion with a vow of perpetual celibacy and the determination to
"attain *samadhi* before I'm thirty." I exchanged confidences
with the beautiful Radha, who had left her tyrannical husband
to pursue her spiritual path. Missing her children, she resolved
to "make it up to them in my next life." There also I encountered the ashram buffoon, Sankara, who was in the habit
of invading the girls' tents at night to complain of how chanting the OM mantra had rendered him impotent, and was
convinced that if only he could find a girl with the right astro-
logical sign. . . .

Searching for secondary sources through the rapidly expanding microsociology of new religious movements, which has
been responding since the sixties to what William McLoughlin
called America's "Fourth Great Awakening," I found only a

handful of "gendered" approaches to the "cult conversion" phenomenon. In contrast to the depth of interest in utopian women's experiences of the past, there has been surprisingly little fieldwork accomplished on alternative patterns of gender in contemporary communes. Yet, while pursuing my interest in nonconventional spiritual groups, I have marveled at their extravagant new forms of marriage and sexuality. I have attended pagan weddings at dawn and watched hyperventilating circles of Sufi "sisters" embrace mysteriously through their veils; I have interviewed a bald ascetic who spoke of the magical effects of celibacy as she raised a sinewy hand to stroke her "third eye." I have participated in Rajneesh therapy groups where voluptuous women therapists warned the red-clad couples who still clung to monogamy that their "energy was stuck!"—that they must "let it flow" because "Bhagwan says marriage is the coffin of love!" Baffled and intrigued by these conflicting role models, I began to wonder what these female "spiritual seekers" were seeking. What were women looking for—or perhaps reacting against—when they voluntarily embarked on these daunting romantic/ascetic/erotic ordeals?

It became increasingly clear to me that the coming of age of my new religious contemporaries could only be understood if viewed against the backdrop of the era they happened to be living in: an era characterized by sexual freedom, gender confusion, family breakdown, and moral ambiguity. From my uncertain perspective, I noticed how pleasant and reassuring it was to be told (whether it was by "enlightened masters," spiritual therapists, or oriental gurus) who I was and how I should behave toward the opposite sex. When Swami preached celibacy something deep inside uttered, "Of course." When Rajneesh argued that women should stop repressing their desires and should explore their sexuality with whomsoever they pleased, I thought, "Yes!" When Reverend Moon exhorted man and woman to love one another as innocent brothers and sisters and to turn to him for the selection of their eternal, spiritual mate, my gut response was "Right on!" I refrained from acting upon their conflicting advice, but became curious about how the women around me were responding to these messages. This curiosity has fueled the work that follows.

Montreal, Quebec   SUSAN JEAN PALMER
January 1994

Acknowledgments

The greatest debt of gratitude is owed to my thesis advisor, Frederick Bird, who was my "initiating guru" into the scientific study of religion. Watching his creative approaches to the data his research team was gathering, I began to discover how exciting the sociology of new religions can be. He has somehow managed, with his extensive knowledge of both biological and spiritual families, to steer me toward finding and finishing this work.

Tom Robbins is an inspiration to many young scholars, and has encouraged this one by sending intriguing material and alleviating the tedium of conferences with his amazing comic gift and general human-ness. Other scholars at these events, particularly Rob Balch, Arvind Sharma, David Bromley, James Richardson, Jim Lewis, Gordon Melton, Catherine Wessinger, Alain Bouchard, and Eileen Barker, have spurred my efforts through showing a kindly interest and, occasionally, by ruthless criticism. Ted Irwin patiently bailed me out of many computer crises.

This work was first conceived of while reading Lawrence Foster's *Religion and Sexuality* (1981), which not only handed me a key to analyzing women's roles in NRMs, but helped me understand the shape of my background in a fifth-generation Mormon family. Although the depth of his insight and unusual synthesis of empathy and objectivity toward nonconventional religion is impossible to imitate, his friendly letters have reassured me that this work is interesting.

My students, who have accompanied me to "cult meetings" and have proved to be gifted and intrepid researchers, certainly deserve credit for enriching the ethnography in this study. My children provided the background noise and trained me to work despite repeated distractions. Steve Luxton corrected my punctuation and takes credit for bullying me to apply for grants. The Social Science in the Humanities Research Council provided a release time stipend so that I could find the time and energy for research.

Finally, I owe much to all those strong, intelligent women on the spiritual path who have tried to help me glimpse their worlds. As one who admires their vision and commitment, I wish to offer a provisional apology to all who find this version of their truths distorted, reduced, or limited, and to admit that it leaves much unsaid.

Moon Sisters,
Krishna Mothers,
Rajneesh Lovers

ONE

New Religious Feminine Roles

Having decided to explore the neglected terrain of women's roles and experiences in new religions, I chose seven groups that offer contrasting gender patterns. Their striking variations in marriage forms and feminine roles will, I believe, convey a more complete picture of the remarkable range of sexual innovations currently proliferating in marginal religions than has been previously painted. Some of these groups—the two institutes and the Messianic Community—are relatively small and obscure and have (thus far) escaped the scrutiny of scholars and stimulated no more than a sporadic or frivolous interest from the press. Others—the Society for Krishna Consciousness, the Rajneesh Movement, and the Unification Church—are well known, international NRMs, whose patterns of conversion and conflicts with secular authorities have been extensively researched. These seven NRMs are all communal in their social organization, except the Raelian Movement, which might be described as a millenarian sect.

The most unusual feature of women's roles that struck me when I first began to attend the meetings of new religions was their clarity, or perhaps simplicity would be a better word. This clarity and simplicity is often achieved by emphasizing one role and deemphasizing, or rejecting, other roles. Krishna Conscious women, for example, are defined as "mothers" by title and by occupation. Even unmarried or childless women are referred to as "mother." Female devotees would never describe themselves as friends or lovers in relation to the male devotees. The sexually expressive Rajneeshee is a "lover" in relation to Bhagwan Shree

Rajneesh (metaphorically speaking), and to the swamis in the commune, but she is not permitted to get pregnant or raise her existing children, and has rejected the role of wife.

"Wives," however, vary greatly in how they interpret this deceptively conservative role; the exemplary "wives" in the Institute of Applied Metaphysics were middle-aged, postmenopausal, and childless "handmaidens" to their much younger husbands. The role of the traditional wife is usually understood to include that of "homemaker," but IAM couples resolutely shared the domestic chores. Women in the Unification Church deviate from this pattern of specialization, in that a wider range of roles is available to them—but only one role at a time. They begin their careers in the movement as celibate "sisters" and then become "daughters" of Reverend Moon when he blesses them in marriage to one of their "brothers." These marriages remain unconsummated for three or more years, during which time the couple continue to live separately. Eventually, "Moon sisters" do become wives and mothers. The role of lover, however, is proscribed.

If one scans the landscape beyond these seven groups to survey what Greenfield (1973) has labeled the "spiritual supermarket," it appears that a contemporary North American woman who is seeking alternative spiritual, sexual, or social experiences is presented with a remarkable range of possibilities. She can be a celibate "sister," a devoted Hindu "wife," a domineering, promiscuous "lover," a pure, yogic "daughter," a veiled "Nubian bride" in polygamy, a sensually aware "playmate," a fertile "procreatrix" ushering in the Endtime, or an asexual shaman (to name only a few). Given this remarkable variety, what factors would condition her choice, and what do women, successful in secular life who define themselves as "feminists," find appealing in these religiously based and often neotraditional models of womanhood?

Utopian Havens for the Family in Transition

The literature focusing on the radical innovations in gender roles found in utopian communes in the antebellum period of

American history provides a rich source of ideas about the relationship between utopian experiments in gender and the corresponding changes in their host society. Lawrence Foster (1981, 234) in his brilliant study of nineteenth-century utopias postulates that these communities were deeply influenced by the "cult of true womanhood" and the antebellum ideals of sexual self-control. He proposes that their "sexual experiments," which ranged from celibacy to polygamy to free love, could be interpreted as responses to the Victorians' ambivalence toward sexuality. Shaker celibacy, for example, "could be viewed as almost a parody of the literature of marital and sexual advice. The Shakers carried the implications of this literature to their extreme, logical conclusion. If sex was basically a dangerous impulse . . . then why not go further and eliminate it altogether?"

The issue of sexual equality is raised continually in communal studies, with conflicting interpretations. Kanter (1973) posits a structural tendency of communal "defamilialization" to enhance women's participation in decision making, social life, and the industrial activity of the community, but Kolmerten (1993, 49) finds compelling evidence in women's letters from New Harmony that, although Robert Owen sought to liberate them from the confines of the nuclear family, he in fact "threatened women's traditional sphere without replacing it with anything but more work to perform." Foster (1981) points out the advantages that Shaker and Oneidan women enjoyed over their Victorian female contemporaries, and even finds aspects of female empowerment within the explicitly patriarchal institution of Mormon polygamy. Kern (1981), who chose to focus on the same three religious communities, takes the opposite view, and argues that utopian concessions to sexual equality were in fact insidious attempts by male leaders to usurp the moral prestige of motherhood and to restore (within the confines of their city on a hill) nostalgic recreations of the patriarchal lineage family. Although both authors present strong arguments, this debate reminds us how complex and subtle and subjective the issue of feminine empowerment can be. These historians, however, share the view that the "sexual experiments" found in nineteenth-century utopian communes represented religious responses to the decline of the lineage family in the antebellum period, and to the subsequent formation of the nuclear family, with its new, unique set of dilemmas.

A careful study of new religious literature demonstrates that contemporary groups are at least as concerned about power and authority in marriage as were their Victorian forebears, and are responding to what they perceive in the larger society as widespread mutual hostility between the sexes. Like the Shakers and Mormons, NRMs hope to achieve harmonious relations between the sexes based on new models of gender that reflect the divine cosmos. Women's spiritual authority, both in the home and in the community, is a prevalent theme in the pamphlets and guides to "better living" issuing from new religions. Woman's priestly role over her children and in the marriage bed, and her officiating function in public rituals, is clearly outlined in new religious literature. Modern prophets exhibit a profound concern for what they deplore as the increasingly secular and materialistic approach to sex and marriage in American society.

This study's approach will be like the historians' cited above, and it will try to understand contemporary utopias by looking at how new and shifting trends in family life are mirrored and expressed in NRMs. To investigate the meaning of these new "spiritual solutions," both for the women who adopt them and as collective responses to social change, we must view them in their twentieth-century context. To this end, we will step back and look at the changing patterns in families and gender roles during the past generation.

Changes in Family Life since World War II

Since World War II there have been dramatic changes in the patterns of family life and in the roles of women in industrialized societies of North America and Western Europe. The trend can be described as a move away from the assumptions basic to nuclear family patterns. These assumptions were the following: (1) the basic family unit was a husband, wife, and about two children living together without the likelihood of divorce; and (2) the husband was the primary breadwinner, the mother was the housekeeper, and the children were raised at home.

Yankelovitch, in *New Rules* (1979), estimated that 70 percent of American households conformed to this model in 1950. By 1981 only 15 percent did so, and many new models of the family prevailed, from single parent, common-law, and childless families, to homosexual couples, double income, and remarried, or "reconstituted," families.

Because of these postwar changes, modern couples cannot simply fall into a well-established set of assumptions about family life. They must choose their own guidelines (Berger and Kellner, 1974). Bromley and Busching (1988) note the increased popularity of premarital agreements and handbooks offering helpful hints on formulating do-it-yourself style marriage contracts.

Larger cultural movements have undoubtedly had their effects on (or been affected by) the modern family. The woman's liberation movement and its emphases on equal work, opportunity, and pay; the homosexual, or "gay," movement; the sexual revolution, which promotes nonprocreative sex; and the increased emphasis on individual happiness and autonomy are outstanding examples.

These changes have taken their emotional toll on individuals, and have created much confusion about the rules governing interpersonal relations and sexual identity. Out of this confusion, and contributing to it, has emerged the "new family."

Glendon's "New Family"

The "new family" is Mary Ann Glendon's term (1985) for the group of changes that characterizes western marriage and family behavior, such as the increasing fluidity, detachability, and interchangeability of family relationships. As Glendon notes, the "new family" departs from the traditional nuclear family in that it is no longer a single model, but represents various coexisting types. For example, single person or parent households, cohabiting couples, married couples without children, reconstituted families, and double-income families have all become common nonnuclear patterns. Besides these changes, more children are spending their preschool years in day care.

In *The New Family and the New Property*, Glendon examines recent developments in family law, employment law, and property law, and finds that they are closely related. She notes that while legal ties between family members are being loosened, the web of relationships that bind a person to his job—and his job to him—is becoming tighter and more highly structured.

The characteristics of the new family that most profoundly affect the roles of women are the fragility of the marriage bond, the relaxing of the parent-child bond, and the increase of women in the workplace. In describing new family couples, Glendon notes two observations that distinguish the modern couple relationship: "One is that modern marriage while it lasts is companionate, its bonding seemingly close and intense; the other that it is fragile, its bonding seemingly unstable" (Glendon 1985, 7).

She notes that the two outstanding features of companionate marriage, its closeness and intensity on one hand, and the interchangeability of its members on the other, appear contradictory. Historian Laurence Stone has made a similar observation and points out that the "intensely self-centered, inwardly-turned, emotionally bonded, sexually liberated, child-oriented family of the late 20th century exists under conditions which lead to the detachment of family members from the home and from each other" (Stone 1977, 693).

The fragility of the marriage bond, then, is one of the features of the "new family" that most threatens women in their traditional roles as wife and mother. Glendon links the instability of modern marriage to the individual's increased power of choice. She notes that "marriage has moved from a situation once characterized by . . . family selection of spouse, to . . . a veto by the child . . . then to unfettered choice, and now to a situation where people may . . . correct their original choice" (Glendon 1985, 32). Bromley and Busching (1988) have pointed out that this "power of choice" is certainly one of the outstanding features of what they term "contractual" social relations.

The attenuation of the parent-child bond is the second characteristic of the new family that most affects women. Glendon cites demographic surveys that reveal that parents today spend less time with their children than their great-grandparents did, that children leave home at an earlier age, and that their psychological dependency on the family ends even earlier.

The third overwhelming problem facing women in the new family is what Glendon calls "woman's triple burden":

It has become common to speak of the "double burden," referring to the fact that the increase in woman's work outside the home had not brought about a corresponding decrease in the share of work they do inside the home. But much more serious for mothers and children in the long run is the increased economic risk a woman takes in becoming a mother in the first place. This risk factor means women carry not a double burden, but a triple burden. Some women have reacted to the risks of vulnerability in and to divorce, combined with the disadvantages at work and home, by declining to have children, in what Joseph Berliner has called "the reproductive equivalent of voting with one's feet." (Glendon 1985, 129)

These three characteristics clearly threaten contemporary women's traditional role within the family. Is it surprising therefore that some women today might feel insecure as a wife, unimportant or undervalued as a mother, and "stressed out" as a worker-wife-mother-housekeeper? For women in this situation with religious sensibilities, the simple and valorized roles of "sister," "mother," and "lover" within the setting of a religious commune might begin to exert an appeal.

But how successful are these "spiritual solutions to love"? The debate we noted among historians about issues of power and equality between the sexes has also been taken up by sociologists interested in contemporary spiritual movements. Robbins (1988), in his survey of the microsociology of new religions, observes that scholars investigating new religious experiments in sexuality tend to fall into two camps: those stressing the *empowerment* of women in unconventional spiritual groups (Neitz 1988; Haywood 1983) and those that view NRMs as a *backlash* against the feminist movement and a regression to patriarchal patterns (Aidala 1985; Davidman 1988; Jacobs 1987; Rose 1987). Compared with scholars of nineteenth-century "new religions" who tend to find their women "empowered," feminist sociologists of NRMs often stress the theme of feminine degradation— a view reflected in the literature issuing from the anticult movement—as summed up by *The Guardian* (1991, 33): "The degrading treatment of women in many religious cults reads like a chapter from the dark ages. Yet 200 years ago, women were leaders of a number of sects, asserting feminine equality (and even superiority) within them. What went wrong?"

Wagner (1986, 178) offers this caveat concerning the study of communal sexuality: "The relationship between gender roles and sexual equality to communalism is an important but complex matter that we are just beginning to untangle; *a priori* statements based on what logically or morally 'ought to be' cannot cut the Gordian knot."

This statement sums up my research experience, for in studying new religions I have found feminine "empowerment" to be slippery. Both the "neo-patriarchy school" and the "feminist school" (Robbins 1988) may present convincing arguments, but are their insights relevant beyond the groups under scrutiny? New religions can be vaunted as the harbingers of women's power if one looks at the Brahmakumaris (Babb 1984), or deplored as the last refuge of male chauvinists and "fembots" if one studies the Aryan Nations (Zia 1991). The seven NRMs described in this study are difficult to categorize, as they demonstrate neither a steady progression toward sexual equality nor a regrettable relapse into what Mary Daly calls the "phallocracy." Instead they confront the researcher with a baffling array of ideologies and life-styles that challenge preconceived notions of sexuality and family. In some groups one may find familiar "sexist" attitudes incongruously intertwined with some of the most enlightened and avant-garde feminist perspectives. Rather than wrestling with the riddle "who is equal, but who is *more* equal?" or resorting to measurements of political correctness, I use a typology to facilitate my investigation.

Three Religious Views of Sex Identity

I have organized the seven groups under three headings: sex polarity, sex complementarity, and sex unity. These headings constitute a typology that highlights three contrasting concepts of woman/man and body/soul relationships, and they propose unique strategies about the usefulness (and dangers) of male-female relationships on the path to salvation. These three types can be observed underlying the rules governing relationships between the sexes in the spiritual communes in the study, and they are reflected, overtly and vividly, in their creation myths.

The labels for these three types have been borrowed from Sister Prudence Allen's comparative study of the philosophical views of Thomas Aquinas and Hildegarde von Bingen on sexuality. Her paper, "Two Mediaeval Views on Woman's Identity" (Allen 1987, 21) proposes a typology of philosophies of sex identity found in the Christian tradition, and her three types are sex complementarity, sex polarity, and sex unity. She outlines them as follows.

By *sex complementarity* I mean a theory which argues for the equality of worth and dignity of women and men while at the same time arguing for a philosophically significant difference between the two sexes. *Sex polarity* . . . accepts the philosophically significant differences between women and men, but this theory argues that men in general are superior to women. In the history of philosophy there is a third general theory of sex identity, or *sex unity*, which argues that there are no philosophically significant differences between the sexes, and as a consequence that men and women are fundamentally equal. . . . Sex unity . . . usually is accompanied by a devaluation of the body.

In attempting to construct a viable typology of gender in NRMs, I have found it necessary to modify Allen's models. Because her typology was intended as a tool to study the developing Christian traditions and its heresies in European history, it is necessary to create a new typology (based on hers and retaining her terms) to explore the inner logic of non-Christian as well as Christian-based and other eclectic strains of spirituality found in the postfeminist 1980s. The two variables in her typology are difference and equality. We will retain the first variable, but we will note that the issue of "equality" is complex, and add the variable of function. In other words, we will ask, "What use are men and women to each other on the spiritual path?" The characteristics of our typology, therefore, begin to look as follows.

Sex Complementarity regards each sex as endowed with different spiritual qualities and emphasizes the importance of marriage for uniting two halves of the same soul to form one, complete androgynous being. The individual's gender and often the marriage relationship might continue on in the afterlife. Marriage and procreation often usher in the millennium. The restoration of true relationships between the sexes, or of the original race at the end of time is a common notion, as is marriage to the dead (e.g., Elizabeth Clare Prophet's "Twin Flames" and Thomas Lake Harris's "Lily Queen"). A dual or androgynous godhead often reigns over this social structure (the Mormon "Heavenly Father and Mother," the Unificationist "One True Parent of Mankind").

Sex Polarity views the sexes as spiritually distinct, separate, and inessential or irrelevant to the other's salvation. Levels of salvation might be quite different for men and women because they are not considered spiritually equal. Usually, men are considered the superior sex, as in ISKCON and the 3HO, but Rajneesh, Dada Lekhraj, and Mary Daly view women as superior to men. The notion of pollution is sometimes present and the sexes are segregated to avoid weakening each other's spiritual resolve. Often the sexes are permitted to engage in limited, highly controlled relationships as a necessary phase in their spiritual development, or to contribute children to the group.

Sex Unity sees the body and its gender as a superficial layer of false identity obscuring the immortal, sexless spirit (e.g., est's *Real Self*). Groups espousing this philosophy might foster unisex clothing and androgynous social personae, or they might play act traditional sex roles while advocating an inner distance from these roles. In shamanistic or neo-gnostic groups there is often the notion that letting go of sex identification can release the power and infinite potential of the "Being" (the IDHHB) or enable it to assume control of its reincarnation cycle (Scientology's "Thetan"). The idea that gender can be chosen or changed is often present through cloning and elective surgery for Raelians, through conscious rebirth for Scientologists and Gold followers, and through metamorphosis into androgynous beings for followers of Bo and Peep (see Balch 1982).

These types are not always found in their pure form; mixtures of two types can be noted in some NRMs; and one type can transform into another type during a group's history.

Two other woman scholars have proposed similar, if not identical, models of gender that they have observed operating in unconventional religion. That all three scholars have proposed similar models independently, with no references to one another's theories, seems to make these categories more plausible.

Aidala (1985, 294), in her comparison of gender roles found in religious (as opposed to secular) communes observes: "Three general approaches to gender roles were found among communes inspired by the new religions: biblically-based understandings of patriarchy, bio-mystical specification of complementarity, and subjectivist denials of gender differences."

Reuther (1983, 99) finds, in contrast to patriarchal anthropologies in Christian history, a recurrence of "theologies of woman's original equality in the image of God, restored in Christ." She distinguishes between three theologies and calls them "eschatological feminism," "liberal feminism," and "romantic feminism," and identifies their characteristics as follows.

Eschatological feminism affirmed the restored equality of men and women in Christ by referring to an original transcendant anthropology that existed before the fall into the finite condition characterized by sexual dimorphism. Male and female were equal in this transcendant state. . . . Liberal feminism rejects the classic notion of the patriarchal order of creation and instead secularizes the doctrine of the *imago dei* and affirms the equivalence of all human beings as finite, historical persons who share a common human nature characterized by reason and moral conscience. Romantic feminism stresses the differences between male and female as representatives of complementary opposites. (Reuther 1983, 100–5)

A comparison of these three typologies suggests they can be combined into one typology. See table 1.

TABLE 1. Three Scholars' Models of Sex Identity

Allen	*Aidala*	*Reuther*
Sex Complement	Bio-mystical complement	Romantic
Sex Polarity	Bible-based patriarchy	Eschatological
Sex Unity	Denial of difference	Liberal

These three distinct notions of sex identity can be found in the creation myths of the NRMs in my study, whose alternative patterns of marriage are often modeled on their leader's revelations about the relationship between the first Man and Woman. After examining the improvisations on Genesis and gender found in the seven groups, their appeal for women dissatisfied with the fuzzy, pluralistic, and secular models of gender found in our society might be better understood.

PART ONE

Sex Polarity Groups

TWO

Mothers and Widows in Krishna Consciousness

I want my daughters to have the hearts of Bengali mothers and the determination of Englishmen!

—*A. C. Bhaktivedanta Swami Prabhupada*

"Mother" is a term of respect for women in the International Society for Krishna Consciousness (ISKCON), and is often prefixed to the Sanskrit names they receive in initiation. Even unmarried women are referred to as mothers. One male devotee of ten years explained. "In India mothers are regarded with great respect. If you think of every woman as a mother it is impossible to think of them as sex objects. After all, no one is sexually attracted to their mother, although, today in the Kali Yuga you can't even be sure of that!"

The History

The Hare Krishna movement[1] might be most accurately described as a denomination of Vaishnava Hinduism, which was imported from India to the United States in 1965. The founder, A. C. Bhaktivedanta Swami Prabhupada (1896–1977), arrived in New York off the boat from India, sat down under a tree in Tompkins Park, and began chanting the name of Krishna accompanied by his finger cymbals. He attracted the attention of many young hippies disillusioned with the drug scene, and within five years had established Krishna temples all over the world.

ISKCON is a highly visible religious minority, for its members adopt Eastern clothing and the men shave their heads—and they are intensely evangelical. They reject American culture and worldly attachments, which are regarded as *maya,* or illusion, and are dedicated to living what they consider the traditional Vedic way of life, based on surrender to Lord Krishna, the Supreme Personality of the Godhead.

They espouse a radical body-spirit dualism, which emphasizes the transient nature of material life and the reincarnation cycle. The aim of the spirit-soul is to advance up the scale of purity until, no longer subject to the laws of karma, the soul (which is female in relation to her Lord) attains a spiritual form and dwells eternally in Vrindavana, envisaged as a garden paradise.

Upon initiation, members must recite before the guru the four vows: the promise to refrain from meat eating, nonprocreative sex, drugs, and gambling. They must also promise to recite the Hare Krishna *mahamantra* daily, which they believe purifies the soul and expresses their love for God.

Gender Roles

It appears that ISKCON men are held to be more advanced than women, physically, intellectually, and spiritually—at least from a Western, sociological perspective. Mother Parvati, a devotee of fifteen years who is in charge of training women and arranging marriages (among other services), explained the relative status of men and women in the movement.

You really notice the difference between men and women in the Krishna Consciousness movement. We both practice Bhakti Yoga, we read the same scriptures, so we follow the same spiritual path. We recognize that the human body is valuable for facilitating spiritual life, but a man's body is a finer instrument for developing Krishna Consciousness and if he remains celibate he becomes very powerful. Within the semen is contained the spirit soul: all children come from the body of man. It takes three cups of blood to produce just one drop of semen and one drop is enough to dispel the thirty-two hundred diseases of the body, according to Vedic medicine. The semen is lifted by the life airs to the brain where it bathes the brain and creates intelligence. We have a saying: "Man has the power of discrimination; woman has the power of inspiration." Since a woman's body lacks this substance, you'll find that they all have a blind spot. I have trained ladies in ISKCON for fifteen years. Our women are expected to act like women and never become masculine. Our ladies are valued and protected because we recognize that a woman needs spiritual protection; she needs an infrastructure to help her advance. It is the duty of men to protect women from abuse. Our women are never beaten, nor used as objects of sense gratification.

From ISKCON's theological point of view, however, there is no significant distinction between men and women—or between the human and lower forms of life, for the material body belongs to the illusory realm of *maya*, or illusion.

Marriage and Procreation

In ISKCON men advance spiritually through celibacy and nonattachment; women advance through motherhood and devotion to their husbands in the tradition of *stridharma*, the wifely duty of submission to the husband and the bearing of sons (Young 1987, 59–103). Mother Parvati described the consequences of male-female relationships on the reincarnation cycle.

If a man becomes too attached to his wife, or too interested in women, he is in danger of coming back in the body of a woman. Women are often men who were attached to women in their last life. It is the opposite for a woman. The more attached she is to her husband, the more devoted she is to him, the more likely she is to advance spiritually and be reborn as a man.

This apparent conflict of interests between the sexes is resolved through arranged marriages, controlled and ritualized sexual relationships within marriage, and through dividing the life cycle into four stages: the traditional Hindu *ashramas* of *brahmacarya, grihastha, vanaprastha,* and *sannyasa*. In the last stage of *sannyasa*, it is customary for the ISKCON man to renounce all wordly attachments, including his family, and to devote himself totally to the service of Krishna. In the early days of the movement, about half the male devotees never entered the householder *ashram*, but remained celibate and took vows of *sannyasa*, often before the age of thirty. This pattern represents a significant departure from the traditional Hindu *ashrama* system.

ISKCON wives cannot renounce their families, and husbands can do so only with their wives' permission. Sannyasins can still see their children after they have taken the vows of renunciation, but must never see their wives again. The wife then becomes a "widow" and wears a white sari; her husband adopts the orange robes of *sannyas*. Mother Parvati described their future relationship as follows.

The widow may ask about her husband and hear of his doings, but he must never ask about her. She can sit at the back of the hall and listen to his lectures so long as he can't see her. By thinking of the husband she will advance, but he must never think of her. Whatever spiritual achievements her husband makes during this time she will make also, because he is her guru and her spiritual protector.

According to the estimates of the temple presidents I interviewed, about one-fifth of the male devotees (since the late 1980s) are not married, a figure that roughly reflects the sex ratio of 4:5 in favor of men. Over 90 percent of the women in ISKCON are married; the unmarried minority are either *brahmacarini* (celibate students, i.e., newcomers to the movement) or "widows." Women usually marry within one to three years after joining the movement; men usually stay celibate for an average of four to five years and often much longer. The recommended age for marriage is over twenty-five for men, but women often marry in their teens and early twenties. In New Vrindaban, the communal farm in West Virginia, girls of fifteen or sixteen were often married. It was also customary for girls in their early teens to become engaged, although it might be years before they have any sort of relationship with their fiancé, the rationale being, "It is important that she knows who her husband is."

Within marriage a high level of austerity is encouraged. Sex is supposed to be for procreation only, to be performed when conception is likely to occur. The couple ask their spiritual master for his blessing on their attempt to have a child. The wife prepares foodstuffs and a garland, and then the Garbadhana Samskara ceremony is performed by the couple. This involves chanting fifty rounds of the *mahamantra* HARE KRISHNA. The purpose of this six-hour ceremony is twofold: to dedicate the pleasure to Krishna and to attract an elevated soul into the body of the child about to be conceived. A child conceived without this ceremony is called a Varnasankara (a soul conditioned by karma).

The inner state of the couple is believed to be important because it will affect the sex of their child. As one mother explained, "If a husband is very aroused they will have a boy; otherwise they may have a girl."

Devotees who wish to marry consult with their temple president. If a suitable candidate is found, the couple is granted permission to associate for six months in the temple. They may sit together at communal meals, the woman may serve the man's food, and he may instruct her in the Vedic scriptures. During this period they will meet separately with counselors and report on their progress. If they decide they are compatible, a legal marriage is arranged and then a traditional Hindu wedding is celebrated in the temple.

It is fairly common for a couple to have a private understanding before they ask for permission to become engaged, and women seem to be active in selecting their husbands. "The women choose the men," one male devotee claimed. It also appears to be customary for the engaged man to put up a show of resistance or reluctance. One *brahmin* (a devotee in the second stage of initiation), when asked about the wedding date, replied, "I'll try to put it off as long as possible." Another *brahmin*, who had just become engaged after twelve years of celibacy, explained his decision.

I was never interested in her until she let me know she was interested in me. Then I began to observe that my mind was agitated after I spoke to her. I could see it coming and was trying to figure out how to escape. I thought of disappearing and going to India, but I had responsibilities here. I had to serve our large Indian congregation and it would be a bad example for the young boys. So I tried to avoid her. Then the night the restaurant burned down, I was up all night trying

to save the furniture. Everyone was running around and I was exhausted. She came over and talked to me and twisted my arm, and I
was too weak to run away. I guess we have really been engaged for a
long time—I just needed time to accept it. Anyway, women need men
to protect them. It's not good for a woman to live without a husband
for too long. I've been in the movement for twelve years and I've seen
what happens to Mothers who live in the ladies' ashram—they go a bit
crazy! And she's been in the movement ten years, and she's a disciple
of Srila Prabhupada, and there aren't so many of us around anymore.
I don't know what I'm going to tell my initiating guru—he's in Toronto, and he has all these big plans for me. . . . I was going to have
to make the decision soon whether I was going to be initiated into
sannyas. After that, you must never think about women, you must
only see them as spirit souls. The standard of purity and perfection is
so high, I wasn't sure I was ready for it.

There appears to be a marked difference between how men
and women respond to the event of an engagement. On one
occasion at the local Krishna restaurant, I watched the male
devotees greeting a newly engaged *brahmin* by making jocular
references to his sudden appearance in white (as opposed to
orange, a sign of his new status as a "householder"): "Hare bo!
Hey, D., you look good in white!" The *brahmin* appeared to
be acutely embarrassed. His fiancée, though, was warmly embraced and congratulated by the other female devotees, who
made quite a fuss about helping her prepare the tray bearing his
tea and dessert, because serving him food was a public declar-
ation of their engagement. For him, it evidently represented a
loss of status; he was giving up the opportunity to become a
sannyasin or spiritual leader. In our subsequent conversation,
he felt obliged to justify his decision as an act of sacrifice for
the good of the larger movement. He explained how, for male
devotees, getting married implied an attachment to one's own
body, and would require a new level of compromise with *karmi*
(secular, or subject to the laws of *karma*) life. They must move
out of the temple and find employment compatible with the
four vows in order to maintain an apartment for their family.
Another recently affianced *brahmin* voiced the regret that he
would be separated from his "godbrothers" living in the
temple, who helped one another along the spiritual path.

Krishna Conscious bride. Courtesy Kristine Kitsikis.

(These "macho" attitudes expressed above are more typical of the early days of ISKCON, before the communal structure declined. Today, a more positive value is awarded to marriage, and ISKCON men have matured in their understanding of women and marriage.)

For a woman, however, marriage represents an improvement in her spiritual/social status. I observed in conversations with devotees that women sometimes offered personal, emotional reasons for getting married ("I liked him." "I felt he was a kind man I could trust."); men invariably voiced altruistic, impersonal reasons ("Women need strong, Krishna-conscious men to guide them," or "My spiritual master feels that we need to raise more children in Krishna Consciousness").

Unmarried men and women live in separate *ashrams* and it could be argued they have developed slightly different cultures. Mother Parvati told a story to illustrate her future husband's exemplary character, but it also reveals how utterly separate these two communities are.

In the early days of the movement, men and women were like this! [placing her hands wide apart]. The devotees were in India and traveling on two buses—all the men were in one and all the women and children were in the other, and our bus driver was a rascal! He was going much too fast and the dust was pouring through the windows. The children were screaming, we were all terrified we would go off the road. Then he *did* go off, and we landed in a ditch. We all got out and the men's bus stopped. I spoke up for the ladies and said, "Why don't one of you *brahmins* come and sit beside our driver and make sure he drives carefully, because he won't listen to us!" The leader made a joke of it and turned around to the busload of men. "Which of you *brahmins* would like to have this wonderful service?" He meant sitting with women. But my [future] husband was there and he realized it wasn't funny—the situation was serious—and he got up and didn't say a word, just went over and sat down in our bus. So, you see, he really understands women and children—he can feel it when we need protection. I thought, He's the only real *brahmin* among the lot!

Sex segregation continues after marriage. The husband and wife may decide to not share a bedroom, lest they "fall down" or "bloop" (which one devotee explained as "the sound the soul makes when it enters the material world"). Although in Canada the initiating guru encourages married couples to live together, the Florida guru demands a higher level of austerity: married men live in the temple but may visit their wives and children who live in nearby apartments during the day. The December 1982 *Back to Godhead* explains the spiritual function of the marriage relationship.

In a Krsna conscious marriage, the husband and wife help each other advance in spiritual life. . . . If the husband is spiritually advanced and the wife is chaste and faithful to her husband, she attains the same spiritual perfection as her husband. In Sanskrit, the husband is called *pati-guru,* "husband-guru" because he acts as a spiritual guide for the wife . . . the wife protects the husband's body from being conquered by material desires, which plunder the body. A spiritually strong wife can help the husband conquer sex desire.

More than 90 percent of ISKCON's *grihasthas* (married couples) live outside the temple and are engaged in secular business. Although Knott (1987) states that ISKCON has adjusted to the necessity of women working outside the home, this researcher did not encounter one instance of a female devotee who worked in the karmi world, except two "fringies" (part-time members) who come to the temple on Sundays. The notion of women seeking employment in the karmi world appeared to be entirely unacceptable to the Canadian married couples interviewed, although devotees from the United States and Europe report they know many prominent ISKCON women devotees who are operating successful businesses.

Women in Work and Ritual

The leadership of the movement was at first composed of single, celibate men, but today almost 50 percent of them are married. When Swami Prabhupada died in 1977, he appointed a board of eleven administrators to govern ISKCON—the Governing Body Commission. The fifteen gurus who perform the initiation ceremonies and function as spiritual masters to the disciples in the movement are also celibate men. So are the *san-*

nyasin, or itinerant preachers, who travel about the temples and hold revival meetings, Krishna-style. The local temple presidents, however, are usually married *brahmins* (the second stage of initiation) living in the *grihastha* ashram. Women cannot hold titles or official posts, but are identified by their husband's title and often assist him in his work.

There appears to be little gender division in domestic work for the unmarried members. Both sexes clean the altar, scrub the floors, and cook the communal meals. Unmarried devotees possess their own plates and cups with which they serve themselves and are responsible for washing. Similarly, each male devotee is accustomed to washing his own clothes. Once they are engaged or married, however, the wife serves the husband his food and washes his dishes and laundry.

Women participate in the *sankirtana,* the daily chanting and dancing ceremony performed in the temple before the deities. The sexes are strictly segregated during the ritual, the men standing on the left, the women on the right. In New Vrindaban, the communal farm in West Virginia, the women stand behind a balustrade while the men are in the forefront, closer to the altar. The practice was explained by the Montreal temple president: "We have a saying: 'Woman is like fire, man is like butter,' so the women keep to the back during *kirtan* so they won't distract the men in their worship." Men are more expressive in their dancing and chanting than the women. A man leads the *kirtan* in chanting, the solo part to which there is an antiphonal response. Men play drums and musical instruments, they jump and spin, chant loudly, and improvise ornamentation. Women are more subdued, often dancing repeated steps in group formation. Many of them hold babies or restrain toddlers. The women cover their heads with their *saris;* the men wear *dhoti,* or loincloths, and may expose their heads, shoulders, and chests, depending on the weather and their officiating functions. It is customary for the altar boys to wear only a *dhoti.*[2]

Women make the garlands that are offered daily to the deities and sew the clothing in which the deities are dressed. Both sexes share the priestly function of *aratrika,* or deity worship, which involves offering food, incense, flowers, flames, etc., to the deities on the altar. During menstruation, however, women refrain from performing *aratrika*, from cooking, offering flowers to the guru, and watering the sacred *tulsi* plant. Menstrual taboos are less forbidding in ISKCON than in India, however, because menstruating women in America are permitted to participate in the *sankirtana*.

Women are actively involved in the missionary work that is one of the major activities of ISKCON. They chant and preach on the street and distribute the sacred texts translated by Swami Prabhupada. The purpose of these activities, besides to recruit new members, is to spread God's word. Those passing by hearing the chant are believed to be instantly purified of all bad karma.

Swami Prabhupada's Hinduism in the West

In examining the influence of the founder on women's roles in the movement, one finds a tension between the patriarchal Hindu traditions that he frequently appeals to and his response to the spiritual needs of real, contemporary western women. He is uncompromising in his verbal support of *stridharma*. For example, when a journalist asked, "Why should women be subservient to men?" he replied:

Not should be . . . they *are*. . . . It is natural for a woman to be a chaste wife and a good cook. It is natural for her to serve her husband lovingly, help him progress in Krsna consciousness, and help him raise Krsna conscious children. In this way she becomes dear to her husband and, by her devotions to spiritual injunction, dear to Lord Krsna. (*BTG*, Mar./Apr. 1991, 53)

However, many older female disciples among my informants (and those quoted in *BTG*) relate vivid memories of Prabhupada's fatherly kindness, of the ways he showed appreciation for women as "spirit-souls," and how he encouraged them to take the initiative in chanting, in preaching, and in exploring their talents to better serve Krishna. Perhaps because he had left behind a wife and two daughters when he took vows of *sannyas* at the age of fifty, he felt comfortable among women. Two reports are unsubstantiated but were repeated (with slight variations) by several older disciples. First, Swami Prabhupada did not expect women to join his movement and was surprised so many women were attracted; he decided he must find husbands for them right away so that they would be protected. Second, in planning the future leadership of the organization before his death, Prabhupada made it clear that he wanted one woman on the Governing Body Commission (GBC). After his death, however, the GBC who were appointed were exclusively male.[3]

Srila Prabhupada sums up traditional Hindu perspectives on women in his commentary in the *Bhagavad-Gita As It Is*. Considering the patriarchal attitudes in "Laws of Manu," Prabhupada's exegeses often seek to make them more palatable for Western devotees. He seems to equate the "demoniac people" of the *Kali Yuga* with contemporary Western culture.

Now, in the *Manu-samhita* it is clearly stated that a woman should not be given freedom, but that does not mean that women are to be kept as slaves, but they are like children. . . . The demons have now neglected such injunctions and they think that women should be given as much freedom as men. . . . But modern education has artificially devised a puffed-up concept of womanly life, and therefore marriage is practically an imagination in human society. . . . Nor is the moral condition of woman very good now.

Unguarded women, he notes, can bring about illegitimate children and social chaos. "According to the Canakya Pandita, women are generally not very intelligent and therefore not trustworthy. . . . On the failure of such varnasrama-dharma, naturally the women become free to act and mix with men, and thus adultery is indulged in at the risk of unwanted population" (*B-G*, 19).

Prabhupada explains how, in the Hindu cosmology, the relationship between spiritual and material nature is the same as the relationship between male and female. "What is material nature? This is also explained in *Gita* as inferior *prakrti*, inferior nature. . . . *Prakrti* is female, and she is controlled by the Lord, who is the predominator" (*BGAII*, 32).

Erotic metaphors are commonly used in the Bhakti tradition to convey the highest expression of devotional love for Krishna.

Stillson Judah (1974, 471), in his article, "The Hare Krishna Movement," describes five stages of devotional love of traditional North Indian Krishna Bhakti, of which the highest, *madhurya*, is the relationship of lover and beloved: "In his meditation the devotee seeks to visualize the amorous sport that Krishna carries on with the milkmaids, and to take part himself in this transcendental experience." Judah cites Prabhupada's warning that spiritual sex life must never be confused with material sex life.

Actually, lust and the sex urge are there in spiritual life, but because the spirit soul is now embodied in material elements, that spiritual urge is expressed through this material body, and therefore it is pervertedly reflected. When one becomes actually conversant in the science of Krishna Consciousness, he can understand that his material affection for sex life is abominable whereas spiritual sex life is desirable.

Gelberg (1983) has pointed to a feminine aspect of the godhead found in ISKCON, since Krishna, like all Hindu deities, has a female consort. Within the movement itself, the feminine dimension of the godhead is referred to in a direct appeal to potential female converts.

She is known as Srimati Radharani, and she is the same as Krishna . . . yet she is eternally different as well . . . without Radha there is no meaning to Krishna . . . in fact, she is worshipped *before* Krishna . . . Radha-Krishna. The word "HARE" is the vocative form of Mother Hara. . . . So the prayer is actually to Radha. . . .

With the most elaborate spiritual tradition encouraging all living beings to follow the example of simple village girls (*Gopis*), and that same tradition giving a detailed explanation of God as the Supreme Female, what would stop a sincere feminist from giving herself totally to a life of God consciousness? (ISKCON pamphlet, *Feminism and the Quest for God* by Satyaraja Dasa; no date)

Prabhupada's official biography contains many anecdotes illustrating his determination to segregate young Western men and women, and to regulate their sexual impulses.

One day, just out of curiosity, I went to witness Swamiji's cooking classes. So I came and stood at the doorway to Swamiji's kitchen. The women were learning how to cook, and Swamiji said to me, "What are you doing?" "Oh," I said, "I just came to see my wife." Then Swamiji said, "Are you going back to Godhead or back to wife?" Everyone was amused. I realised I wasn't welcome, so I left. The incident made me reflect on Swamiji's seriousness. For one thing, I learned that I shouldn't be so attached to my wife, and secondly I learned that his relationship with the women and what he was teaching them was actually very sacred—not like the sometimes frivolous association between husband and wife. Because he spent many hours in the kitchen teaching them, they were very inspired. (Satsvarupa dasa Goswami 1981, 70)

This story indicates that Praphupada invested much effort in educating his American devotees in traditional Vedic gender roles. He insisted that human love should be subordinated to divine love. His response to one disciple's hesitations about arranged marriage was, "You want a girl? Pick one. There is no love in this material world. . . . Love is for Krsna" (Satsvarupa dasa Goswami 1981, 85).

The "Woman Issue" in ISKCON Literature

ISKCON literature occasionally addresses feminism or "women's liberation," perhaps intending to attract women who define themselves as feminists, and who might otherwise be "turned off" by the traditional and subservient position of women in Krishna Consciousness. The 1982 "Special Issue" of *Back to Godhead* (16–18) features an interview with Miss Denmark, Anne Schaufuss, who is a devotee and has donated her earnings from modeling to build a *gurukula* on the Hare Krishna farm near Paris. Her views of the limitations of the feminist movement are as follows.

Many unscrupulous men are promoting the term "women's liberation" to exploit women. Krishna conscious men are self-realized. They don't regard us as objects of sense gratification. Krishna Conscious women . . . don't have to live in constant fear of being cheated by men. If women's liberation is to be successful, it must have a spiritual foundation.

In response to the question, "Can you be a liberated woman in the movement?" she responds:

Yes. Liberation goes beyond social or economic freedom. It frees you from your *karma*. One who understands and realizes this transcends superficial identification as male and female. The Krishna conscious woman is not constantly distracted by men. She doesn't waste her valuable time trying to attract them. This is possible because Krishna conscious women have attained happiness within. *That* is real liberation. (*BTG* 1977, 17)

The December 1982 *BTG* elaborates on the same theme in an interview with Sitarani dasa.

First let's try to understand the core concern of the women's liberation movement. If you look beyond the standard criticism that society has failed to grant women social, political, or economic equality, you discover . . . a deeper concern. . . . Women are protesting that they're not respected . . . they are viewed as mere instruments of male gratification, as sex objects. The gross or implied idea that women are meant for pleasing the senses of men pervades our culture. . . . What is demeaning is that the woman *herself*—whether as a psychological being or a spiritual being—is not taken seriously. She becomes, in a sense, a nonperson. All that's important is her *body,* as an exploitable commodity.

The aspects of secular "women's liberation" that ISKCON women congratulate themselves on leaving behind are listed as follows: "What have 'equal rights' and 'high profiles' brought women anyway? Exploitation, broken families, broken marriages, an animalistic chain of uncaring sexual partners, abortion, children bereft of parental love, and, above all, no time for Krsna consciousness" (*BTG* Mar./Apr. 1991, 53).

An issue of *Back to Godhead* (Jan./ Feb. 1991, 11–13) features an article on "The Role of Women in the Hare Krishna Movement." The fact that five women openly voice their complaints about what they consider the male devotees' misinterpretations of woman's role, "the Prabhupada way"—and, moreover, that these criticisms have been published—suggests the movement has begun to adopt a more egalitarian attitude toward women.

Pranada Devi Dasi, initiated in 1976, notes the frequent assumptions by male devotees that women are less intelligent than men, and more materialistic. She refers to an apocryphal story that Prabhupada had, before he died, recommended that women should become initiating gurus as well as men: "How do we understand Srila Praphupada's statements, in several letters, that his women should also initiate?" (*BTGH* 25.1, 42).

Sita Devi Dasi is a "widow" whose husband took vows of *sannyas* when she was only twenty-five, and she has since taught in the *gurukulas.* She expresses concern over the fate of the family in ISKCON, and suggests that, when Swami retired from administrative duties, the young men who relieved him lacked his spiritual maturity, and in their struggle to "handle their new attempts at celibacy," might have "institutionalized patterns of behaviour that to some extent made our family relationships dysfunctional." She voices the hope that because women are meant to be protected by men, the society should "make sure it protects women from serious social neglect, make it hard for men to abandon their wives and children . . . provide counseling to help devotees keep their marriages together . . . and see to it that devotees take their vows of marriage and *sannyasa* most seriously" (*BTGH* 43–44).

Visakha Devi Dasi, a wife and mother, tells a story about a three-year-old boy in an ISKCON nursery school who told her daughter (who had just volunteered to lead the singing), "You can't lead because you're a girl!" She eloquently deplores the contradictions found in ISKCON between a "philosophy that acknowledges the spiritual equality of all living beings in all forms of life" and community practice in which women were "shackled with 'can do's' and 'cannot do's' based on the particular body the soul was housed in." She contrasts the male devotees' "mean swami syndrome" to "Prabhupada's gentlemanly dealings and sweet exchanges with us women," and notes that her guru had often encouraged women to lead the singing even at "programs with literally tens of thousands in attendance." She nostalgically recalls a "relationship free from any mundane romance or anti-woman sentiment": "Srila Prabhupada, being free from sensual desires, did not feel his vow of celibacy threatened by his young female followers. And, being free of false ego, he had no need to assert male superiority or dominance."

Even more outspoken in her attack on "sexist" attitudes in ISKCON is Manasa Ganga Devi Dasi. She describes herself as a former feminist and Marxist-Leninist who, in her search for a truly harmonious society in which all people could live with mutual respect and flourish to their fullest potential, had joined the society in 1986. There, she was struck by the irony of finding herself in a situation where, "instead of me seeing men as the enemy, they saw me as the enemy, as 'Maya Devi,' or illusion personified." She goes on to explain how this placed obstacles in her spiritual path.

Because I was seen as a temptress first and a devotee second, I was subtly or overtly denied or discouraged from a host of spiritual activities that I understood to be given to me by Swami Praphupada. . . . On one hand I was welcomed to clean, to cook, and make flower garlands, services I enjoyed. But, on the other hand I was told that because I am a woman I would disturb the minds of men (that is, sexually agitate them) if in their presence I chanted *japa* in the temple room, led *kirtana*, stood up near the deities during *arati*, offered *puja* to Srila Praphupada, gave *Srimad-Bhagavatam* class . . . and so on. This dichotomy made me feel excluded and a little schizoid, because I wanted to excel in *all* activities, not just those stereotypically designated as female.

Yadurani Devi Dasi is Prabhupada's earliest female disciple and the foremost painter and illustrator in the movement. She is one of the few (perhaps the only) women in America who preach and give classes. She is confident that impediments caused by gender can be overcome by becoming "transparent instruments for Krsna's will." She cites the *Bhagavad-Gita* teaching that "every living being causes his own happiness and distress." She affirms that women "can use all situations to our advantage in becoming pure devotees." Her message to women is: Don't worry about men's attitudes, focus on your own and stop identifying with the body. "Who knows?" she warns. "A man who mistreated women in his last life may come back in this life as a mistreated woman" (*BTG* 25.1:56).

ISKCON's Appeal for Women

Having described ISKCON views of gender and marriage in some detail, it is now necessary to ask if it is possible to generalize about what kind of women are attracted to this movement, and why women are attracted at all.

When one looks at the information available on membership in North America, both the figures supplied by the Montreal temple president and the statistics collected by scholars in the past, one finds that men consistently outnumber the women and that new converts tend to be between eighteen and twenty-four. In 1978 the ratio of men to women was 2:1, according to Johnson's study (1976) of the San Francisco temple. Today the ratio is more equal, from 5:4 to 6:5 in favor of men, according to an estimate made by senior members at my request. Between 15 and 20 percent of male devotees are celibate and, except for the *brahmacaris,* these are the leaders. Judah (1974), Johnson (1976), and Rochford (1985) have all noted that young people in their late teens to early twenties tend to join. Out of the twelve interviews with women devotees collected by my students and me, ten were between eighteen and twenty-four when they joined, one was twenty-eight, and another thirty-five. Their social backgrounds vary greatly, so although Johnson's study indicates that devotees are from white upper- middle-class backgrounds, recent research indicates that the appeal of Krishna Consciousness is no longer confined to one class.

When questioned about their reasons for joining ISKCON, most devotees, female and male, would offer theologically correct answers, demonstrating their familiarity with sanskrit texts. This is not to say that many of them did not join because of the most rigorous philosophical investigation or the highest religious motivations. Many devotees appeared to lack psychological insights, some resented what they perceived to be sociological reductionism, and others had absorbed the Krishna worldview so thoroughly that they could understand their former life only in terms of materialism or *maya.* Although a few women described excellent relationships with parents and husbands whom they had reluctantly left behind in their quest for spiritual realization, many women interviewed described difficult family situations that they had managed to escape or resolve by joining ISKCON.[4]

Concerning female patterns of conversion, Rochford (1985) has observed that women convert women in ISKCON, that female recruits tend to encounter the movement through same-sex networks of friends. This appeared to be true of our informants also, and another interesting finding was how many women mentioned having sisters (in the biological sense) in the movement. Because women live in a separate society, or *ashram,* in this NRM, before and after, and (in many cases) even during their married life, it is tempting to speculate that at least part of the initial appeal this spiritual path holds for women is the prospect of living in a peaceful, cooperative feminine society—and not having to deal with men. Mother Parvati describes young women from the counterculture undergoing purification and healing in the women's ashram in 1969.

When I joined the temple in Vancouver, my present husband was then the president, and he asked me to train the women. We were all newcomers then, but I was an older person and I wasn't a hippie. I was able to organize and train the women in *sankirtan,* preaching, and book distribution. When they first came in, they were wearing makeup, chewing gum, and had their bikini marks tattooed to their skin. I trained them in the Vedic rules of cleanliness. Also, some of them were very depressed—they'd been taking drugs, or split up with a boyfriend, so I was a counselor too. They needed to be taken care of—it was almost like a hospital—until they got their spiritual identity.

She paints a vivid picture of the excitement, adventure, and the intense feeling of *communitas* experienced by ISKCON women during their evangelical activity.

We'd go out on book distribution, traveling and preaching all over North America. I did that for six years and was the first woman in ISKCON to head a cross-country expedition for women. I had a Winebago and my own deities inside it. I traveled around with between six to fifteen girls, and we had lots of fun. We were always getting arrested and spent lots of time in jail. . . . They would always let us go. They were easy on women and never afraid of them. . . . We would go to big events like the Calgary Stampede so we could distribute our books nicely. . . . There were six of us in the van living very simply. We each carried a small bag and had no attachments. All the places we went looked the same—the same Holiday Inn, the same

parking lots, chain restaurants—there was rubber stamping all across
the land. The people looked all the same too. . . .
    I had a wonderful time. I remember driving into a strange town
and all the girls were sleeping. There was a tape of Swami Prabhupada
chanting. There was a big full moon and it was very low—sitting right
on the horizon. I felt like I was driving right into the moon.

Another theory worth investigating is that ISKCON provides
refuge from family conflicts, sexual problems, and career pressures. There were a few informants whose stories, related
below, supported this thesis.

Linda, an apostate in her early twenties who had lived in the
Montreal Krishna temple from 1968 to 1969, explained that she
had left home at the age of fourteen because her mother was
arranging to have her committed to a mental institution. Wan-
dering homeless around Montreal, she had encountered some
devotees, and they had persuaded her to stay in the temple and
eventually to become initiated. She enjoyed the way of life,
particularly the morning chanting, but had defected when the
temple president began pressuring her to marry him.

Satisvari, a current devotee and married woman with a baby
girl (interviewed by Dawson student Gemlyn Lewis) gave the
following account of a most unsatisfactory family life, which
had led her to leave home and become a hippie, experimenting
with drugs and living with her boyfriend:

My father was always traveling around the world and was never home.
He had seminars in other countries. My two brothers and four sisters
were always fighting with each other, and also I was involved in every
fight. When my father did come home, he and my mother had fights
about money. And yet, they had enough money, but were always fighting over it. I thought it was maybe because they had too much. I
became a hippie and used to take LSD and many other drugs, and I
used to have sex, but it had no meaning for me. I was never satisfied
with life itself from when I was very young—there was something
missing. I was very confused and frustrated with my life and wouldn't
listen to anyone.

When she was nineteen, her boyfriend took her to the Krishna
temple to visit his friend who had become a devotee. They both

stayed for a year, then became initiated and were married in a traditional Indian wedding.

Devaki relates a similar tale of a flight from a dysfunctional family in her interview with Dawson student Christine Garcia. A twenty-four-year-old married *brahmin* expecting her first child, she joined at the age of eighteen and is still hiding from her wealthy parents. She described her unhappy childhood.

I was born in Vancouver and was an only child. I went to seven private schools, lived in three provinces, and moved five times. This was because my father was a franchise operator for a major national bank. . . . My parents were very materialistic people . . . I always had the best of everything, best schools, best clothes, lived in the best neighborhoods . . . I mean, you name it—I had the best of it! I don't know, it's as if there was always something missing in my life . . . I couldn't help but feel that I was unwanted. I mean, my father had a terrific job . . . this meant my mother could have stayed at home to raise me, but she *needed* her own "identity," so she worked in the personnel department in the same company as my father, making it easier for her to relocate when he got transferred. But for me it was never easy. Well, every time we moved, not only did I get a new nanny . . . but I had to make a whole bunch of friends, often in the middle of a school year, which for me wasn't a very easy thing to do. I was always a very shy and introverted child and I guess that all those feelings of frustration . . . had to channel their way out of my system somehow.

After getting involved in a fast crowd at fourteen in a public school in Manitoba, her parents sent her away to a private school in Connecticut. When her grades declined they sent her to a psychiatrist ("I didn't need a shrink, I needed to be shown that I was loved and wanted!"). Then she stayed at home for a year with a private tutor but, at sixteen, her parents decided to move again, to Quebec City, although no one in the family spoke French. Five months later they moved to Kingston, Ontario.

I would sneak out of the house after my parents were asleep and go and meet my so-called friends and come back home at two or three in the morning. What did we do? Drugs—any kind you can think of I have done. They figured out what was going on about a year later. We had moved from Kingston to Toronto and I was almost eighteen . . . and I decided to drop out of school. The fights . . . went on for ever, but finally they . . . offered to get me a job in their company, but I told them I wanted to make it on my own. Actually, I wanted to be as far away from them as possible because at this point I was a fully-fledged addict. So, to the utter disgust of my parents, I got a job in a bar-salon. It was a shabby place. I was a waitress, got high on my breaks, and after work went out with the gang from work and got completely stoned. . . . My parents . . . tried to force me to go to a drug rehabilitation program. . . . I refused and ran away from home.

I quit my job . . . and moved in with a guy from work, the cook, whom I'd been seeing secretly for about a month. I sold the brand-new Audi that my father had bought me to go to work in so that they wouldn't be able to trace me and I could pay my half of the rent. . . . Now I had plenty of time to get stoned and I did. Soon the money ran out and my boyfriend would threaten to kick me out if I couldn't pay my share, he beat me and I was pregnant.

Well, I definitely had to get away from that guy, so I went to look for this girl who used to work in the bar-salon about a year ago who I knew lived alone, and she had once told me if I ever needed anything not to hesitate to ask her for help. To my surprise, she no longer worked there and I was told she had joined a religious organization called ISKCON. I found out that they were the ones who called them-selves Krishnas. "How weird" I thought at the time. So, I went to see her at the temple on a Sunday at the feast.

When she saw the condition I was in, she took me to a type of infir-mary room. There I was examined and I found out the child I was carrying was dead. She brought me to the hospital incognito to have the child removed. [Why incognito?] Because I was sure my parents were still looking for me and the last thing I wanted was to return to that life of wealth and loneliness. Well, luckily, I was brought there in time so that after the operation I was still able to have children.

I went back to the temple with my friend and decided to stay there for a while until I could get my life back on track again. But the longer I stayed there, the more I felt at peace with myself. I learned a lot about the religion, I stopped taking drugs . . . I had long sessions with the temple president, which was a great influence on my progressively growing peace of mind, and I even started reading the Vedas. . . . Slowly, I began integrating myself into this society, and even though I wasn't theoretically a member yet, I felt, for the first time in my life, as though I truly belonged to a family.

Kamala, another devotee of twenty-four, who had recently married in ISKCON, described her unhappy former life in an interview with Adele Banarjea, student at Concordia University. Her father was a Sicilian immigrant and carpenter, her mother a French uneducated housewife. Both parents would beat her and her sister and, as they themselves had also been abused in childhood, they believed this was the correct way to raise a family. Kamala complained: "I could not speak to them about anything without feeling their rancor, but I was much more afraid of my father. My mother, I dared to ask her about small, practical things. I trusted them to provide me with material necessities, but I was not happy, so at eighteen I left home." She went to a university and achieved good results in pure and applied science, but said,

Everything that I tried was not successful in making me happy: family, school, friends, drugs. I had a great need to understand the meaning of life, but drugs were not helpful—the problems of existence were not solved. Then I became involved with a Yoga group and found that meditation was the first thing I had tried that could alleviate my suffering.

She lived with a young man for two years and when he left her, this broken relationship caused her to revert to the "stressful and anxious state I had been in during my whole childhood. It was the feeling of helplessness, when my father made all the decisions and my mother had to agree. I decided that I did not want to enter into another relationship and wanted to join a religious community." She considered moving to New York to join a Yoga group, but did not have the money and was afraid of living there alone. She then encountered the devotees of Krishna and was attracted by "the perfection of the philosophy which answered all my questions." About her husband, she said:

We have a friendly, trusting relationship. It happens inside a structure of authority that I am familiar with, so I know what to expect from him. He does not surprise me, shock me, like my father did to my mother. I can accept being guided by him because he is more knowledgeable, more enlightened and he guides me according to the teachings of an unbroken line of spiritual masters.

One of the apostates interviewed appears to have joined because she found much joy in *sankirtan* and in serving the

deities at the altar, but the rigid sex roles and the strict segregation of the sexes bothered her so much she rebelled and
made a scene, which led to her defection. In response to the
question, "Was it possible to talk to the men in spite of the
rules?" she answered:

Yes, but it was dangerous. Once I did lose control. I was so embarrassed! That is when I started to think about leaving, for I wondered
what I was doing here—if I stayed I was probably going to attack him.
When it happened, I was behind the altar. The altar is the holiest
place. You have to be really clean, proper, and always have good
thoughts. A *gudjari* was standing up at the altar—he's the guy whose
job is to offer flowers and food at the altar. He was at the second level
of initiation. Anyway, he was a real devotee. Well, he said something to
me, and I answered back with a joke! I also gave him a tap on the
shoulder . . . then I got scared! He didn't say anything. He simply
looked at me, smiled and seemed to wonder. He was nice. The others
would have screamed and made a big scandal out of that. Really, I
don't know what happened, for I split after that.

A recurring theme throughout some of the interviews was
that in looking back on their former lives, ISKCON women saw
themselves as neglected or abused children. Although only two
devotees interviewed claimed their parents had actually beat
them many referred to other devotees who had supposedly
suffered physical or sexual abuse as children at the hands of
male relatives. Ironically, the brainwashing allegations and lawsuits launched by apostates were often explained as the result of
an abusive relationship with their parents. Robin George's
famous multimillion-dollar lawsuit was explained as follows:
"We felt sorry for her, and offered her asylum after she told us
how her parents used to tie her to the toilet and beat her, so we
let her stay, even though we knew she was only 13. Was that
brainwashing?"

Joining the movement, for some women, involved a conscious rejection of their mother as a role model. Many of the
married women voiced a disappointment about their mothers
who had chosen to join the work force instead of being home-
makers, and they expressed a deep satisfaction in choosing to
stay home with their children. Another theme was the sense of

security women felt living in a highly structured society. The ISKCON perception of women as weak, fragile, and in need of protection seemed to resonate with the early life experiences of some of these women. The married women interviewed appeared to accept their husband's superordinate position in the home with good grace because, in their view, it was linked to an unbroken line of discipline succession and therefore their use of power was not (unlike their male relatives and boyfriends in their previous life) based on selfishness and individualism. For this reason they trusted male authority in ISKCON as essentially altruistic and benevolent.

New Opportunities for Women's Leadership

Woman's role in ISKCON has been strictly circumscribed by what American devotees interpret as the "ancient Vedic" way of life. In reality, the patterns of sexuality evolving during the ISKCON's early phase in America were by-products of its emphasis on asceticism and evangelism, and often caricatured Hindu family patterns. The "traditional" *ashramas,* for example, were speeded up in a dramatic fashion. A man could pass through the "householder" phase of life in six years or less—just long enough to father a son and turn him over to a *guru-kula* at the age of five—permitting the ambitious *brahmin* to renounce his wife and enter the *sannyasa* stage before thirty. Since Prabhupada's death in 1977, however, the rate of conversion has declined sharply, more women are joining, and the average age of members is in the early thirties. There is far more emphasis, as a result, on family life and the raising of children. According to estimates made by local leaders, in the mid-seventies around 40 percent of the men were married; today the figure is closer to 80 percent.

There are signs that ISKCON is responding to the needs of married couples and is placing a higher value on the family. Since 1987, the GBC has taken measures that slow the *ashramas* down. Men must wait until the age of forty-five to apply for *sannyasa,* and married men must wait until fifty. It is no longer entirely acceptable for a husband to leave his wife and children for several months to serve Krishna. For example, a local *brah-min* recently decided to accompany the traveling chariot festival for a four-month tour, leaving his wife and two small children in Montreal. His friend described the responses of ISKCON husbands, who warned him it might place a strain on his marriage, and referred to cases in which the husband's long absence had resulted in a marriage breakdown. Another indication of ISKCON's new concern for healthy marriages is a growing tendency for couples to go in for Christian marriage counseling, for there are no equivalent services in ISKCON. In moving away from communalism into familialism, the movement's patterns of sexuality appear to be moving closer to the mainstream.

Recently there have been signs that women are beginning to play a more prominent role in ISKCON'S leadership. This phenomenon appears to arise from three factors: the high attrition rate among the membership, recent setbacks and scandals occurring in the movement, and the opening up of eastern Europe.

The High Attrition Rate. ISKCON's "dropout" rate, which has been estimated as high as 80 percent over a two-year period (Bird and Reimer 1982), awards (by default) spiritual authority to the senior female disciples of Prabhupada over the younger males initiated by the second generation of spiritual masters. One devotee claimed, "Swami Praphupada initiated eight hundred disciples, but less than two hundred of us are left." These early disciples in their forties are less likely to be regarded as temptresses by the men. Mother Parvati responded in her interview to the question, "Isn't it unusual for a woman in ISKCON to have the responsibilities and influence which you have?" as follows.

I am in a unique position because I came to the movement much older than my godsisters. I had experience in business, in organizing programs, and there was a need for my services. . . . I have been jokingly called the "temple president." I was not given that title, but have had that capacity. However, I do not have the capacity of my husband. He has been with the movement longer than I—for eighteen years. . . . Right now, we're the administration of the temple. [My husband] is training the young men and does the book-keeping. . . . While he is away I take over his job and handle the men. Some of the more macho boys don't like being ordered around by a lady, but some of them like it because they see me as a mother. I'm generally accepted by the men as an older, senior devotee in Krishna Consciouness.

Throughout my interview with Parvati, while she was instructing me in woman's role in ISKCON, young male devotees kept coming to her for orders, which she issued in a confident and authoritative manner. "You'd better get to the bank before it shuts or you'll blow our whole plan!" she warned one young *brahmacari*, who backed out of the room, hands clasped in *namaste*, saying, "Right away, Mother Parvati, Hare Bo!" She then resumed her monologue. "Women are weak and less intelligent than men. . . ." As we left her room after the interview, one of the *brahmins* joked, "I see you've been talking to our temple president." Mother Parvati explained serenely, "I do not have that title but I have that capacity."

Recent Schisms and Scandals. The movement has suffered some serious setbacks in the 1980s because of scandals, lawsuits, and schismatic movements resulting from conflicts between the GBC and the initiating gurus. The most dramatic of these involves the murder trial of Kirtananda Swami Bhaktipada, founder of the large farming commune, New Vrindaban, in West Virginia (Rochford 1985; Gelberg 1990). This guru was expelled from ISKCON in 1987 and formed the League of Devotees International. In 1988, he began to initiate women into the *sannyasa* order, a role forbidden them in the Vaisnava tradition, and by 1992 roughly half of the *sannyasis* in the League of Devotees were women (Bozeman 1992, 4–5). As many historians and feminist scholars have noted, during periods of national emergency, or during phases of intense religious persecution, women are more likely to take over men's work and play a role in leadership. ISKCON today evidently needs competent, loyal leaders regardless of their sex. Yadurani Devi Dasi was the first woman to preach in public in the Montreal temple in September 1990, and she was also the first woman to attend a meeting of the GBC (Nov. 3–4, 1990, in Los Angeles). She reports that there are three other "mothers" who preach in public and lead the *kirtan:* Urmilla in Detroit, Kanalini in East Lansing, Michigan, and Jamuna, a "widow" (whose cookbook, *Lord Krishna's Cuisine,* recently won a *New York Times* book award.

Evangelical Activity in Eastern Europe. The opening up of eastern Europe with its "spiritual vacuum" has resulted in a flurry of new (and old) religious evangelism. Yadurani, the most senior female disciple of Swami Prabhupada, has completed two tours of the Balkan countries and eastern Europe, and reports that currently three women are temple presidents in Germany and one in Yugoslavia. One of the most successful missionary tours of the Balkan countries has been a European Bhajan Band composed of six women and a girl who play harmonium, cymbals, and drum and sing devotional songs to Krishna, and perform Indian dance.

Conclusion

The view of gender in ISKCON clearly belongs to what Allen (1984) called the "sex polarity" type. Although the spirit-soul is essentially genderless, once it inhabits a body and moves in society, men and women are viewed as unequal and profoundly different. They live in segregated *ashrams* and pursue different spiritual paths. Women are lower in the scale of purity and evoke pollution fears in the men. Women lack the advantage of semen, and the men believe if they can retain it within the body, it will transform into a powerful fuel facilitating their spiritual advancement.

Women joining the Krishna Conciousness movement tend to be young—in their late teens to early twenties—and tend to be from middle- to upper-middle-class families. Judging from the interviews, they remember their family life as materially privileged but dysfunctional, and themselves as abused or neglected children. Many of them appear to be exchanging the uncontrolled, arbitrary patriarchy of their fathers' rule for what they consider a benevolent system of male protection based on the authority of an ancient lineage of guru succession. The ISKCON community, therefore, beckons to these women as a safe haven where masculine tyranny and passion has no place; where they will find protection and will not be sexually exploited.

Because women tend to join through networks of female friends and relatives (Rochford 1985), there is reason to suggest that one of the initial strong attractions is the segregated woman's *ashram,* or spiritual community. Mother Parvati's metaphor of "driving into the moon" as she traveled with the women's missionary *ashram* eloquently conveys the magic of her own experience within the Krishna-conscious sisterhood.

THREE

Lovers and Leaders in the Rajneesh Movement

Every woman can become an arrow towards godliness—her grace, her beauty, her love, her devotion can show you the way to higher realms of being, great spaces of consciousness.

A woman is not only capable of giving birth to children, she is also capable of giving birth to herself as a seeker of truth. But that side of woman has not been explored at all. I would like my rebellious people to explore that side too.

—Bhagwan Shree Rajneesh

Rajneesh women reject the roles of wife and mother and assume the role of "lover." This role not only has a high cultural value within the movement but is considered a valid spiritual path. Although many Rajneeshee are involved in long-term relationships (particularly the older members and leaders), the most prevalent pattern in the Rajneesh communes (now disbanded) was for men and women to engage in short-term, pluralistic, heterosexual relationships. Because this pattern is unusual among NRMs (particularly the "oriental imports," which tend to arrange marriages or promote celibacy), and because a stigma is attached to sexually promiscuous women in the larger society, the central question in this chapter will be, Why did women choose to live in the Rajneesh communes, which demanded the renunciation of motherhood and marriage and offered a life-style that might be described as a never-ending series of short-lived, intense, and overlapping love affairs?

A close look at the membership reveals data that appear relevant to this question. Rajneesh women are older (about thirty-three to forty) than women in ISKCON and the Unification Church, and are more likely to be recruited from the upper and upper middle classes and to hold graduate degrees. Many of the women interviewed for this study had already achieved success in their professional life before joining the Rajneesh movement, a characteristic that corresponds with the findings of Carter (1987) and Braun (1984).

A second clue to this NRM's appeal for women can be found in discourses of Rajneesh; these exalt women over men and paint utopian visions of a new age based on a radical restructuring of relations between the sexes. Rajneesh provides glimpses of a new spiritually liberated woman, a female Buddha, who is physically beautiful and sexually expressive, who shall rule in the new millennium after two-thirds of the world's population has been decimated by AIDS, and who will build a society characterized by ecological harmony, technological advancement and meditative consciousness. Considering this striking material and on the basis of the interview data, it is worth investigating the possibility that one of the main attractions of this NRM is Rajneesh's philosophy of sexuality. Several *sannyasins* who had encountered Rajneesh while on the "guru circuit" in India noted approvingly that he was unique among Indian gurus in that he did not put down women or insist on celibacy, but, on the contrary, emphasized that sex is the path to enlightenment.

Considering this and other sources, I would argue that this movement attracts a *type* of woman: the middle-aged, upper-middle-class woman who is accustomed to independence and a lucrative employment, and who tends to be childless, unmarried, and highly educated. Moreover, this type of woman chooses to participate in this NRM because it offers an alternative philosophy of sexuality that is consistent with her previous life-style, and that validates her life choices. Finally, it will be argued on the basis of data found in the interviews that the role of "lover," as defined by Rajneesh, is perceived by these women as offering *religious* solutions to problems of intimacy and family life that they have encountered in their previous life.

To present a coherent picture of Rajneeshee sexuality we must first look at the history of Rajneesh's movement, and then describe his philosophy of sexuality and the sex roles and sexual relationships that developed in his communes.

The History

The founder-leader of the movement, Mohan Chandra Rajneesh, was born in 1931 to a Jain family in Kuchwada, India. A former philosophy professor who claimed to have achieved enlightenment at the age of twenty-one, Rajneesh traveled throughout India giving lectures in which he expounded his eclectic and controversial ideas. Statements such as "Never deny the body" and "Sex is the first step to superconsciousness" led the Indian press to dub him "the sex guru." He settled down in an *ashram* in Poona in 1974 where he attracted large crowds of western disciples. Visiting therapists from the human potential movement were invited to set up "groups." Among them were Paul Lowe, founder of Europe's first growth center, Quaesitor; Michael Barnett, author of *People Not Psychiatry;* and Leonard Zunin, a Californian psychologist on the American Board of Psychiatry and Neurology. Their *sannyasin* names were, respectively, Teertha, Somendra, and Siddha. According to Rajneesh's devotee-biographer, "these therapists had given up all the rewards of wealth and prestige . . . because they found in Bhagwan . . . the only spiritual master who fully understood the concept of holistic psychology . . . a means of bringing individuals to higher levels of meditative consciousness" (Joshi 1982, 124). In 1975, the ashram offered encounter and gestalt groups. By 1979, sixty different therapies were offered as well as Eastern meditations such as yoga, vipasana, Sufi dancing, and tai chi.

The therapy groups were a major source of income for the movement. *Time* (Jan. 16, 1978, 57) reported that between 1975 and 1978, more than fifty thousand "seekers" had visited Poona to try out the famous groups. According to a lengthy study in the *Oregonian* newspaper, "For Love and for Money" (1985), they drew from one to two thousand participants a year, and claimed in a financial statement filed with Maharashthra state charity officials in 1980 that therapy accounted for $188,253 of the movement's savings.

In 1981, Rajneesh withdrew his physical presence from the evening *darshan* and went into silence. The *ashram*'s head therapist, Swami Anand Teertha, began to perform the initiation ritual of "taking sannyas," and presided over blessings and "energy darshan" as a "medium for Bhagwan."

In 1981, Rajneesh and his core group moved to the United States where they bought a ranch in Oregon and began to construct the city of Rajneeshpuram based on the utopian ideals of sharing, equality, meditative consciousness, ecological harmony, and sexual communism. It was woman-ruled and grew at an extraordinary rate in land cultivation, tourism, and building construction, mainly because of the regimen of "worship"—the twelve-hour day of unpaid labor in which not the task itself, but the consciousness brought to a task was emphasized.

Sheela, Rajneesh's personal secretary, took over the leadership of the commune after he became silent and apparently attempted to usurp his spiritual authority, conferring upon herself the title Boddhisattva and wearing what were later burned as "Sheela's pope's robes."

The twenty-seven head therapists raised money for the city by conducting groups at RIMU (Rajneesh International Meditation University) for visitors to Rajneeshpuram. They also toured the international Rajneesh communes, which had begun to sprout in 1983 in Germany, Japan, Australia, Holland, England, and Montreal, where they were enthusiastically received as ambassadors of the utopian society at Rajneeshpuram. They offered groups that were attended by local *sannyasins,* commune members, and outsiders. These therapy groups were not unlike revival meetings, and the therapists inspired and revitalized the local religious communities as mediums for "Bhagwan's energy."

In 1984, Rajneesh came out of silence and began to predict the death of two-thirds of humanity through the disease AIDS by the year 2000. *Sannyasins* were advised by the Rajneesh Medical Corporation to wear condoms and rubber gloves while love making, and to refrain from kissing.

Rajneesh held a press conference on September 4, 1985, in which he announced that Sheela had defected after attempting to poison three core group members, bugging his private chambers, and leaving the commune $55 million in debt (*Rajneesh Times* September 20, 1985, 1). Rajneesh was arrested, charged with various illegalities, and pressured to leave the United States as part of a plea bargain. After a world tour, he settled down in the old Poona *ashram* and "left his body" in January 1990. International *sannyasins* continue to gather at Poona to participate in meditation courses, and communicate daily through a computer network. Since the communes disbanded in 1986, the group's patterns of sexuality have become less extreme. There is a higher proportion of male leaders, women can have babies, the AIDS precautions are left up to the individual's discretion, and "free love" appears to be going out of fashion.[1]

Rajneesh's Philosophy of Sexuality

Rajneesh's ideas on sex roles and sexuality can be found throughout his discourses and (in a more concentrated form) in *The Book* (1984), which is a codification of his thought listed in alphabetical order. *A New Vision of Women's Liberation* (1987) also offers a coherent picture of his philosophy of sexuality, the main components of which can be summed up as follows.

Rajneesh equates sexual with meditative states of consciousness and recommends exploring one's sexuality as a spiritual path leading to enlightenment, the "cosmic orgasm": "Meditation is a by-product of orgasmic experience. . . . What happens? Time stops, thinking disappears. . . . To be exactly true, meditation is a non-sexual orgasm" (*NVWL*:28).

He states that people are naturally polygamous and that women have more sexual "energy" than men, hence are spiritually more evolved: "Women are capable of multiple orgasms, man is not. Sexually man is very poor compared to woman. . . . She had not even started and you are finished—that is very embarrassing. Because of this fear man has repressed women all over the world" (*The Book,* see "Woman").

He advocates "free love," calling marriage "the coffin of the love" (*The Rajneesh Bible* 1985). He views marriage as man's attempt to own and control women, and also as the cowardly attempt to cling to love, which is, as he sees it, essentially ephemeral and changing.

He emphasizes the individual's autonomy and the necessity for nonattachment and solitude on the spiritual path. He claims that women are more self-sufficient and independent than men.

He recommends living in communes and renouncing the family: "The biological family must be destroyed. Only the spiritual family will remain" (*The Sound of Running Water* 1978).

He discourages parenthood and pregnancy for three reasons: because of the overpopulation of the planet, because it degrades woman to a baby factory, and because it interferes with individual self-development. He approves of test tube babies as a method of eugenics for the future: "The scientific thing would be for every hospital to have a sperm bank . . . and a couple can have an absolutely definite choice about what kind of child they want. . . . And the sperm should be provided by the hospital and injected into the woman, so from the very beginning the idea of possessiveness is cut. . . . This is getting out of the imprisonment of biology. . . . The father is unknown and the mother has only provided her womb; the child belongs to the commune . . . possessiveness is out of the question . . . within a few years . . . eggs from the mother can also have a bank in the hospital, and the womb can be mechanical. It will look inhuman at the beginning but it will create a far better society" (*NVWL*:86).

As the passages above illustrate, Rajneesh has developed a philosophy of sexuality that is quite as radical and elaborate as those of Ann Lee, Joseph Smith, and John Humphrey Noyes. The latter's ideas on "philopropogativeness" resemble Rajneesh's notions of parenthood expressed above. Moreover, like these millenarian prophets of the past, and the Reverend Sun Mying Moon today, his ideas on sexuality are inextricably bound up with his unique version of the new millennium.

My own vision is that the coming age will be the age of woman. Man had tried for five thousand years and failed. . . . It is enough! Now feminine energies have to be released. . . . And unless women become enlightened they cannot be really free because enlightenment is the ultimate in freedom. The freedom of women cannot come through stupid movements like Women's Liberation. . . . If we can create a few woman Buddhas in the world then woman will be freed from all chains and fetters. . . . Love is going to be her meditation . . . that is going to be her path towards light, towards godliness. And out of love woman will have a new birth. She will become a child of light, a child of moonlight. . . . And you can see that thousands of women are gathered around me. It has never happened before. It has always been a male-dominated quest. (*The Book,* see "Woman")

   Rajneesh's model of gender could be categorized as *sex polarity.* By stressing the difference between men and women but also their inequality, he clearly fits Allen's first type. However, in insisting on the natural superiority of women, rather than men, Rajneesh belongs with Mary Daly (1974) and Lesbian Wiccan leader, Zsussana Budapest (1978) in a relatively rare subtype of this category—what Allen terms "reverse sex polarity."

   The following story appears in a collection of Rajneesh's taped discourses, entitled *A New Vision of Women's Liberation,* in which he expounds his views on women.

But that God is also a male chauvinist. In the Christian trinity there is no place for a woman. All are men: the father, the son, the holy ghost. It is a gay men's club. I am reminded that when God first created the world He created them equal. But, looking at the world, you can understand—whoever has created it is a little stupid.

   He created man and woman, and made a small bed for them to sleep in. The bed was so small that only one person could sleep in it. They were equal, but the woman insisted she would be on the bed— he should sleep on the floor. . . . You will be surprised to know that the first night in existence was the beginning of pillow fights.

   They had to go to God. And the solution is very simple—just make a king-sized bed; any carpenter could have done it. But God is a man, and is just as prejudiced as any other man: he demolished the woman, destroyed her. And then he created Eve, but now woman was no longer equal to man—she was created from one of Adam's ribs; so she was just to serve man, to take care of man, to be used by man. Christians don't tell you the whole story. They start their story from Adam and Eve—but Eve is already reduced to a state of slavery. And since that day woman has lived in slavery in thousands of ways. Financially she has not been allowed to be independent. . . . Educationally she has not been allowed to be equal to man. . . . Religiously she has not been allowed to read the scriptures. . . .

   Woman's wings have been cut in many ways. And the greatest harm that has been done to her is marriage, because neither man nor woman

is monogamous; psychologically they are polygamous. So their whole psychology has been forced against its own nature. And because woman was dependent on man she had to suffer all kinds of insults. . . .
   To satisfy his polygamous nature, man created prostitutes. Prostitutes are a by-product of marriage. . . . And to destroy a woman by making her a prostitute is the ugliest murder you can do. (*A New Vision of Woman's Liberation* 1987, 22–23)

Obviously this tale is not a serious treatment of Genesis, but would be understood as a lighthearted parody of the Old Testament story. Nevertheless, it does convey a vivid sense of Rajneesh's ideas on gender. Rajneesh appears to be extrapolating on Jewish legends of Lilith, which addressed the problem of the two contrasting accounts of Creation (Philips 1984, 38). According to *Midrash Rabab*, Lilith refused to be subservient to Adam, because she and he were created simultaneously. When Adam tried to force her to lie with him in the "missionary position," she spoke the name of God and escaped to the Red Sea, where she lay with demons (Ginzberg 1937, 65–66).

The first woman, Rajneesh tells us, was strong, independent, and incompatible with Adam. Contemporary woman, modeled on Eve, is weak by comparison. She is out of touch with her wild, rebellious nature, condemned by the Christians to be a slave and prostitute, a shadowy projection of masculine desires. He is urging women to join his commune, where they can throw off their shackles, discover their true strength, indulge their polyandrous tendencies, and as the "pillars of his temple," assume positions of leadership to usher in the New Age of Woman.

Gender Roles

Before attempting to describe Rajneeshee sex roles and sexual mores, it is important to note the following impediments to accuracy and clarity. First, Rajneesh often contradicts his own statements and this could have some bearing on the fact that different *sannyasins* express widely different interpretations of what "Bhagwan says." Second, patterns of family life have changed throughout the movement. They were at their most extreme during the Rajneeshpuram era (1981 to 1985), and since the communes have disbanded these patterns have become less deviant, more "mainstream." Finally, although the international communes were modeled on Rajneeshpuram, they were by no means identical in their patterns of sexuality and leadership to it or to one another.

True to Rajneesh's vision of women as "the pillars of my temple," women dominated the leadership of the movement (except for Bhagwan "Himself"). Braun notes that women controlled more than 80 percent of executive positions in Rajneeshpuram. In the Montreal Rajneesh commune in 1985, the work was divided into ten departments, or "temples": kitchen, construction, cooking, cleaning, reception, restaurant, secretary, graphics, and accounting. Eight of the department heads were women. Both communes made a self-conscious effort to abolish sex divisions in work roles. Rajneeshpuram women were conspicuous in their operation of heavy earth-moving equipment used in the massive construction program. *Penthouse* admiringly describes beautiful, scantily clad, teenage girls driving bulldozers, and the videocassette *The Way of the Heart* shows Maneesha directing building wearing a hard hat and work boots. In Montreal, a swami ran the commune's day care and the directors of the commune were women, Paras (1983–85) and Kudai (1985–86). Woman and men worked side by side in a playful and flirtatious atmosphere. Female coordinators were called "moms" and in Rajneeshpuram the core group was referred to as the "supermoms." Swamis interviewed would explain the female leadership as a means to achieve true equality because "Bhagwan says woman are much more in touch with the heart, more receptive and grounded, less likely to get caught up in power trips."

Women in Ritual

Women were dominant in ritual and were considered to have superior charismatic qualities to men in that they were more receptive than men, therefore a better receptacle for "Bhagwan's energy." Rajneesh was constantly accompanied by his core

group of attractive women, who surrounded his chair during the evening discourses. Belfrage (1984) describes the participation of Vivek, Maneesha, and Laxmi during the initiation *darshans* in Poona. The women who danced around Rajneesh's chair as he sat enthroned during his silence were mediums. The mediums performed the *energy darshans* and exhibited charismatic gifts; "they would whirl around filled with Bhagwan's energy and then they would touch us and zap!" A former *sannyasin* claimed their function was "to transmit Bhagwan's *Shakti* to his disciples." Former mediums claimed to have hàd sexual contact with Bhagwan for the purpose of "stimulating our lower chakras," "rewiring my circuits," and "orchestrating our energies" (Gordon 1987, 79).

Sexual Identity

Although Rajneesh emphasizes that men and women possess very different spiritual qualities, there was a tendency to undermine sexual distinctions in the Montreal commune. This was evident in the unisex look in clothing and in the living arrangements. In Poona, women and men both wore loose shifts and waist-length hair (Gunther 1979, photo essay). Once the group moved to America, members abandoned the hippie look and men and women cut their hair short and wore loose elegant trousers and tank tops. When I first began to visit the Montreal commune I was struck by the men's fashion for earrings and perfume and low-necked T-shirts, which, to the untutored eye, might be mistaken for the "gay look." Unlike the Unification Church and ISKCON, there was no segregation of the sexes in living arrangements. Bathrooms, bedrooms, and dining tables were shared by both sexes.

Commune life appeared to foster close friendships between the sexes. Men and women would confide in each other and receive advice and comfort about their love affairs. Men were physically affectionate with each other in a manner unusual in North American culture, and were constantly hugging, roughhousing, and wrestling on the floor. It was not unusual to see a man sitting on another man's lap weeping and the other stroking his hair. Women embraced each other constantly and it was customary for women to sit facing each other, one on the other's lap with her legs locked around her waist to be rocked like a child, particularly after "heavy" time in a therapy group.[2] Homosexuality, however, was not encouraged. Commune members claimed there were no homosexuals among them, except for a bisexual Lesbian couple. Several members claimed that when the group moved to Oregon, Sheela had announced that all the homosexuals had to leave. However, homosexuality is not considered sinful or abominable (as in the UM or ISKCON), but a cowardly "cop out." Teertha's response to a self-confessed Lesbian in his therapy group was, "You are trying to hide from the terror of the unknown. Your own sex is a small puzzle, the opposite sex is a big puzzle."

Sexual Relationships

The Montreal commune could be described as an ongoing sex therapy workshop in which short-term, pluralistic sexual relationships were the norm. This pattern was based on an ideal of communal sharing and equality in love and on Rajneesh's emphasis on sexual expression. There were various control mechanisms in the group that reinforced and regulated this pattern of sexual behavior. The Rajneesh therapy groups, which aspiring initiates were obliged to participate in, employed exercises and techniques that encouraged members to release inhibitions, express sexual feelings, and learn new patterns of sexual relating. The ritual "hug" with which members frequently greeted each other and resorted to in order to refresh their spirits during their twelve-hour workdays encouraged physical intimacy among members, but was understood as reinforcing their spiritual identity and revitalizing their "connection to Bhagwan," whose "energy" was immanent in the community, or *sangha*. Sexual feelings were interpreted as charismatic indications of Bhagwan's presence flowing between his disciples. It was common to see a man and woman seated opposite each other in the café, holding the other's hand pressed against their chests with their eyes closed and breathing deeply. When I first inquired about this behavior I was told they were "feeling the heart connection."

Although there was a strong pressure exerted by the community on the individual to behave in a way that would probably be considered sexually hyperactive and promiscuous in the larger society, there was also much evidence in the interviews that members enjoyed some degree of choice and autonomy in their private lives. For example, one of the female directors informed me that for her first year in the commune she had remained celibate. The other director had been with the same lover for seven years. I noticed that the older and more established members, particularly the leaders, seemed to be involved in long-term relationships.

This appeared to be the pattern also in Rajneeshpuram, where many of the supermoms and therapists were married or lived with long-term lovers. Exclusive sexual relationships, however, were frowned upon. One swami outside the commune, who admitted to being happily married for fifteen years, added, "I couldn't stand being married to a woman who was faithful!"

While interviewing commune members, I received the impression that long-term lovers were *secretly* faithful to each other. It was a prevalent notion that "sharing energy" with others enriched one's love affair, and that one's lover would lose interest, the "energy" would become "stuck," if one were too devoted and exclusive. For those suffering from jealousy, the recommended panacea was to find another lover, which might succeed in renewing one's original lover's interest. Judging from accounts in interviews and public confessions in therapy groups, the members' love lives appeared to be a never-ending struggle between maintaining a strong diadic relationship and integrating it with a group that demanded communal sharing.

Couples joining the movement or entering the commune seemed, almost inevitably, to split up and find new lovers. Many members claimed to have been with many lovers the first year or two in the commune but eventually settled down with one person. Women, who outnumbered the men by a small margin and tended to be slightly older, were encouraged to be the sexual aggressors. One swami, who had lived in Rajneeshpuram, said, "It was pretty common to have a woman come up to you on the street and say, 'Look, I've seen you around the last couple of days and I find you very attractive.' And then you'd go off for coffee and probably end up in bed." It was not uncommon to see couples in the commune in which the woman was at least ten years older than the man; there was a conscious effort to abolish ageist attitudes.[3]

Love and Therapy

In many ways Rajneesh lovers seem to view their sexual relationships as therapy rather than as marriage. Self-expression takes precedence over mutual cooperation. The peculiar compromise between intimacy and autonomy found in the Rajneesh lover relationship appears to have its origins in therapy. In the early 1970s the Rajneesh movement began to offer an eclectic range of Esalen-style therapies to visitors in the Poona *ashram*. Therapists from the Human Potential Movement conducted "groups" that emphasized Reichian and "tantric" techniques for releasing sexual inhibitions, and forged new patterns of self-other relating, including a new code of sexual ethics (Palmer and Bird 1992). Attitudes and qualities fostered in encounter groups, such as "trust," "being open," and "sharing," were also applied to initiating and maintaining a sexual relationship. There was a ritual aspect to the sexual confessions and problems revealed in therapy groups. Commune members were not just being honest about their problems, they were responding to what got a positive response from the group or the therapist. Some kinds of problems, such as jealousy or uncontrollable sexual attraction, received enthusiastic applause; others, such as physical revulsion or Lesbian impulses, evoked a poor response. Hence, those on the hot seat were seeking acceptance, and perhaps a sense of what Kanter (1972) called "communion" with the whole group, the charismatic community.[4]

Bellah, Madsen, Sullivan, Swidler, and Tipton (1985) have described the therapeutic relationship in terms that might be applied to Rajneesh lovers. They characterize the communication between therapist and client as "peculiarly distanced, circumscribed and asymmetrical," and quote a patient's view of her relationship with her psychiatrist.

The focus is really on one person, and there isn't a relationship outside of the circumscribed one. And yet it's a relationship with a very narrow and a very, very deep nature. And so there can be a kind of frankness that isn't possible with a more sort of vested interest. And yet the distance is exactly what makes it possible to reveal so much. (Bellah et al. 1985, 122)

Bellah et al. go on to examine the benefits of the asymmetrical aspect of the therapeutic relationship in that it "encourages people to see . . . the relationship as a means to their own ends, not an end of which they are a part or an enduring set of practices that unifies their ends" (Bellah et al. 1985, 122). They note the absence of moral values in this kind of relationship, for the therapist's authority rests on his/her psychological insight and clinical skills.

These authors have suggested that the therapeutic relationship provides the kind of training needed in a complex, functionally differentiated society, particularly in professional and managerial life, for "we often have to relate to others briefly, specifically, and sometimes intensely and it is here we need to be 'better communicators'" (123). Because many Rajneesh women have held management positions or worked at successful professions, and have also been enthusiastic participants in the Human Potential Movement, it appears likely that they would be familiar with the therapeutic relationship before entering the commune. Many members interviewed described commune life as "personal growth" or as an opportunity to develop interpersonal skills. "I have found that *relating* is more important than having a relationship. The main thing is to be authentic in every interaction as opposed to trying to form a permanent attachment."

Several *sannyasins* expressed the notion that through cultivating intense and honest relationships with others in the commune, they were able to establish a deeper, more authentic relationship with themselves. One woman claimed she even went so far as to "fall in love with myself."

When my lover left me I was very sad and I cried and talked to my friends, but after a while I began to realize, well he was beautiful, but I am beautiful too. Here I was, pouring out all these painful emotions, and my friends were saying, "We think it's really beautiful, what you're going through." And then I realized that that was what I had learned from Bhagwan—that I could love myself exactly as I was right that moment—that I could even fall in love with myself!

One recently initiated *sannyasin* describes his bafflement in having to adjust to new expectations in his relationship with women inside the commune. His frustration focused on the expressive and cathartic approach his Rajneesh girlfriend adopted toward their relationship, while he was expecting her to cooperate in establishing rules that would guarantee their mutual satisfaction.

It's like living in the twilight zone—there's never any resolution. Like, it's considered perfectly okay for a couple to live in the same house and not speak to each other for two weeks because they need the space.
I took U. to a restaurant last night and I was trying to tell her all the frustrations I felt in our relationship—how I never knew what to expect—whether she'd come back each night or whether she'd disappear for days, and I looked at her and her eyes were shining in total admiration. She said, "I love it when you express your energy—I feel all this passion coming from you"—and I realized she hadn't listened to a word I'd said, but was simply admiring the way I was expressing myself as Bhagwan says you should from the heart. She had no interest in changing her behavior to make our relationship work. When we go to the Saturday night party at the center, U. likes to go off and be her own woman. I'll be dancing and suddenly look up; and she'll be gyrating in the corner with some handsome young devil or sitting on someone's lap. This beautiful woman wanted to sit on my lap and I was really uncomfortable and she asked what was wrong, and I said, "I don't want to hurt U.'s feelings" and she looked surprised and gave me a lecture about following my own impulse in the moment and said if I didn't get centered in myself, U. would lose interest in me. So I began fondling her and she was right. U. came over and started paying attention to me again.

By "surrendering to Bhagwan" and living in a commune, it could be argued that the disciples of Rajneesh have overcome some of the narrowness and limitations of the therapeutic relationship that Bellah et al. describe. The unique combination of intimacy and autonomy, the compromise between individualism and collectivism, between closeness and distance that the Rajneesh communes have developed was eloquently expressed by a female *sannyasin*.

> We are individuals who accept our aloneness joyfully. When I feel an impulse to hang on to someone else, I just watch it. At times I feel so empty inside, but Bhagwan says, when you feel lonely, don't run around trying to find someone, just stay at home and celebrate your loneliness! Of course, we don't have a lot of time to sit and be lonely. Most of the time we are working shoulder to shoulder doing things. . . . In the commune the emphasis is on the individual, away from roles and relationships. We are no longer identified with our roles, our skills, our talents.

The Members

If one compared the members of the Rajneesh movement with those of other communal-style NRMs, which are the most likely groups to develop alternative sex roles and patterns of family life, one finds that the Rajneeshee tend to be older and to have more female members.

Previous studies suggest that the average age of a Rajneeshee is between thirty-five and forty. Kirk Braun claims that in 1981 the mean age of Rajneeshpuram residents was thirty-seven (Braun 1982, 71). Fitzgerald cited a survey by the University of Oregon's Department of Psychology, which found the average age of Rajneeshpuram residents to be thirty-four in 1985 (Fitzgerald 1986, 58). Carter notes that Rajneesh members do not fit into Levine's rite de passage theory of cult conversion (Levine 1984) because:

> Rajneesh are almost uniformly older and at a later stage in their lives before turning to the movement and rather than chance recruitment by strangers as described by Levine (1984), sannyasins indicate an active pursuit of Rajneesh training after referral by friends. Some have been drawn by advertised therapies. (Carter 1987, 164–65)

TABLE 2. Montreal Rajneesh Commune
Membership Data, 1985

	Women	Men
Average age	34.25	32.71
Number of members	31	28
Youngest	22	24
Oldest	55	47

The statistics in table 2 were given to me by Khudai, the director of the Montreal commune.

The Montreal residents are younger in mean age than the Rajneeshpuram residents (in their early, as opposed to late, thirties). This is perhaps because of their attracting many recent local converts; Rajneeshpuram was established by the older (in years of involvement) core group of disciples.

Rajneesh recruits tend to come from upper-middle-to middle-class families. They conform closely to Donald Stone's typical participant in the Human Potential Movement, who tends to be thirty-five, single or divorced, and "never having had children" (Stone 1976). Because most Rajneeshee continue to live in the world after initiation and tend to join later in their lives than ISKCON devotees, they are far more likely to hold postgraduate degrees or to have established themselves in their careers, as Fitzgerald and Braun have noted. "Eighty percent of the disciples came from middle-class or upper-middle-class backgrounds; their fathers were, overwhelmingly, professionals or businessmen. Some eighty-three percent of the Rajneeshee had attended college; two-thirds had bachelor degrees, and twelve percent had doctorates" (Fitzgerald 1986, 58).

Carter's research project at Washington State University arrived at a similar conclusion about the social background of *sannyasins*.

Initiates are almost uniformly drawn from the apparently successful either aristocratic Europeans or accomplished professionals from Europe, the United States, Canada, Japan, India. Members include attorneys, physicians, writers, artists, academicians, and other professionals. Many sannyasins characterize themselves as the "dropouts" from the top of society and indicate disillusionment with bureaucratic institutions and industrial societies. (Carter 1987, 163)

The ratio of women to men has fluctuated during the different phases of the movement, and there are conflicting reports. However, it is clear that women in the Poona *ashram* outnumbered the men. A photo-diary of Poona published by the RFI, *The Sound of Running Water,* states, "Women outnumber the men three to one. In this way our group resembles the following of Buddha and Lao Tzu whose disciples were mainly women" (1980).

Hugh Milne's estimate is less dramatic. He writes: "Of the thousand or so sannyasis at least six hundred were women, and nearly all were sexually active. All who come, female and male, had been attracted at least in part by a guru who advocated sexual experiment of the freest kind" (Milne 1986, 134).

The discrepancy between these two ratios, 3:1 and 6:4, is probably accounted for if one assumes that the first estimate refers to the permanent residents of Poona, and the second includes the visitors. Neither account makes this clear.

Milne complains about the shortage of women in the Chidvilas *ashram* in New Jersey, and during the first winter on the ranch, but once Rajneeshpuram was established and began attracting visitors to its summer festivals, women again outnumbered men by a slight margin, according to former residents I interviewed. None of them, even a woman who had been in charge of statistics, could quote any exact figures.

Two long-term residents at Poona and Rajneeshpuram guessed that there were 15 percent more women there. Montreal commune members sometimes commented on their fortunate situation in having almost an equal ratio—31:28 in favor of women.

The inevitable question that this sex ratio and portrait of members raises is, What is it about the Rajneesh movement that attracts women, and women of the single, childless, financially advantaged, middle-aged variety in particular? To answer this question it is important to look at studies of the dilemmas, social, emotional, and "romantic," that confront this class of women in America. The theories of Glendon (1985), Berger and Kellner (1974), and Bellah et al. (1985) are relevant to understanding recent changes in family patterns and women's roles.

The Appeal of the Rajneesh Communes for Women

As a casual reading of *A New Vision of Women's Liberation* will demontrate, Rajneesh has some interesting things to say about sexuality and spiritual life. He presents in his discourses visions of a new society based on woman's sexual, social, and spiritual liberation. His movement is aspiring to realize his vision through fostering new attitudes toward sexual relationships and family life. Among the more striking aspects of this new religion that distinguish it from other movements are:

1. The number of women in positions of authority
2. The discouraging of exclusive couples and the rejection of marriage
3. The fostering of immediate intimacy with no courting stage
4. The ban on pregnancy and childbirth and the loosening of parent-child bonds.

The inevitable question arises. What does all this mean in terms of its significance for individual female adherents, and as a response to, reflection of, modern family life?

Recent changes in sex roles and family life have come about as a result of the woman's liberation movement, the homosexual movement, the sexual revolution with its emphasis on nonprocreative sex, and the increased emphasis on individual happiness and autonomy (Stone 1977; Glendon 1085). These changes have taken their emotional toll on individuals, and have created considerable confusion concerning the basic rules governing interpersonal relationships and sexual identity. It is reasonable to assume that those individuals who have chosen to remain single and childless are among the most sensitive to these trends, and perhaps the most affected by anomie. Rajneesh's message attracts exactly this kind of individual: the

Sannyasins in the Montreal commune. Courtesy Montreal Osho Meditation Center (MOMC).

childless, single, sexually active adult. Why? One answer might be found in the therapeutic effect of his message, which validates and lends religious meaning to a sexually permissive lifestyle, and thus reducing his followers' sense of anomie. The reassuring and therapeutic aspects of his thought are reinforced in the movement's institutions in several ways.

First, the Rajneesh International Meditation University encourages new members to participate in therapy groups that offer cathartic techniques designed to purify them of guilt and to release repressions. By this means, feelings of failure or inadequacy at their inability to conform to their parents' and society's expectations—and their expectations of themselves—are purged.

Second, the sexual drive and nonprocreative sexual relationships are elevated to a high status and endowed with religious meaning. The inability of many contemporary women to form lasting relationships with men is no longer viewed as neurotic, but is interpreted as a restless longing for union with the Absolute/Bhagwan, and as one of the inevitable pitfalls on the path toward enlightenment.

Third, a provision of support mechanisms in the community assists and educates women in handling the emotional divagations of a sexually promiscuous life-style. The availability of counselors, therapists, and the considerable influence of the group over couple relationships are means by which the individual can share, exorcise, or reinterpret feelings of rejection, jealousy, inadequacy, and rejection.

Having described Rajneesh patterns of sexuality and examined the statistical evidence for determining what kind of woman joins, one might begin to address the question raised at the outset of this chapter: What attracts women to these communes that demand the renunciation of marriage and motherhood and foster short-term, pluralistic sexual relationships?

Four "Spiritual Solutions" to Woman's Changing Role

On the basis of interview data and impressions received as a participant observer, I will propose that the Rajneesh communes offer women four main "solutions" to the confusion and dilemmas arising from changing male-female relationships in the larger society. These four solutions are:

1. A female-dominated leadership
2. An opportunity to reject or gain a distance from traditional feminine roles
3. A solution to the problem of aging and remaining "attractive"
4. An environment in which the role of "lover" is clearly defined, validated, and "spiritualized."

A Female-dominated Leadership. The Rajneesh communes allow women to participate in an experiment with matriarchy. Considering that women hold more than 80 percent of leadership posts, and that more women join than men, it seems fair to assume a relationship between these factors. Descriptions of the "Power Ladies" at Poona, or the "Supermoms" in Rajneeshpuram, portray women who were highly educated and accustomed to jobs that involved responsibility and authority, and were well acquainted with the ideologies of the feminist movement (Braun 1982; Belfrage 1982; *Oregonian* 1985). One suspects that these women might feel less at home in the male-dominated Unificationist or Krishna Consciousness movements.

A Distancing from Traditional Feminine Roles. A recurring theme throughout the interviews with women in the Montreal commune was their ambivalent feelings about motherhood and their disillusionment with marriage. For many of them, joining the commune appeared to be a way of resolving inner conflicts about these roles, or a means of absolving themselves from guilt resulting from their inability to live up to their parents' expectations, or their own internalized preconceptions of women's roles. For example, one thirty-seven-year-old resident described the conflict she had experienced in trying to juggle career, love affairs, and the possibility of parenthood, and how she had resolved these conflicts by entering the commune.

All through my twenties I was preoccupied with marriage and babies, but I never found a suitable partner. . . . So I decided three years ago to go back to school and get my master's and train for a profession so I would be able to support my kids but then I went to the ranch in the summer of 1983. I was talking to Arup about my strong desire for children, and she explained to me that that was not what was happening there. They didn't have the facilities for small children, and that was not the way the energy was moving. I was disappointed, and I sat down and asked myself, "Is this the most important thing for me?" . . . and then I realized that the most important thing was being a *sannyasin.*

Another woman, a forty-one-year-old former teacher, explained how living in the commune had resulted in her renouncing the maternal role.

For a while my nine-year-old son was living with me in the commune, but he freaked out one day when we had this group. Everyone in the house was screaming and bashing pillows and running around crying—letting it all out—and he phoned his father and said [imitating a child weeping], "Papa, venez m'amener chez toi!" . . . I don't blame him, I know how he felt; if I had someone I could call up and say, "Come and take me away," I would do it. So, since then he lives with his father.

For one thirty-one-year-old woman, who had led an idyllic life in the country with her husband and child making leather shoes and bags, joining the commune was presented as a solace and a means of rejecting roles that had painful associations.

When I read my first book of Bhagwan, I was feeling very desperate. My two-year-old daughter had just died of leukemia and I had spent months watching her die. We were very close and I was breast-feeding her. Right after she died, my husband, whom I'd lived with for ten years, left me. When I found Bhagwan it was as if I had been dying of thirst and someone had come along and offered me a long, cool glass of water. I became initiated right away. I have my lover here and I will never be married again. I will never have children.

For this woman, moving into the commune was a radical solution to her grief and disillusionment with marriage: "When I moved into the commune, I knew there was no other path for me. It was suicide or *sannyas.*"

Several women presented commune life as a therapeutic environment in which they could heal emotional wounds inflicted by their experiences in family life. For example, one thirty-nine-year-old woman told the following story.

I had been interested in spiritual matters since I was a child. I was singularly unimpressed with life as it was lived on a material level. . . . My natural parents were always fighting, always unhappy. I watched their games and their hypocrisy and saw that they were completely unavailable to love. . . . They weren't married, and first my mother split and then my father decided he couldn't handle me and left too. I remember how we were living in a high-rise and he took me over to the next door apartment and asked them to watch me for minute—I was only four. I looked him right in the eyes and I knew exactly what he was doing and why and I remember feeling sorry for him that he couldn't be available to love.

This woman presented commune life as an alternative family environment: "Living in the commune, I get plenty of mothering—the whole place is run by mamas. There is space in the commune to heal; the focus is on personal growth and I feel support. People here are open to love." Her decision never to have children was explained as a therapeutic recapitulation and healing of her deprived childhood: "I never want to have kids. I'm too much of a kid myself. I need to take care of myself and fill my own gap first."

Many women expressed relief that they no longer had to cope with traditional female roles. One member of the Montreal commune, who was arranging to have her fallopian tubes tied, commented, "I have finished with conventional life. It has no meaning anymore. The idea of being a wife or a mother . . . it would be a dead end, a drag on me." Another member, who had left her family to follow Bhagwan, shared her unpleasant memories of conventional motherhood: "I was like a robot, always so tired, always cleaning, cooking, changing diapers—too tired to make love. I was spiritually dead. How could I be good for my children feeling like that? Now I see them on Saturdays and I am so alive, spontaneous with them." This theme is found throughout the movement's literature. "I am just so *relieved* to be on my own . . . and just be able to do what Bhagwan puts me to do and what feels good to me and not to have any responsibility to anyone else. . . . It's so much cleaner;

how freer, more spacious and. . . . It just gives me the *creeps* to think of all that work of babies and kids" (*Blessed Are the Ignorant* 1979, 311).

Although I found my *sannyasin* informants generally held negative views on parenthood, an exception was one of the female coordinators of the Montreal commune, Ma Prem "Arup," who stubbornly managed to reconcile her maternal vocation with commune life. A landscape gardener and single mother of one when she first "fell in love with Bhagwan," she had become pregnant with her *sannyasin* lover and decided to have an abortion. As she entered the clinic, however, she reported hearing "a tiny voice inside me chanting 'Keep me, keep me!'—so what could I do? I had to keep him." She attended a summer festival at Rajneeshpuram, although it was against the rules for pregnant women to enter the city. When she joined the Montreal commune in 1984, her two toddlers joined also, living in one room with three other children. For the next two years she saw them only on Wednesday evening and on Sundays, because the "kids' commune" was overseen by rotating adult male guardians. When asked about her children's adjustment to communal life, she replied:

They are blossoming! It is so good for them living here. Every day when they come home from the day care, they have a delicious meal with a flower beside their plate. They get to know so many people! And my son—he is two now—he is very protective of me. We went for a picnic on the mountain last Sunday, and someone picked up my plate. He said, "No! Arup!" He was guarding my plate like my little lover. Although I don't see him so often as when I used to come home exhausted from gardening all day, when I do see him we are both very alert, very conscious, and I fall in love with him all over again.

When the commune disbanded in April 1986, she moved into an apartment with her children and two other *sannyasins*. I would meet her frequently at the same *garderie* where our children were enrolled, and we would sometimes walk home together. I received the impression that, apart from her Rajneesh rhetoric, Arup's style of mothering was not so very different from other single mothers in the "mainstream."

A Solution to the Problem of Aging. Rajneesh women have espoused a philosophy and a life-style that reinforces a self-image of permanent young adulthood. They are surrounded by a circle of friends of the same age who are adventurous and playful. They have found a way to become sexy and attractive without depending on their youth. In contrast to the Christian tradition in which a woman, turning her back on "the world" and seeking an intense inner spiritual life, was *renouncing* her sexuality, in the Rajneesh *ashrams,* women who meditate and cultivate trance states are reassured that these practices can only enhance their sexual appetite and attractiveness. "Sexiness" is no longer a by-product of youth or an accident of genes; it is defined as a mysterious, inner, spiritual quality. In this way, women approaching mid-life, who find the roles in our society available to middle-aged women unattractive and depressing, can join a Rajneesh commune and maintain their self-image as a woman who is young, desirable, and carefree, and at the same time they can follow a spiritual path.

As for the problem of aging and declining beauty, women in the Rajneesh communes are vegetarians and physically active through dance and work and tend to preserve their youthful figures, particularly because they avoid pregnancy. During the communal phase they wore revealing clothing in bright shades of pink, orange, maroon, adorned their faces with makeup, wore crystal jewelry, and even glued New Age sparkles to their cheeks.

A Validation of the Role of Lover. Rajneesh's philosophy and the ethics underlying communal life not only validate the role of "lover" but also present a sexually promiscuous life-style as a spiritual path. Rajneesh offers his disciples a highly elaborated theodicy of sexual love. In his system the emotional pitfalls of a sexually promiscuous life-style are given a transcendental meaning: jealousy, sexual rejection, abandonment by one's lover—all are explained as inevitable stages on the path to enlightenment. The close, confidential friendships between commune residents who are inclined to share every detail of their ongoing love affairs with each other constitute a support system that enables women (and men) to safely navigate the perilous divagations of their emotional life.

In the larger society it is likely that a woman over thirty-five who identifies with the role of "lover" and is sexually promiscuous would generally be considered an object of moral censure, pity, or ridicule. The Rajneesh movement, however, confers a high spiritual and structural status upon exactly such women. Women are the leaders in the movement and their sexual expressiveness is not only socially acceptable but is often interpreted as charismatic. The problems facing middle-aged women who seek emotional satisfaction and social prestige through a series of short-lived love affairs in the larger society are daunting. She is likely to confront social censure, sexual exploitation, emotional insecurity, and the anguish of her own declining physical attractiveness.

In the Rajneesh culture, however, these problems have, to a great extent, been overcome. Sexual promiscuity is the norm: women are encouraged to be sexually aggressive, so they can hardly be described as exploited. Love affairs occur in a group context, a communal situation, so that women receive emotional support and advice from their fellow residents. The swamis are trained to be "open" and "vulnerable" so that women do not face the kind of rejection, indifference, and alienation that women in the larger society might experience during their love affairs.

One way of understanding women's choice to become "lovers of Bhagwan" is to regard it as a solution to the loneliness facing childless professional women in mid-life. A series of articles issuing from the popular media explore the phenomenon of women who have achieved success in their careers at the expense of their private lives, and label the problem "the emotional fallout of feminism" or "the feminization of loneliness" (*Newsweek* Mar. 31, 1986). "At age 40, most women cope alone with the lack of intimacy, sexual expression, children, social life and the deepening crisis of facing old age alone." This situation is blamed on the excesses of the first wave of feminism "whose emphasis on equality sometimes crossed the line into outright contempt for motherhood." Another article, "The Dilemmas of Childlessness," states that 25 percent of college-educated working women between thirty-five and forty-five are childless. These "baby busters questioned the moral imperative to reproduce and instead forged ahead in the male-dominated work force." Feminist Gloria Steinem—a role model for this type of woman—is quoted making a statement that echoes the quotation from Rajneesh that heads this chapter: "I either gave birth to someone else . . . or I gave birth to myself."

Kirk Braun's interview with Ma Mary Catherine, one of the Rajneeshpuram "supermoms," offers a glimpse into the conversion of a woman who closely fits the "baby buster" portrait above. At the time of her decision to take *sannyas* in 1979, she was a professor at Reed College and the head of Portland's Neighborhood Associations.

She was preparing for a trip to Japan, and while standing at her desk she asked herself if this—a desk, office, mind, work, administration—was going to be the rest of her life? She didn't feel she was actively searching for spiritual depth, it was just that spiritual depth was lacking. When it came time to book the ticket to Japan, she added a few extra days (15) at Poona. After she arrived in Poona and "did a few groups" she came to the realization that she belonged there. (Braun 1984, 82)

Many of the women I interviewed were in their mid-thirties, childless, and had been successful in their chosen careers. Although not wishing to imply that their spiritual experiences were inauthentic, or to reduce their religious motivations to mere emotional yearnings, I must persist in defending my analysis of NRM alternative patterns of sexuality as "spiritual solutions" to social change. By becoming "lovers of Bhagwan" many of my informants succeeded in resolving dissonances between their public and private lives. They chose the only contemporary religious commune (to my knowledge) that offers women leadership, physical intimacy, an intense meditative and communitarian life, and unlimited sexual expression.

PART TWO

Sex Complementarity Groups

FOUR

Sisters in the Unification Church

Since the Unificationist views man as the manifestation of God's masculine nature and woman as the manifestation of God's feminine nature, the man and woman are viewed as essentially equal in the sight of God.

—*Reverend Sun Myung Moon*

Unificationist women are the spiritual "daughters" of Reverend and Mrs. Moon as well as "sisters" to each other and to their "brothers" in the movement. The committed member takes up communal residence in a Unification center and performs volunteer work to further the goals of the church as a hardworking missionary, fund-raiser, and organizer. Members abstain from tobacco and alchohol and live in celibacy for three or more years. This process qualifies them for the "Matching"—a ceremony in which Reverend Moon chooses the marriage partners for the next mass marriage. Members call themselves "the family" and look across sex lines at siblings, and not at potential lovers or spouses. Unificationists believe that woman is spiritually equal or even more advanced in the spirit than man, and that she is essential for his salvation. Her equality—and indispensibility— derives from the bisexual nature of God, who is "The One True Parent of Mankind," and her importance as a wife derives from the key role marriage plays in Moon's eschatology.

The History

This movement originated in Seoul, Korea, in 1954 when the evangelist Reverend Sun Myung Moon founded the Holy

75

Spirit Association for the Unification of World Christianity (HSAUWC). Born in 1920 to North Korean Buddhist parents who converted to Presbyterianism during his childhood, Moon received a revelation in his sixteenth year that Jesus bestowed upon him the mission of fulfilling God's plan of physical salvation on earth as the Second Coming. After establishing a reputation as an evangelist, Reverend Moon was placed in a labor camp in 1948 when the Communists took over North Korea. The church's official accounts of this period stress how he overcame extraordinary suffering through compassion for his fellow prisoners—and even for God.

> To compensate for the physical deprivation, Rev. Moon resolved to bolster his spiritual strength. He gave away half his meager food allowance to other prisoners. . . . He felt sorry that God should have to witness his desperate plight. . . . so he resolved not to pray to alleviate his own predicament, further grieving God. (*People Serving People* 1985, 6)

When the American troops liberated the prisoners in 1950, Moon and his band of disciples escaped from the fighting in North Korea over the mountains, Moon carrying a friend with a broken leg on his back during most of the trek. Arriving in Pusan, they built the first Unification Church out of rocks, mud, and cardboard boxes.

Unificationist missionaries arrived in the United States in 1959, but not until Reverend Moon's Day of Hope tour (1972–74) were members in America inspired to quit their jobs, solicit contributions on the street, and engage in full-time proselytizing activity. Publicity and political liasons were sought, and Reverend Moon was photographed with influential politicians, including Jimmy Carter and Richard Nixon. Since the 1970s the church has been involved in anti-Communist activities on an international scale, holds ecumenical conferences, and operates lucrative businesses in the East and West. Bromley and Shupe (1988, 36–37) comment on the church's "curious mix of bureaucracy and charismatic leadership" and describe it as "not one monolithic organisation, but an extremely complex conglomerate of loosely-related incorporated enterprises that seek to accomplish different goals that answer to the same executive board of trustees, and that, (whatever the Church's enemies might think) frequently operate in ignorance of each other's activities."

Reverend Moon's Philosophy of Sexuality

Reverend Moon's revelations on Creation and the Fall are recorded in the church's sacred text, *The Divine Principle*. In this text, God is presented as an androgynous being, the "One True Parent of Mankind" who physically gave birth to Adam and Eve as His/Her children. Moon's ideas on gender and marriage derive from his unorthodox understanding of the Fall, in which the Archangel Lucifer, jealous of God's love for His created children, seduced the youthful Eve during her engagement to Adam. Because of this "abuse of love," Man has fallen from his original state as a child of God and has become a child of Lucifer. Jesus Christ was a true child of God, but failed in his mission because he was killed before he could find the perfect woman and father a new race of God's children. Jesus restored mankind on the spiritual level; Reverend Moon has come to restore us on the physical level and to complete Jesus' original task, which was to marry and populate the earth with a new race of God's children.

To accomplish this task, in 1960 Reverend Moon married a seventeen-year-old Korean woman, Hak Ja Han. Out of this millenarian union, thirteen offspring were born, declared the first of the pure race of God's children. He explains the millenarian significance of his 1960 wedding in *God's Will and the World* (1985, 141).

In 1960, 14 years after I began my public ministry, I performed the Holy wedding—the marriage of the Lamb that the Bible had predicted. In 1960, therefore, the first heavenly family was established on earth. That was equivalent in significance to the very moment of the crucifixion of Jesus. . . . This was a life or death matter. Under very adverse circumstances I won the first and most important victory. I consummated the heavenly plan. This was the most historical day in the history of God. This was the day that the Heavenly Son came to earth, restored the base, and welcomed the first bride of heaven.

Reverend Moon's ideas on gender represent an uneasy compromise between traditional Korean and contemporary Western notions of marriage. The following speech suggests that he disapproves of Western "liberated" women and prefers the oriental style of womanhood.

> In this country women have a commanding voice at home. In the typical American home the wife is master of the house, while the husband is like a servant; his shoulders are hunched over and he is always checking to see what his wife's mood is. . . . All you sisters, would you like to be recognized for being feminine and charming, or would you like to be known for being very courageous and tomboyish? (*God's Will and the World*, 394)

Moon defines woman's liberation in spiritual terms only: "The greatest responsibility and glory that a woman can assume is that of an empress or queen of the kingdom of God." He finds evidence in nature that woman was created to inhabit the domestic sphere.

> God thought a lot about how to create woman. Instead of making her taller than men, He made them a little shorter, but with bigger hips. Why? Because women are to assume two roles. First, in giving birth to children women need a strong foundation, and second, they will be living most of their lives in a sitting position, so God provided built-in cushions. Men have narrow hips without cushions, because men are supposed to take the initiative and always be in action. A woman is to be objective, receiving grace from her husband and always sitting at home comfortably waiting for him. That is the way it should be. (*God's Will and the World*, 576)

On the spiritual level, however, Moon regards woman as more highly developed than man. "Women are more creatures of the heart than men. Therefore, it is not unusual to see them go ahead in spiritual experiences. Men should follow them in this case" (*Master Speaks* 2, 2965:6).

Unlike most of the other groups in this study, Unificationism permits women to experience a wide range of roles. After a minimum of six years of celibacy, they do eventually marry and have children, but they pass through each role slowly—and one at a time—and the emphasis is on the inner spiritual purification or preparation for marriage and motherhood, thereby fulfilling Reverend Moon's plan to "restore" a society based on "God-centered" families. Thus, a "typical" career for a female Unificationist would involve working for three to four years as a celibate "sister," then becoming "blessed" as the "daughter" of Reverend and Mrs. Moon, then cultivating a sibling relationship with her husband in separation, and finally, consummating her marriage and beginning her life as a wife and mother. One sister explained that a mature woman is seen as embodying all feminine roles. "We believe a wife should be able to be everything to her husband, a mother when he needs a mother, or a daughter, if he feels like protecting her, and a sister and friend when he needs companionship." Grace even notes a brief phase in which the woman becomes the mother of her fiancé; she is "*in a symbolic way* the bride of the Messiah . . . and finally the woman takes the role of mother in relation to her fiancé during their engagement period, an essentially 'subject' role" (Grace 1985, 101).

The life of male and female Unificationists is virtually identical during the phase of "co-ed monasticism." They perfom the same tasks, live by the same standards, and are equal in ritual. After marriage, women tend to assume the traditional, domestic role, particularly wives of leaders in the church. For couples lower down in the hierarchy, the allocation of bread-winning, child care, and domestic tasks seems to be worked out by the individual couple. Keith Cooperider, director of financial affairs for the American movement, presents a traditional version of gender roles. "It is my opinion God made us different on purpose. The woman is caught up in the home, and the man is caught up in his mission. It's the creative, loving dialogue between the two of us that enables us to accomplish both at the same time" (*Unification News* July 1, 1982).

His wife, Sara, who assists in the co-op nursery, says Keith wins most of their arguments " because he's smarter than me so he's more convincing."

An alternative view was expressed by Hal McKenzie, an editor of the *New World:* "I do a lot of the domestic work. There's no need for roles or that macho stuff. We're in this together" (*Unification News* July 1, 1982).

Grace (1985) suggests that there is some discrepancy between men and women's expectations of married life— the women tending to emphasize cooperation and partnership, and the men tending toward Reverend Moon's ontologically based chauvinism. This insight was supported by one of our female informant's egalitarian view of marriage and affirmation of the church's exalted view of woman:

The Ideal Woman is a reflection of God's femininity. For us, God is both male and female, and the One True Parent of mankind. When I first heard this I was inspired; for in Christianity always the male is emphasized and the woman is a lesser being who caused the Fall. In our movement the woman and man are equal but different, and they need each other in order to mature. In order to find spiritual fulfillment they must love each other. When I heard this I was touched because it elevated woman beyond anything I ever heard of before; this idea that a man needs a woman in order to be perfect. Women and men are no longer judged as inferior or superior but must come together in order to create a whole picture. Seeing the Father and Mother aspect of God, we are trying to find it in ourselves to see the world from God's point of view. Through the years we have been trying to put this vision into practice. As women, our value lies in being the daughters of God and we are maturing into true wives and mothers.

The Marriage Blessing

The most significant ritual in the Unification Church is the "Blessing," popularly known as the "Moonie Mass Marriage." The theological meaning of the ritual is closer to baptism than to the Christian sacrament of marriage, because the couples who participate in the wedding are believed to be purified of original sin and reborn as children of God. The Blessing restores men and women from their satanic lineage, brought about by the Fall, to their heavenly lineage. This ritual is also an initiation into the movement and formalizes the devotee's relationship with the spiritual master, Reverend Moon. This spiritual connection is conceptualized as the parent-child relationship.[1]

The Blessing is not only a path to individual salvation, but it is the church's means of establishing the Kingdom of God on earth, a goal known as the "restoration." Each successive Blessing involves a larger number of couples, and Moon's aim is to unite all races and nationalities and to raise moral standards through this ritual. As he explains, "I did not come here to fight communism. What I love to do most and what I came for is to marry people" (videocassette, *Holy Wedding*, 1982).

The *Unification News* sums up the key role of "Perfect Families" in bringing about the restoration:

The divine scheme of love and family is laid out in the "four position foundation" . . . God, Husband, wife and child. The pure and perfect relationship with God helps to establish the perfect relationship between husband and wife, and then between parents and children. The spiritual and physical kingdom of God, the total salvation that God intended in sending the Messiah, will be achieved by the ever expanding network of such God-centered families.

Thus Unificationist weddings present a paradox: what has traditionally been a rite of passage into the life of a sexually active adult becomes for Moon's followers a symbolic rebirth as a child whose innocence and purity is restored. At this stage, the bond between "Father" and his spiritual "children" is of far greater importance than the bond between husband and wife. The Blessing is also a legal act, for Reverend Moon has a license to perform marriage ceremonies and the Blessed Couples are advised to go to city hall to pave the way for obtaining visas when the time comes to live together.

Before Unificationists can realize God's plan, however, they must pass through a long ritual purification and inner, psychological preparation, of which the Blessing is just one stage. There seem to be at least six distinct stages of preparation for married life in the church.

Qualifications. To qualify for the Blessing the member must have been a fully committed Unificationist for three or more years, and have worked full-time for the church, and be over age twenty-five. They must fill out an application form describing their career in the movement, attaching their photograph, and stating their racial preferences.

The Matching. On this occasion Reverend Moon chooses the marriage partners. The candidates assemble in a large rented

Wedding of Mr. and Mrs. Duffy with Reverend Moon and his daughter.
Courtesy R. Duffy.

hall, and Reverend Moon begins the proceedings by offering a prayer and then wanders about the hall, assisted by his close disciples. He calls up men and women and introduces them to each other as future husband and wife. He is believed to be under divine inspiration, possessing the ability to see into the spirit world, so that he chooses partners according to their ancestry and to the future generations they will create. This point is emphasised in *God's Will in the World*. "I clearly know what conditions will be the most beneficial for people in the spirit world, for those presently alive, and for future generations. Thus, I have clearly understood the providential significance of your Blessing."

One sister explained the logic behind this system of arranged marriage.

Reverend Moon is able to see all the ancestors of the person so he will match people to improve the relationships of their ancestors. For example, he will see that the ancestors of a black man are very angry at whites, so he will marry him to a white girl, and through the love the couple have for each other, the ancestors will learn to forgive and love also.

Moon's modus operandi appears to vary. Sometimes he consults lists put out by local leaders who recommend matches, and then calls out names, or he might glance around and beckon spontaneously, "You there, with the red tie!" One Englishman who attended the Matching at the World Mission Center in December 1980 described Moon's manner as outrageous and humorous.

We were all standing there, so nervous, and he was so funny! He pretended to be a fat black lady with one leg, and was hopping around asking us all, "Will you marry me?" I was laughing so hard my nervousness vanished and I was ready to marry anyone he chose! So I put up my hand and said, "I will!" and then he introduced me to this beautiful Japanese girl.

This anecdote underlines the notion that by marrying Moon's choice, one is marrying Moon himself. It also echoes traditional folk tales about the princess who kisses the frog, or the prince who marries the old crone who turns into a young maiden. Judging from both written and verbatim accounts of participants, this appears to be an extraordinarily anxiety-provoking occasion—a veritable ordeal. The waiting candidates immerse themselves in silent prayer to control their emotions and wish for an acceptable mate. Many of my informants seemed to have entered an altered state of consciousness through the preparatory techniques of fasting and prayer, so that when they opened their eyes and beheld their future spouse, they experienced an instant bonding, or falling in love—not unlike Conrad Lorenz's baby geese. "Then I heard him say, 'Do you swear to love this sister,' and I looked up and saw Susan. Bam! There was an instant attraction!" (videocassette, *Holy Wedding* 1982).

Reverend Moon often introduces the prospective partners by saying to the man, "Do you swear to be a good husband to this sister?" This suggests that even as an engaged couple their primary relationship is (like Adam and Eve before the Fall) a sibling one. The couple then bow to "Father" and to each other, then join hands and go to a corner where they converse, usually between five and twenty minutes, sometimes with the help of an interpreter. Some conversations between newly matched couples were reported as follows in the *Unification News*.

Janice: He sat down and said, "All I ask is that you love God more than me." I thought that was fine, then I asked him how old he was. He noticed that I was taken aback when he said twenty-four, and asked the obvious question, "How old are you?" There was an awfully long silence after I said I was thirty-two.

Kate: After exchanging names, I asked Kazuo, "What does Kazuo mean?" to which he answered, "First Man." Then I said, "How about Tsubata?" and he answered "fertile farmfield." I couldn't help blurting out, "How many children do you want?" to which he replied with admirable equanimity, "As many as you wish."

Almost all Unificationists accept their leader's choice of spouse, but some refuse. Of the twenty-two Canadians who attended the Matching ceremony before the 1982 wedding in Madison Square Garden, two rejected their partners: one because the man was ten years her junior (she was thirty-four) and the other because she considered him a risky prospect because he was still a part-time student, so she had misgivings about his commitment to the church.

Members can turn down their chosen partners with no loss of status, but then must wait for the next Matching. One of the Canadians mentioned above is still unmatched today. Reverend Moon urges his followers to be compassionate rather than fastidious.

We are all brethren. If you have a disabled person among your brothers and sisters, it is proper that compassionate love should well up in your heart and you should sacrifice yourself to care for that individual. Parents feel that way, so . . . following the example of the parents is the way to filial piety. This is the principle. . . . In this situation, if you stand in our position and look on your spouse-to-be, who may not be good-looking, who may be of below-average intelligence, and very short in height, you should feel very loving towards that "child" of ours. It is the parents' heart to view a child from the standpoint of the heart of heaven and to love that child more than anybody else. (*God's Will and the World* 1985, 448)

The Holy Wine Ceremony. This ritual is both an engagement ceremony and the first stage of purification from original sin, or Satan's lineage. The chosen couples bow to one another and Reverend Moon stands in the position of Adam as he offers a cup of Korean wine made from "the elements of creation" to the woman who stands in the position of the fallen Eve. As she drinks of it, she becomes the Restored Eve and then passes it to her fiancé, who stands in the position of the archangel, who is forgiven for his transgression as he drinks of it.

The Marriage Blessing. The Blessing in Madison Square Garden of July 1, 1982, was recorded on videocassette and shown to me at the Montreal center. It opened with a flag bearers parade, and then twenty-four older couples (Blessed in 1961) formed an archway through which Reverend and Mrs. Moon proceeded to mount their separate platforms. Father and Mother were dressed in stiff white imperial robes and glittering white crowns. The 2,075 couples passed between them, four sets at a time, the brides wearing identical Simplicity pattern dresses.

Father and Mother sprinkled holy water over the couples, baptizing them as their adopted children, and thereby restoring their heavenly lineage. Brothers and sisters recited identical vows and exchanged identical rings.

Postmarital Celibacy. After the Blessing the couples separate and usually return to their centers to continue to work in missionary activity, fund-raising, and rally organization. They also are required to find three "spiritual children" during this period, which means they must be responsible for bringing three converts to the church. Reverend Moon explains the religious meaning of this rule.

The foundation is indemnified when your three spiritual children serve your physical children even in the womb. In that way, you can restore the earthly foundation of the three archangels willingly attending Adam while he was being created. . . . Unity between our spiritual children and physical children means unity between the spiritual world and the physical world. (*God's Will and the World* 1985, 84–88)

The couples communicate through prayer, letters, and telephone calls, and strive to perfect their spiritual love for each other and to become the "Ideal Man" and "Ideal Woman" so that when they do eventually consummate their marriage physically, they will be perfect wives, husbands, and parents. Three years is the official period of separation, but the couples married in the 1982 ceremony deferred their union for an extra year out of deference to Moon, who was in jail and separated from his family. Exceptions are made for older women who are approaching the end of their childbearing years, and they are allowed to unite with their husband forty days after the wedding. The theological significance of this period of postmarital celibacy is to reverse the consequences of the Fall, which was caused by a premature sexual relationship.

This phase is reminiscent of the distant, idealized, and unconsummated love affairs of the medieval troubadours, and the women interviewed described romantic experiences through dreams, premonitions, and telepathic communications. During this period the spiritual love between spouses is meant to mature, and members see themselves as undergoing an inner purification that will enable them to become "ideal women" or "ideal men," so that eventually they will create perfect families. One informant described her separation in marriage as a time of intense spiritual growth.

Waiting through the years I feel we've established an understanding, an openness and confidence. I can be myself with him as I could never be with someone who was condemning, possessive, jealous, and demanding. Our relationship has the potential for something greater than ordinary marriage. When I pray to God I ask Him to help me use this period to develop those qualities in myself that will enable me to be good for my husband and my future children.

One brother, who was born on a Quebec farm in a family of eleven chidren, boasted that his was the only successful marriage in the family. He produced a photograph of a pretty Japanese girl whom he had last seen three years ago, in the 1982 mass marriage. She did not speak French, and his English was minimal. He described their relationship in terms of sibling love.

We have the perfect relationship. I don't see her very often, as she lives in Vancouver and I am here in Montreal, but as I work closely day by day with my sisters here, and grow to love and respect them as a brother, my love for my wife as a sister increases every day. We have been married three years now and have never once had a quarrel! Now, *all* my brothers and sisters had bad marriages and they are all now divorced!

The Three-Day Ceremony. After a seven-day fast, the husband and wife consummate their marriage in the following ritualistic manner. The handkerchief that wiped the cup after the Holy Wine Ceremony is produced to dry the couple after their shower. They kneel in prayer to invoke the presence of God. For the first two days the wife must assume the "subject position," or initiate their sexual relationship, while the husband remains passive. On the third day he assumes the subject position. This symbolizes a reversal of the seduction scene in the Garden of Eden. The mature, Restored Eve initiates the sexual act instead of the teenage Fallen Eve, who was passively seduced. The husband stands in the position of Lucifer until the moment of consummation, then he takes the place of the Restored Adam (Wood 1979, 163).

Women in the Leadership

Women's leadership and success in evangelical activity was outstanding in the initial stages of the movement. In the early days in Korea, Moon's followers were almost exclusively women, and there are indications that the church functioned as a sort of liberation movement for women, a means of opting out of parental control and arranged marriages and providing opportunities for leadership and travel. Mr. Won Pil Kim, an early follower, wrote that women joining the group were instructed to "live like virgins" until their marriages had been blessed by Moon, and noted that husbands became suspicious of Moon and denounced him as a heretic who disrupted family life (Kim 1982, 2).

The late Oon Young Kim was a professor at Ewha Women's University and became the first missionary to the West. By 1960 she had gathered twenty-one members, including two women who had renounced their husbands and children for the cause, creating some anti-Moon sentiments in the neighborhood (Lofland 1977). In 1965 Miss Kim moved to Washington to work with Colonel Bo Hi Pak, founded the Freedom League Foundation in 1969, and spent her last years teaching at the Unification Theological Seminary in Barrytown, New York. As a scholar who wrote her Ph.D. dissertation on Swedenborg at the University of Toronto, and who later assisted Reverend Moon in writing his revelations, it has been suggested that Miss Kim's interests in metaphysics and the spiritual realm have influenced Unification eschatology (Barker 1985; Lofland 1977). Another major female missionary is Yun Soo Lim ("Ooni"), who conducted a highly successful mission in Japan and then moved to the Bay Area and married Mose Durst in 1974. The couple ran the Oakland Family, an active recruiting center whose controversial methods were criticized in *Moonwebs* (Freed 1980).

An American woman, Doris Walder, founded the church in Britain in 1968, and she and her British husband, Dennis Orme, have run the British Family for ten years. The Canadian movement also was founded by a woman, Linna Rapkins, who was succeeded by Catherine Bell. By the mid-eighties, most Canadian members were blessed, and there was a growing tendency to appoint couples to direct the centers, the husband playing the dominant role. "Man is the initiator, woman the supporter," members explained.

Mrs. Moon's most significant contribution to the movement is in providing a role model of the ideal wife and mother. Until recently, she has rarely spoken in public, although she has an important dramaturgical role as Father's consort. The following speech from the April 1985 *Conference on Eve* given by Mrs. Mal Sook Lee suggests that Mother is revered by Unificationist women.

Mother cares for 13 children and leads the Church now, but she never complains or shows her struggle. . . . She is not lazy. Father is so busy, but when he goes to his room, Mother talks to him even though she is tired and gives him proper advice. . . . Mother comes to breakfast at 7 A.M. every day, always so neat and cared for. She doesn't spend so much, she is a saving person. . . . After Mother wakes she checks each child to make sure they're up. After breakfast the leaders report and she catches it quickly and gives advice. Then she reports it all to Father. Whenever Mother is upset or angry you can hardly tell it, even when she is tired. She's peaceful and quiet. Better not show your angry face to the children. So when I look at Mother, I am so happy she is our True Mother.

Mrs. Moon's authority in the church appears to be waxing. On June 24, 1991, in Coburg, Ontario, Reverend Moon inducted his wife into the "messianic mission," which endowed her with the spiritual authority to take over the leadership when he should "pass away." This ceremony was witnessed by four wives of the Japanese leaders and, on the same occasion, Reverend Moon explained to them Mrs. Moon's role in the mission for word peace.[2]

A new woman's organization, headed by Mrs. Moon, was founded in 1991 called *Women For World Peace.* The first Canadian WFWP meeting was held in Montreal on March 22, 1992; it featured a film documenting the large WFWP rally in

Japan the previous year. Mrs. Moon delivered a speech congratulating Japanese women on choosing to stay out of public life to "protect your families," and she credited Japan's economic success to their dedication. She predicted that Japan would promote peace and selfless service in the world community. Then she urged Asian women to expand their influence beyond their homes, to turn their faces toward other nations, and, as "Mothers of Asia," take part in saving the world.

Membership and Sex Ratios

During the early phases of the movement in Korea, women greatly outnumbered the men (although no statistics are available). Once the movement began its expansion in the West, however, men began to outnumber women. According to Barker's estimate (1984), the sex ratio in Britain and the United States was 2:1 in favor of men. Grace (1985) also found that there were twice as many male Unificationists as female in the United States, and he suggests the movement's stronger appeal for men was related to the opening up of leadership positions for men. It seems safe to say that in the East (Korea, Japan) more women join; in the West, more men join.

The church claims 3 million members in 120 countries, but Barker (1984) offers her "guestimate" as less than 50,000 full-time worldwide. Bromley and Shupe's figure for U.S. members is "no more than two or three thousand members in the 1970's." Mike Kropveldt, "exit counselor" of the Montreal Hillel Cult Information Center, claims there are as many as 7,000 Moonies in North America, and up to 300,000 worldwide. Because of the mobility of the mobile teams, and the tendency of both church officials and anticultists to inflate membership figures, it is impossible to provide exact figures.

According to the Toronto Unification Center's records,[3] there are 139 adult Unificationists in Canada; 88 of them are married, with 58 children. The average age of adult members was 33 (women) and 37 (men). Unificationists in Canada, therefore, tend to be significantly older than Barker's sample

TABLE 3. Marital Status of
Canadian Unificationists

Marital Status	Number
Blessed Couples	(44) 88
Individuals Separated in Marriage	7
Singles Eligible for Matching	20
Singles Ineligible for Matching	24
Total	139

in Britain in the early 1980s—in their mid-thirties as opposed to their mid-twenties. Only 26 out of 139 members are Canadian-born. Because the Canadian church is not a center of evangelical activity, these are not recent converts, but a stable population of long-term members who are currently having babies and reorganizing their community to accommodate children. Of the 26 Unificationist male children in Canada, 20 are of mixed parentage (and they are under age 10), and the 6 teenagers are Korean or Japanese. Of the 32 girls, the four oldest (ages 16 to 21) are Korean; the remainder, all under 12, are of mixed parentage. The marital status of the 139 Canadian Unificationists is as follows: blessed couples, 88 (44 couples); separated in marriage (SIM), 7; singles eligible for matching, 20; singles ineligible for matching, 24.

Toronto is the headquarters for the Unificationist community in Canada. This researcher noted during her visit in 1983 that the eight couples living in the Toronto center shared a communal kitchen and dining room. By 1985, each of the four couples had installed their own kitchens in their apartments and ate with their families. Of the sixteen couples of the Toronto Unification Community in 1985, four were living communally in the center and twelve were living in independent households. By 1992, the center was sold, and everyone now lives in independent households.

Portraits of Four Unificationist Women

Only a few Unificationist women in Canada are Canadian-born. I interviewed women from Japan, Korea, the Phillipines, England, Norway, New Zealand, Pakistan, and Uganda. Presented with this bewildering array of cultural backgrounds, it was difficult, if not impossible, to formulate any conclusions about their former experiences with family life. Concern over the dissolution of the modern family was a dominant theme in the interviews, and appeared to be a popular topic at their women's rallies if only to set off a lively discussion among women from such varied cultures.

Women's accounts of their reasons for joining belie the popular "brainwashing" myth. Many of them were idealists actively seeking like-minded idealists, or were already devout Christians and natural mystics who found in Moon's theology a language that corresponded to what they had spontaneously experienced. Many expressed dissatisfaction with the "mainline" churches: their secularization, lack of intensity and discipline, and, above all, their failure to provide an adequate theodicy for suffering in the modern world. In many respects, Unification theology is peculiarly "relevant" to contemporary life: it dispenses with eternal damnation and the glorification of Jesus' torture on the cross, it boasts an androgynous Godhead, it refrains from blaming Eve, it makes sense of the cold war, and it encourages political activism.

Hortense[4] is an outstanding example of a woman who appeared to experience a "pure" ideological conversion. A French Canadian in her mid-forties, she is a leader in the Canadian movement who pioneered the centers in Sherbrooke and Quebec, and directed the Montreal and Quebec City centers. As a former nun, her rigorous training in Christian theology and knack for explaining philosophical concepts are a valuable asset to the church in missionary activities. She grew up in a small village near Quebec city in a family of eight children. Her father was a construction worker, an alchoholic, and was frequently unemployed. Her mother was a devout Catholic, devoted wife, and sympathetic parent. She claims her interest in spiritual matters was stimulated by a near-fatal illness suffered in her childhood. "When I was seven years old I had meningitis and they expected me to die. I was in hospital for a year, but I recovered and I've always asked, 'Why did He save my life?'" At the age of eighteen Hortense entered a religious order, the Grey Nuns (1964 to 1966). She explained her reasons for leaving.

Living the religious life is not easy. I felt cut off and wanted to help people. I did social work; visiting poor families, distributing children's clothes . . . but it wasn't enough. Also, I worked in a house for men to come and have a meal, and when they asked for a second serving, I had to say, "No!" This made me feel bad, because at the convent we lived like queens with three-course meals. I used to wonder why the Kingdom of God never came on earth. Between 1965 and 1967 everyone began leaving—it was just after Vatican Two. It was a new age. Even my best friend left, and I used to look up to her as teacher. So then I thought, How can I stay? And I left.

At twenty-four she married an army officer and lived in New Brunswick, then Ontario, and worked throughout her marriage in an office. Her marriage broke up in 1979, after eight years, and she left her five-year-old daughter with her father and moved to Toronto to work for a translation company, visiting her child on weekends. She painted a depressing view of her life-style as a swinging single career woman about the time she first encountered the movement.

I was thirty-two then and living the life of a liberated woman. I was going to parties, drinking, sleeping with men, but still believed in God—although I was not practicing. I asked Him, "If You are really alive, then what are You doing?" I had an ideal about marriage, and wanted to find a religious man who had prayer in his life. As a single woman, people try to take advantage of you. One day I stayed up finishing a work of translation until four A.M., so I decided to stay home the next day. I was drinking a bit, and I said to God, "If You exist, where are You?" I had money and I wasn't happy, so I knew that wasn't the purpose to life. I couldn't sleep that day, so I went for a walk, and I . . . saw a couple who looked like they were lost. So I asked if I could help them. They started talking about unity and I said, "There is only one man who could unite the world, and that man is the Messiah."

Hortense began going to the center to study the Principle, and she makes it clear that she did not join for social reasons, but that she found the community unappealing. "At first I didn't like the Moonies—their communal life did not appeal to me after being in the convent, but I kept going to the center although I was working very hard and was very busy. I don't know why, I found the people strange. . . . I had a prejudice about the English." Then she went to the church-owned farm for a seven-day course and experienced an ideological conversion.

I was deeply touched by the Principle of Creation. I would pray to God and say, "What do you want from me?" . . . The next day we studied the Fall of Man and I saw my whole life, my parents' lives, run before my eyes like a movie. I realized my ideal about marriage—as a union of the spiritual with the physical body—was true! I'd had spiritual experiences when I was young which I now understood! I *knew* we weren't here to suffer, but I *did* suffer, and why was this so? On the third day the lesson was on Jesus' mission. . . . When I was sixteen I used to pray and ask Him, "Why was Papa an alcoholic? Once Jesus Himself appeared to me and said, "Your father is a child of God. Everyone like him is a child of God." I did not understand. It did not make sense—until I heard that lesson. Then I knew that Jesus should have lived. Did He save the world? Well, just look at the situation!

After much thought and prayer, she accepted Reverend Moon as the Messiah, but still hesitated to join. "I was too old to get involved, I thought. My life was not straight enough." Finally she moved into the center, quit her job, and began her career as a pioneer in the church. She worked on the anticommunist newspaper, *Canadian Unity Freedom Federation,* and was editor of *Notre Canada.* She pioneered the Unification center in Kingston and Montreal. In January 1985, she opened a center in Quebec City. She was in charge of visiting the estranged parents of members "to bring them to an understanding of our work," many of whom became friends and visit the center often. She became involved in Home Church and cleaned houses for elderly people in the poor districts of Montreal ("but the purpose of my visits is not to convert people").

One of the attractions to Unificationism for Hortense appears to have been the members' receptivity toward her paranormal experiences and Swedenborgian travels in the spirit world. These have been recurring throughout her life, but were sternly rejected by her family, Catholic priests, and her Mother Superior, who condemned them as heresy, spiritual pride, or suggested she see a psychiatrist. Her first vision, received in her teens, uncannily anticipated Reverend Moon's unorthodox interpretation of the crucifixion.

I met Jesus one day when I was sixteen, on a Good Friday while I was praying in our field of corn. I had a question that had always bothered me, and I used to ask my mother, "Why did Jesus have to die on the cross?" My mother would explain it was to redeem us from our sins, but I did not think that was a good answer. Jesus appeared to me that day and I saw that He was very handsome. He looked Jewish. He had dark curly hair and a big nose. But His eyes were blue. . . . Jesus told me that His death was a mistake. He said, if His disciples had not fallen asleep in the Garden of Gethsemane, He would not have died on the cross. . . . When I asked a priest about my experience, he did not believe me. I never spoke of that experience again.

The spirit world is an important element in Unificationist cosmology, and the ability to see spirits is interpreted as a charismatic gift—a sign of one whose five spiritual senses are open, and on the way to becoming "restored."

Hortense, like the other woman informants, admitted to feeling disillusioned in love when she first visited the church, and found members' spiritual approach toward sex and marriage moving.

Before I was married I wanted to be pure, a virgin, for my husband. Then, after the divorce, and even while I was married, we had a very liberal, open marriage and so did our friends. But I was disillusioned— I saw people living like animals. In the movement I see the desire of men and women to live their life and find complementarity in [their] roles. I look forward to the day when I shall meet my spiritual partner and receive the Blessing. But now I am one of the oldest in the Canadian movement and men are like my little brothers.

Hortense had attended several Matching ceremonies, but has not yet been introduced to her mate. As she explained it, "What can Reverend Moon do? *He* wasn't there!" Because she is now in her forties and is infertile, owing to a medical problem, and most male Unificationists are in their late twenties and aspiring to fatherhood, it appears her "choice" is limited. She is reassured through dreams that her husband-to-be exists on earth, and one of her "sisters" received a vision of him, an Englishman in his fifties working in Africa. She is confident that "even if I do not meet him in the physical world, we will be married in the spirit world for eternity, so there is no big rush to get together."

Gudren[5] is a thirty-seven-year-old Canadian of German parents who were nonactive Lutherans. She attended an art college in Toronto where she studied printmaking and stained glass and lived in a "common-law" relationship with her boyfriend. Through an intense appreciation of the beauty in nature, she began to receive mystical experiences and felt the presence of a Creator. She began to ask religious questions and, lacking any religious training, began to study the Bible. She experienced a difficulty like Hortense in accepting the notion that Jesus was crucified for our sins. "I went to church one day with a friend, and they were singing a song which said, 'Thank you, Jesus, for dying for us.' When they sang that song I felt so upset I just burst into tears. My question was, 'How could we thank someone for *dying* for us?' Then I heard some man on the radio thanking Jesus, and I thought, How could we take it all so lightly if someone dies for us?" She began investigating different Protestant churches, and made a "desperate prayer" to God. "Please let me meet people who are serious about their faith." After college, her boyfriend moved to Kingston to live in a residence at the university, so she decided to visit her godmother in Germany. She found work as a chambermaid, and met some Unificationists selling their newspapers on the street. She claims that their high moral standards and self-discipline is what she at first found attractive. "Everything he said was just so clear and right. In the church you are not allowed to smoke and I'm a nonsmoker, and that was strange because I went to a Christian church and saw the minister smoking and drinking and I thought, This is so wrong. They have no control over their rules, they just do what they want. They don't follow what they say." Moon's advice concerning premarital celibacy resonated with decisions she had already privately made. "I started to read the *Divine Principle,* and everything in it was so perfect, so right—and then I thought it is not right to live in common law with my boyfriend. My boyfriend doesn't believe in God, so it doesn't matter to him, [but] God is a reality which means there are consequences to how you live."

For three years she traveled across Europe with the mobile fund-raising teams. She describes this period as one of personal growth: developing social skills, learning to love, and feeling close to the other sisters.

I really enjoyed it. You get to understand faces and characters, it's not just the money. Of course, the money is important, but getting to know people is more important, and it teaches you how to love regardless of face, color, or clothing. Our goal was to love. I traveled around in a van with seven girls, and we went from city to city. Sometimes we slept in a convent, we slept in the Salvation Army, in a barn on a farm, in a hospital. They always made us comfortable and it was a lot of fun. The girls were great. . . . In the morning we would say a prayer. The girls were all German, but the leader, she was French.

Gudren was married in 1982 to an African from a Muslim background. She spent her separation years in Alaska, while he worked in New York. They are now living in Montreal, and he is supporting the family by selling cosmetics while she stays at home and looks after their two-year-old girl in the company of other Unificationist mothers. Her husband directs a church project of sending educational books to Africa; she designs posters and banners for the new Women for World Peace rallies. She notes that when her family is old enough she would like to find a job in design, but meanwhile does not regret giving up her career in art because "we believe the soul is immortal, so I will have all eternity to develop my interest in art. Right now it is more important to help humanity."

Anthea is a thirty-one-year-old British woman, and was married in 1982 to a Japanese brother. At the time of this interview (1985), they were still separated, as they lacked one "spiritual child." Anthea grew up in a small village in Cornwall, England. Her father was a toolsmith and she described an orderly, Anglican working-class upbringing.

Anthea attended Reading University, where she liked the studies, but was disillusioned by the students' low standards of morality. She seemed to be shopping for a cause: "I liked to check out different groups." These included a feminist, a Marxist, and a Christian youth group.

I was not impressed by the way people were living. . . . I had hoped to find serious, responsible students. I had one or two boyfriends, but these were not deep relationships. My aim was to become a career woman, a psychologist. I had no intention of marrying right away. I saw my girlfriends marry early and divorce early . . . it was a permissive time, I was open in my views . . . I meant to stay a virgin until I married, but tried not to judge others.

She volunteered for community work in old people's homes. Then, one April afternoon while she was window-shopping, a Moonie approached her saying, "I'm with a community and we share a new revelation from Korea—a man named Sun Myung Moon. Are you interested?" After attending workshops and praying, Anthea decided to move into the Unification Center when her term ended. Her parents were upset by her dropping out of the university and she reports, "It was not easy for me to explain the depth of the teaching, the scope of the movement." Because of her close relationship with them, she claims, they eventually accepted her new life.

After working in England, she came to America in 1973 to travel in teams to help set up the Day of Hope Tour. In 1975, she organized rallies all across Japan for a year. She met Moon on Yoido Island in Seoul during World Rally of Korean Freedom. She worked in France and Italy for three years as a house-mother in various centers. She communicates regularly with her Japanese husband (who speaks English fluently) through letters and phone calls. During the period of separation, "I ask God to help me develop myself to be good for him; to prepare to be a good wife and mother. She described her relationships with other members as "not friendship," but based on "working closely," and claims her relationship with men in the Unification Church is an improvement over her previous romantic entanglements.

> I know their intention is not to chase after me, so this tension is removed and there is trust. I feel towards them as brothers and friends. It gives us a certain freedom. We have shared values. There are certain limitations—what we can discuss, for example. With women we can reveal our inner feelings, so we make closer friendships with each other, but with men we stick to general topics. We don't spend time alone with a man, and don't get too personal.

(Anthea is currently living in New York with her husband and their son, and continues to play an active role in the church.)

It appears from both interviews that the desire for deep, "serious" relationships, particularly with the opposite sex, is a strong motivating factor in conversion. This was also a prominent theme in Ayesha's interview.

Ayesha is the daughter of a wealthy insurance agent in India, and she and her other sisters were brought up to be strict Muslims who prayed and fasted regularly. Even as a child, she was aware of the inegalitarian nature of her parents' relationship (based on a traditional arranged marriage), and this disturbed her.

> It was very formal; there was not much personal contact or sharing. My father was boss, my mother had no decisions. I often felt there should be more equality, that the balance was wrong. My father was a good man; he worked hard and was concerned about his family, but I knew I wanted a different kind of husband—there was no room for my mother to be herself.

Her father sent her off to a prestigious English girls school, at age eleven, against her mother's wishes. She felt intensely lonely in this new situation. "I missed my family and my home for a long time. There was no one to turn to. Suddenly, I was left alone to make all my own decisions. I was at Malvern for seven years, and in the last six months, when I was eighteen, I met the movement."

She then described herself as disillusioned and worried about her relationships with men. When she was fourteen, an old friend of her family in his late twenties visited her in Yorkshire and persuaded her to sleep with him. Although she had been taught that sex before marriage was wrong, she was deeply in love with him, very lonely, and convinced that he was her husband-to-be. After much resistance on her part, they finally went to bed together. The next day he informed her coldly that she was not the "right woman for him." She reports, "I felt the deepest regret. He was insensitive to my feelings and thoughts. I was just another woman for him. He was much older and so experienced. And I was innocent and had admired him so! I cried every day for months."

When she was sixteen she began to have a series of boyfriends, for as an older student she was permitted to leave the school on weekends, but she found her new freedom problematic.

I had a boyfriend for about eight or nine months, and still saw him after we broke up, but I wanted a *friend*, a brother, and he was going back to Bermuda, so he suggested we break up—he wasn't interested in trying to maintain a friendship. After a few relationships I was disappointed. I couldn't understand why it was so difficult. Either you had to have sex, or they would want to split up. I usually gave in just to make *them* happy. What is true love? I wondered. Is it just a sexual attraction or is there something more? I had always longed to have a brother my own age—just a friend to share things with. That's what moved me when I met the movement—that we live like brother and sister. We share the same values, there is no ulterior motive—we relate in a pure way. It was like the big families we have back home.

She reports that, on attending her first Unification workshop, she was deeply moved by Moon's theodicy of love, which accounts for all suffering and evil as the seduction of the young Eve by the mature Lucifer.

The *Principle* tells us that Eve was innocent and growing, and Lucifer enticed her. She was intoxicated by the beauty of the universe, and trusting, but he took advantage of her. She felt the same fears, the same regrets. This misuse of love, it's the most detrimental to a person's life. It can destroy a person! And it didn't just happen four thousand years ago. It's something we live every day.

Ayesha was married to a Puerto Rican in 1982, but during the separation, her husband left the movement. She was deeply distressed, but after two years of active service and constant prayer, she was rewarded in a Matching ceremony with a husband from the Phillipines, who is adept in the martial arts. Currently, they direct the Vancouver center, have opened a successful karate studio, and have produced two "blessed children."

Conclusion

It appears from these interviews that Unificationism appeals to idealistic young people who, in many cases, already felt the vocation to serve humanity before encountering the movement. The church offers them a highly organized, varied, and well-traveled career as a missionary, social worker, and political activist. During their volunteer work they develop a wide range of entrepreneurial skills, social graces, and often a facility with languages. What is less evident is that the church offers women wounded in the "dating game" or appalled by current standards of sexual morality a revitalized tradition of romantic love—with its religious roots exposed. In turning their backs on individualism and self-interest, Moonies are expressing a deep distrust for the process of coming-of-age in America. Through joining the church and participating in its initiation rituals, Unificationists regress (at least symbolically) to a childhood innocence and receive a second chance to "grow up right." Through temporarily renouncing their sexuality and serving others, they hope to be rewarded with the not un-American dream of meeting "Mr. Right" and living "happily ever after" in "Perfect Families."

Barker writes, "Moonies do not appear to be rejecting the values that were instilled into them during their childhood;

they appear, on the contrary, to have imbibed these so success-
fully that they are prepared to respond to the opportunity
(which society does not seem to be offering them) to live
according to those very standards" (Barker 1984, 210–11). This
observation appears to hold true for Andrea, who came from a
secure family life in a small village and was horrified by the permissiveness of the students at the university. Ayesha, also, might
be seen as attempting to re-create the arranged marriage and
extended family system of her Indian parents.

The "heretical" aspects of Moon's theology appear to hold a
strong appeal for sensitive, committed young Christians. The
church's intense evangelical fervor, its millenarian, communal,
and celibate life resemble the social forms of the early Christians (Pagels 1987). At the same time, Moon is in tune with
modern sensibilities and social issues. The value of marriage is
elevated above the goal of personal happiness to become a
means of uniting humanity, ushering in the millennium, and
guaranteeing personal salvation. Because of its religious basis
and the impossibility of divorce, Unificationist way of marriage
promises young women stability and permanence in their
chosen career as wife and mother.

The Unification Church combines elements of "traditional"
models of close, patriarchal families and modern themes, such as
"feminism," globalization, and racial integration. The modern
tendency for women to establish themselves in a career before
eventually settling down to marriage and motherhood in their
late twenties or early thirties is also found in the Unification
Church, but while the secular woman chooses her mate on the
basis of past sexual experience, the mature Unificationist accepts
an arranged marriage. While the secular woman cultivates a
wage-earning profession to quarantee a degree of independence
after marriage, the Unificationist engages herself in voluntary
work to prepare herself, spiritually and psychologically, for a
domestic career *inside* the family.

The "traditional" domestic roles of wife and mother, however, are also highly valued spiritual offices and public roles in
the Unification Church. Although motherhood is held to be
woman's highest vocation, Unificationist women often (tempo-

rarily) leave their children to attend rallies, such as Women for World Peace, and to deliver public speeches. Motherhood endows them with authority to speak for humankind and represents a public identity, extending far beyond the white picket fence. This view of womanhood is remniscent of the nineteenth-century women Christian reformers who sought to extend women's domestic role into public life, as represented by the slogan, "A new broom will sweep up city hall." Reuther (1983) emphasizes the feminist aspect of this movement, and categorizes it as "conservative romantic feminism."

As mothers and wives, Unificationist women are entitled to leave their kids in day care, and travel apart from their husbands to make the world a better home for their families. The wife of the Montreal director of the Unification Church left her husband in charge of their five children while she traveled to Toronto to chair the WFWP rally. Nora Spurgin noted back in 1978 that although she was a mother of three children, "my mission did allow me to do many exciting things, did free me from the day-to-day of children" (*Blessing Quarterly* 2 (Spring 1978): 41). The role conflict that women in this situation might feel is eased by the belief that the parent role and the mission role are parts of God's plan to restore the world.

The main dilemma Unificationist women in Canada face today is not uncompatible marriages. I received the impression the "Moonie" marriages were at least as solid as those in the mainstream. At present, Unificationist women in Canada appear to be coping with financial problems. Many of their husbands are recent immigrants from Asia or Africa and have spent their youth working for the church rather than compiling an impressive job record and training in a profession, and some of them have complained of racial discrimination in the workplace. Many Unificationist family men in Canada work for minimum wage or start their own small businesses, and the wives prefer to stay at home with their young children. After years of living communally, supported by a wealthy organization, Unificationist families today range from "well off" to poor and struggling. This situation is likely to change, however. When one considers such factors as the high value placed on industry and sacrifice, the church's financial and business creativity, its positive approach to the material world, and tradition of mutual cooperation, it seems likely that in fifty years or so, Unificationists will be regarded by the wider public as just another right wing, respectable, family-oriented, and upwardly mobile Christian minority church, not so very unlike the Mormons or the Seventh Day Adventists.

FIVE

Actualizers in the Institute of Applied Metaphysics

Before sexual division occurred each bisexual unit was in perfect affinity.

—Winifred Barton

Woman in the Institute of Applied Metaphysics (IAM) was defined as a complementary half of a yin-yang unit (married couple), and the "actualizer" of her husband's dreams and visions that he received in meditation. Marriages in IAM ritually expressed the reunion of two halves of the same soul separated since the beginning of time. The ideal yin-yang marriages were considered those contracted between young men and postmenopausal women. IAM couples were childless because of obligatory vasectomies for men joining the commune. The yin-yang units were held immortal by the female founder because they were the Chosen Ones who had witnessed her version of the End of the World. Husbands and wives worked side by side as teams organized under four "colors," or departments, and participated in ongoing workshops that fostered close, therapeutically orientated friendships between the different sets of couples.[1]

The History

The Institute of Applied Metaphysics was founded in 1963 by Winifred G. Barton (born circa 1919), a British immigrant living in Ottawa with her husband, Ernest, and their four sons. On descending into the basement of their suburban home to fill the washing machine, Barton (known as "Win" by her followers) encountered a spirit, Loliad R. Kahn. Loliad introduced himself as a metaphysician from Lost Atlantis, currently reincarnated as an insectlike alien on the planet Vringg, but Win recognized him as the "ringmaster" of her shamanic dream-visions, experienced during her tonsilitis operation in early childhood.

Inspired by Loliad, her "spirit guide," Win set up classes in metaphysics in her basement. By 1965, she had established a small following with local branches across Canada and was publicizing her courses. IAM was granted the status of a nonprofit, charitable organization in 1967, and proceeded to purchase three residential schools, or "campuses," in Madoc, Ontario (1972), in Nominingue, Quebec (1973), and in Gravelbourg, Saskatchewan (1974).

Loliad's revelations were written down by Win in a series of ten books, which explore an eclectic range of topics, such as dreams, astral travel, auras, psychic phenomena, ghosts, UFOs, and Lost Atlantis. Traditional Christian doctrines are combined with New Age themes, and her richly mythologized Universe is ruled over by a patriarchal "master." Although no information is available about Win's background in occult groups, Loliad resembles the "ascended masters" of the Theosophical tradition, and the name of her organization suggests a connection with the Great I AM of J. G. Ballard (Stillson Judah 1963).

IAM was presented in Open Houses and in a conference series across Canada (1974–76) as offering courses in which the student could realize her/his full human potential through meditation, dream analysis, keeping journals, and exploring the esoteric meaning of world religions. This training laid the foundation for the Applied Metaphysics course during which, it was understood, students would directly experience the spiritual realm and be reborn into it.[2]

Having established herself as a teacher of spiritual techniques and director of a thriving institute, Win began to escalate her charismatic claims and to demand a higher level of commitment from her students through her next spiritual innovations.

The Psychic Explosion. In 1973, Win began to predict a "psychic explosion" through confidential memos sent to senior students. In September of the same year, during the two-week Applied Metaphysics course at Madoc, students reported experiencing intense feelings of love and ecstasy, which were explained as a major breakthrough of spiritual energy on the planet (Morris 1986). During the psychic explosion, Win fell in love with Pierre Levesque, a handsome twenty-two-year-old student, thirty-two years her junior. Soon afterward she left her aged British husband and announced to her students that she and Pierre were two halves of the same soul, reunited after eons of separation into a yin-yang unit.

Win's next revelation was that the true identity of Pierre was Loliad, the cosmic lord in charge of planet Earth. This meant that Win and Pierre were now claiming to be the Messianic Couple, or the spiritual queen and king of the planet.

Yin-Yang Weddings. Between 1974 and 1976, students were strongly encouraged to form yin-yang units, which would become formalized in bucolic group weddings during the summer. The organization of IAM was restructured in a hierarchical fashion, the Messianic Couple ruling over a "theocracy," and four couples titled the "Four Beasts" placed in charge of four "colors," or departments: administration (yellow), teaching (blue), domestic work (green), and marketing (red).

The philosophical view of gender in IAM is an excellent example of sex complementarity, in that it combined the notions of equality and difference. Morris describes the philosophy of sexuality behind IAM's alternative marriage pattern. "According to IAM's doctrines, a man and a woman were two parts of the same spirit—a Yin and a Yang component. Only when two Yin-Yang halves were rejoined would a whole spirit and full spiritual power result."

One informant raises an important point, that originally the yin-yang marriage was presented as unique to Win and Pierre and related to their messianic status, but that by 1976, it was expected that *all* the citizens find and marry their yin-yang.

Of course Win and Pierre's wedding was a big deal. I remember thinking, Out of all the souls in the Universe, after eons of separation, these two great spirits have finally found each other. Wow! . . . I never thought it would happen to the rest of us. Well, all of a sudden, someone would walk off the street, take one course, meet someone in the workshop and bam!—another spiritual marriage one month later. When Win and Pierre got married it was *never again on Planet Earth!*—but then, *everyone* had to get married, *everyone* had to find their yin-yang.

Win had always emphasized the sanctity of marriage and the importance of fidelity to one's spouse. She offered courses in which couples presented conflicts and sexual problems and received spiritual advice. In Win's view, conjugal sex was "energizing and rejuvenating," and reinforced the essential spiritual interplay of yin and yang. One informant noted, "Win talked about sex . . . as the ultimate in coming together. It was like having flashes of eternity, of realizing that you were two halves of the same soul." Presenting an (unconscious) challenge to Rosabeth Moss Kanter, the same informant, Cora, saw this reinforcement of the diadic relationship as related to the need to strengthen the commune.

Then, a lot of Win's classes were about how to get along with your mate, about respect . . . you have to remember she wasn't *stupid!* When a whole bunch of people were living in such close quarters— and when you hear the word "commune" you think everyone sleeps with everyone else—things could easily have got out of hand. . . . Oh! it could have been chaos! So the concept of yin-yang was good in itself, but it was also a way of ensuring that people didn't sleep with each other's husbands. I thought, That's smart! I think she wanted to keep the institute *straight.* It was very frowned on for couples to live together, and there were a lot of hippies taking our courses, so when they moved in they had to get married—and it wasn't only a spiritual marriage, it was also legal.

Couples already married before joining would acknowledge their spiritual relationship in a yin-yang wedding. Single members were assigned work teams and told they "worked so well together," which often resulted in a yin-yang unit. One woman from the Winnipeg IAM center described how the leaders facilitated these matches, and noted her resistance to being treated as a "unit" rather than as an individual.

So, Luke and I became the local leaders, and I noticed how everyone seemed really happy that he'd found a woman at last. Win and Pierre wanted a couple to run things and they constantly set things up so that we were together all the time. . . . One day I took Pierre for a long walk, and I told him that I was sick of Luke, that I felt stuck with him. I felt I was no longer a *person*. I was always introduced as "Luke's girlfriend." I'd say, "Hi, I'm Edna!" but no one called me by my name. I'd always been a strong person; it didn't seem right not to have a name. Once people got to know me in the institute they would talk about "Luke n'Edna" . . . never "Edna n'Luke"—not even "Luke *and* Edna." I told Pierre I wanted to stand on my own. Anyway, Pierre never really answered me. He just went off on a long speech about how man and woman need the strength and balance of the other half. I was left feeling manipulated into being a unit. We weren't people in the institute, we were *units*. For example, we'd say "thirty couples" instead of "sixty people."

The same informant came to terms with Win's efforts to arrange her marriage through experiencing a "mystical moment."

Then I had a mystical moment on an airplane. I was on the way home from a two-week course at the Madoc center, and I'd got to know a guy; he was the most unbelievably gorgeous man, and he appeared to be interested in *me*. . . . I was sitting on the airplane thinking about him and listening to this song by Joe Cocker, "You Are So Beautiful to Me," when I had this experience. I suddenly knew I was linked with Luke and that we were meant to be together. When I arrived . . . Luke was there to greet me, and he drove me home. He had filled my whole room with lilacs. I realized that he had had the experience too. We never really discussed it, but we ended up having a yin-yang wedding.

In a manner resembling John Humphrey Noyes, who denounced what he termed "selfish love," Win militated against what she called "sympathetic relationships," such as a close friendship based on liking rather than on mutual cooperation over a task. She insisted that the selection of spouses was supposed to be spiritually predetermined (yin-yang) rather than based on personal preference.

The ritual format of IAM mass marriages was described by a participant in the yin-yang wedding celebrated in the summer of 1977.

I remember there were six or seven couples, and we were standing in a circle in a wheat field and the sky was a brilliant blue. It must have been summer. We were wearing off-white tunics and loose pants. Luke and I were; the other couples had their own colors. Win and Pierre stood in the middle of the circle and said something about the sacred and eternal quality of marriage and then they blessed us. . . . Oh, and we got hugs. They always hugged each couple. . . . It's funny, I can hardly remember anything, just the golden wheat and the blue sky with enormous fluffy clouds. I can't remember the wedding vows at all. . . . We had to look into each other's eyes and Win and Pierre had a special message for each couple; and then after the ceremony we all went back to the center and had a party.

The "End of the World." Win began to hold seminars in hotels across Canada featuring herself and different speakers on eco- logical and New Age issues. She was attending the United Na- tions Habitat Conference in Vancouver when she announced during an interview broadcast over the radio on June 7, 1976, that the world would end at noon, June 13. IAM students were ordered to gather at the rural campuses, bringing money and gas, to "be prepared for anything." One informant presented her version of this event.

Anyway, we all decided to go to the country campuses for the week- end. There were about one hundred and fifty of us gathered at the center in Nominingue. Winifred's warning was broadcast on the ham radio, and people were calling in to ask about it, but nobody knew what was going on. There were no details about how it was going to end. The police came looking for Win because the radio stations were calling her and doing interviews and there was a big panic—there was a big reaction. The faith in her was quite something.

On Sunday morning it was coming up to the deadline. Is some- thing going to happen? At ten o'clock suddenly Win arrives. She just came in and went to the front and started meditating. There was music playing and we all meditated. An hour passed, then suddenly it was twelve o'clock. We were still here. What had happened? Then I heard people around me saying, "Wow! Did you feel that?" A lot of people definitely felt something, that something spiritual had hap- pened. Certainly, nothing physical had.

Winifred maintained, after that weekend was over, that the world as we knew it (and now the stress was on the phrase "as we knew it") had, in fact, come to an end. This ending, she said, would become apparent in time and would manifest physically within a maximum of 3 1/2 years (Morris 1986, 15–16).

An interesting example of the stimulating effect of millenarian expectations on the mating instinct was provided by one informant's story about a member's brother who had never taken an IAM course, but on hearing Win's prophecy remembered a girl he had met briefly in Europe the previous summer. He thought, If the end is coming, I want to share that moment with her! He drove to her home in Alberta and persuaded her, despite her parents' protestations, to accompany him to Nominingue. They witnessed Barton's apocalypse, became a yin-yang unit, lived in the commune until it failed, and are (by all accounts) happily married today.[3]

The Communal Phase. Within the next four months the structure of the organization changed dramatically. What had begun as an urban institute offering courses to a large but transitory body of students transformed into four postmillennialist utopian communes in rural areas composed of a small but stable population of couples. Win and Pierre had followed up the apocalyptic weekend by inviting members to become "Citizens of the Kingdom of Heaven on Earth." This required students to marry their yin-yang unit, sign over all their assets to the institute, and live communally in one of the three rural locations. Citizens were also required to sever the "genetic link" by writing to their parents informing them that they would not be in contact again, for they were devoting their lives to God. Husbands were instructed to undergo vasectomies, because the millennium had arrived and the yin-yang units were immortal. Members who expressed difficulty in accepting this notion were advised by Win not to struggle with doubts, but to "put them in the neutral file." Morris writes: "Once citizenship was instituted, the total number of citizens quickly reached, and then stabilized at, around two hundred" (Morris 1986, 17).

These communes cultivated vegetable gardens and kept cows, chickens, and horses. Couples lived in "yurts," or small, muffin-shaped huts, dotted among the trees on the hills overlooking the main house, and thus enjoyed some privacy, but bathrooms, dining room, and the large living spaces were communal. Cigarettes, caffeine, and alchohol were forbidden. The institute made dandelion coffee and brewed beer, which was alcoholic but described as "undrinkable."

About thirty children were brought into the commune by their parents, but they were bused to a separate community called "le Jardin du Soleil" in Gravelbourg, Saskatchewan. The local school refused to take them, and they did not learn to read or write in the commune. By the following account, it appears they were seriously neglected. "They weren't taken care of. . . . In Nomininque I remember six of them were all living in a tiny room. When they brought them back to Ottawa, they found out they were just like little animals. They didn't know how to use a fork or a knife, they couldn't read or write or say their ABC's. They had no manners."

Life for the adults, however, was more pleasant. The citizens worked hard in maintaining their farms, renovating and building their houses, publishing their magazine and Barton's writings, and enjoyed leisure activities, such as traditional singing and dancing to the music of fiddles and guitars. Win periodically held workshops in which Citizens explored their inner life and the esoteric dimensions of their friendships.

The Charismatic Duo

Winifred Barton started out as an exemplary prophet (in Weber's terms), or as a teacher of techniques, characteristic of apprentice-type NRMs (Bird 1976). By marrying Pierre, she was claiming a new status as an ethical prophet, or a messiah who demands from his/her devotees total surrender. Win in the early phases of her career was described by her former students as a dynamic group facilitator with techniques for improving interpersonal communication. After she declared Pierre the Second Coming, she kept him insulated from casual, daily contact with her followers. In this way she succeeded in creating an aura of mystery around him, which she (as his yin partner) participated in, thereby enhancing her spiritual authority.

Some interesting insights into how the charismatic duo offset each other and functioned as parent figures to their followers were noted by former citizens.

Well, Win was a powerful leader, but I'm not sure about Pierre. . . . Physically, he was very much in the background. She would be teaching and he would be sitting in class not saying anything. The idea was, she was out there fighting but he was the Vibe behind her: that he supplied the energy to keep her going. It was always "Pierre's in meditation" or "Pierre's had a dream." He was the inspiration, she was the actualizer.

Another citizen noted the use of dark glasses as a "transcendance mechanism" (Kanter 1963). "He used to walk around with dark glasses because the light was supposed to destroy his Vibes. But, later we found out he was always smoking hash. . . . So it was probably to hide his eyes, so we wouldn't notice he was *gone*." All the informants emphasized his striking beauty and the erotic quality of his charisma. "We women used to fantasize about him. He was extremely handsome. I had erotic dreams about him, and so did some of the other girls . . . but none of us ever got to know who he really was. Win was his interpreter. All her decisions were because Pierre had a vision, Pierre had a dream." One woman's psychologically astute observation was that the charismatic duo became parent figures to their followers, and that Pierre played the role of the absent father.

But he had a larger impact than she did. There was a fear, an excitement when he came around. There was a bigger emotional impact. Win was like our mother—she was easier to get to know, more ordinary. We used to sit around with her and smoke and drink coffee and chew the fat. It was like my vision of the old days when Daddy went out to work and Mummy stayed home. He was mysterious, he came and went, and he was the disciplinarian. It was that mystery, that mystique that made Pierre so powerful.

Many of the innovations in sexuality and authority that followed were a result of the charismatic duo's effort to mould their followers' relationships into patterns resembling and re-

flecting their messianic marriage. IAM couples responded enthusiastically to Win and Pierre's innovations as cryptic messages, which promised to unveil the hidden significances of
their conjugal relationships.

The Angels of Armageddon. One of the unusual features of
IAM sexuality was the union between men in their teens or
early twenties to women in their late forties, fifties, and sixties.
These couples were presented in the literature as endowed with
special spiritual powers, and Win heaped praise on them, referring to them affectionately as "My Angels of Armageddon."
Pierre writes of the internal struggle in "His Own Case" by
which he came to recognize his yin-yang with a woman thirty-
two years his senior.

In My Own Case, Yin had been around for many years before My ar-
rival. Her personality circle was extraordinarily strong—success at
home, leisure and business life left few weak spots. Age and fading
sexual attractiveness were Ego's only recourse of manipulation, for we
had both been raised in the traditions of romantic love and this was
difficult programming to reconcile. Initial shyness and clumsiness in
role was My chief mortal difficulty, as man and God wrestled together
in their integration process. All exercises in unification were designed
to bring weaknesses to the forefront of mind where they can be consciously dissected in the spotlight of spirit. Pushing these things further back only gives strength to The Rival. . . . For many, cutting
through the thicket of biased sexual attitudes was a formidable task.
(*IAM The Book of Life,* 1979, 2:68–69)

The matchmakings of the Angels of Armageddon were described as follows:

There were at least eight units in Nomininque where the woman was
considerably older. There was H. amd M.—she was at least thirty years
older than he was. In those cases, Win usually acted as matchmaker. . . .
She would send them out on a project together. It was somehow manipulated. People would start telling them they looked alike . . . how
well they worked together. Then she would strongly suggest they were
yin-yang. But the couple themselves would have to decide. They would
have to have some kind of mystical experience together. . . . They
sometimes had it separately like me and Luke, but it was supposed to
happen at the same moment. The problem was, there were all these

young men attracted to the institute, but for some reason, the average age of the women was much older. I remember one summer a group of about twenty teenage men joined. They were great workers! I was worried because we didn't have any young women for them. Most of them ended up with older women. Obviously, some of these people were not meant to be together.

The union of older women with younger men served a millenarian function. The passage below is written in Winifred Barton's inimitable prose style, and it is evidently intended to be read as a testimonial to the superior quality, both spiritually and sexually, of marriage between callow youth and postmenopausal women.

The success story of M. and H. is typical of the eventual realizations we reached. It truly captures the essence of Yin-yang. "Good sex" was normal for this loving and open couple. . . .
Then one night during intercourse Marcel found himself centred in the midst of a huge, brightly lit bubble—much like a circular movie screen. . . . He watched the formation and reformation of all his fantasies from childhood on. . . . The pictures were bionic, pounding on and off like modern TV advertising, growing in emotional intensity with every other move. He saw the essence of his every love, his mother, sisters . . . swirling and dancing together in the theatre of mind.
The pace, both physical and mental, quickened, in his moment of orgasm Marcel experienced the point where all the bionic pictures melted into one—that of his wife, H.—and in that second he experienced the emotional realization that all the essence of love ever experienced before was distilled into that one being—his Yin-Yang cosmic bride.
As the orgasmic thrill subsided, still in their own universal bubble, H. and M. watched pictures of all the people on earth smiling from the screen. For their lovemaking had gone out to everyone. Mankind had received the reverberations of their love—as indeed it was meant to be. Such lovers contribute their all to the Universal Sea, so contributing to the upgrading of all life on the planet. . . . Our beloved M., together with his lovely wife, was indeed the Angel of Armageddon. The Rival was deposed. They had arrived. United they had entered the Kingdom of Heaven. The sword of truth had cut their path to love, to the total conquest of their combined 360 circle of I am Yin-yang unity. (*IAM The Millennium* 1979, 2:69–70)

One can only speculate on Barton's motives for imposing this unusual sexual innovation on her followers. One plausible explanation ex-members offered was that it was based on expediency (there being a dearth of young women and an excess of older women). The most obvious explanation, however, is that she wished to spiritually legitimate her unconventional relationship and undermine ageist attitudes among her flock.

Pierre's Double. To protect Pierre, who "as the Second Coming was necessary for the survival of Planet Earth," the citizens shielded him from the view of outsiders, and no photographs of him were taken. One day a student appeared in an institute course "who looked phenomenally like him," so a plan was hatched to use the unwitting student as a "front man" for Pierre. The citizens "knocked themselves out to keep him" and he was called "Pierre's Double" behind his back and reportedly never realized "why we all were being so nice to him."

Commitment Mechanisms

Besides these striking innovations, techniques were introduced by Barton that aimed at forging strong, therapeutic friendships and marriages. These were tried out in workshops held at the IAM communes in the 1970s.

The Microdots. The Microdots experiment, conducted in a workshop at the Madoc, Ontario, rural "campus" in the spring of 1979, could be interpreted as a first tentative step toward adopting a "free love" ethic, which was quickly retracted. On the basis of my informants' accounts of this event, its function appeared to be to enrich and cement friendships between men and women outside the yin-yang unit. It might also be explained as a Kanterian commitment mechanism in that it reinforced the individual's sense of belonging to a whole community rather than to a dyad. It introduced a playful, spontaneous element into a network of relationships that were withdrawing from—and closing out—the outside world. Because IAM citizens had recently "severed the genetic link" and were now cut off from family and past friendships, it seemed necessary to find new avenues for exploring relationships within the commune. Carol describes the Microdots workshop.

We were told that our consciousness was like a big TV screen and the picture was made up of tiny dots of red, green, yellow, and blue. We needed to have a full slate of experience—to have *all* colors of microdots. You would need a minimum in real life experience to become spiritually fulfilled. So, we were to take a look at the past and see what we had missed out on. If you'd never had a relationship with your father, or mother, or never truly been in love, or lacked a sister. . . . What I felt I had never experienced was *puppy love*. So, I was told to go off walking in the woods with Bob, and pretend we were twelve and he was my first innocent puppy love. We spent all day together for a week—just playing and having fun, but I had to put an end to it because of [my husband]. It was driving him crazy—he felt so much pain, he told me he couldn't stand it, so I stopped. But I *did* feel a little resentful that he was interfering with my microdots.

The ABWA Concept. The ABWA concept was introduced in 1978 in one of Win's workshops, and might be explained in Kanterian terms as a "communion" mechanism. It resembles Scientology's "confrontation" technique, which uses eye contact to promote a sense of a hidden, powerful spiritual identity. Informant Carol describes how it enhanced her friendships with both male and female communards.

I remember in one workshop Win told us, "You should ABWA with people." My first ABWA I had was with Jules, and we were doing past life therapy. I was sitting on the rocks facing Jules, and it was as if I was hypnotized by him. I conjured up a vision of myself as Cleopatra! It was like taking LSD, and I think it was somehow induced by him. And his features changed and I felt we were spiritually akin, as if we'd once been married. I think the purpose of it was to have a spiritual experience together and unite in the spiritual realm. But then, later, it became an excuse to not do anything—or to take a break when you were tired or bored. I would be working in the kitchen all day, and Edith would suddenly say, "I've got to ABWA with you!" Then we'd go sit on her bed facing each other and we'd just—talk. I remember it was really fun, we'd laugh and we'd just say whatever came into our heads and get really silly . . . but it was OK to waste time and drop our cooking because we were doing something spiritual—we were ABWAing!

Both the ABWA experiment (an attempt to see into past lives) and the Microdots workshop (inventing a mythical childhood with an IAM partner) might be analyzed as part of a psychological task of *replacing* the rejected bonds with family and friends by constructing an alternative "spiritual" or surrogate emotional history involving one's fellow communards.

The White Knights Course. The White Knights Course, which took place at the Madoc farm in August 1979, appears to be a striking example of what Kanter (1972) called *mortification*. Mortification enhances the individual's commitment to the community because it "provides a new identity for the person that is based on the power and meaningfulness of group identity; they reduce his sense of a private, unconnected ego" (Kanter 1972, 103). Worseley's insights (1977) into the ritual breaking of taboos among Melanesian cargo cults also seem relevant here. Georg Feuerstein's study of "crazy wisdom gurus" (1991), who seek to shock disciples into awareness and jolt them out of preconditioned patterns of thought through ritual obscenity, also springs to mind.

I remember . . . all the men were told to go out in the woods, form bands and fight each other—just with sticks, no one got really hurt. We girls used to hear them roaring. . . . Anyway, we were all waiting one morning in the classroom, and I looked out the window and I could see Win coming down the path carrying a pink towel, and Marjorie (one of the Beasts) was walking behind carrying a big pail and a wooden toilet seat, and I was thinking, What is she doing with that?

So Win comes in, puts the toilet seat over the pail, pulls down her pants and sits right on it and pees! We were shocked, we couldn't believe it. Then she got up and launched a harangue against us, complaining about our lack of commitment and that we should "pee or get off the pot." So, everybody had to do it—and it was pretty embarrassing. But Marcel, he not only peed, he shat into the pot. We all thought that was pretty funny!

Sex Every Day. Although sex before or outside marriage was forbidden in IAM, there were no restrictions on the sexual relationship *within* marriage (beyond the vasectomies), but the couples in the Nominingue commune complained that for several weeks there was "*too* much sex." This situation appeared to arise from a misunderstanding, described as follows.

Well, I'm sure it was all a mistake. It started out because the Yellow Couple were having problems. He wasn't sexually attracted to her. She was considerably older than him—by about twenty years. They went and consulted Win and Pierre, who told them they should make themselves have sex every day, whether they felt like it or not. Somehow, when they got back to Nominingue and told us about it, it was misinterpreted, and we got this idea that *every* couple had to have sex every day. So we set aside an hour after dinner when everyone retired to their bedrooms . . . it was ridiculous! The walls were paper-thin and you could *hear* everyone. Luke and I agreed we'd just take a nap if we didn't feel like it. We all believed that this was the Master's Will, but then when Win visited, she asked what was going on, and when we told her she said she had only meant that advice to apply to the Yellow Couple.

Sympathetic Friendships. Although Winifred officially condemned "sympathetic friendships," two of my informants described enjoying an intense, satisfying friendship, which continues today.

I was so excited when I finally met her, because we'd been hearing so much about each other and had corresponded about various projects. The minute I saw her I just loved her! We used to find some pretext to go to Ottawa for the day on business, but we'd just take it easy, sit at our favorite cafés, and enjoy good coffee, not the dandelion stuff we made in the domes . . . we'd have a ball! Carol would always buy me a bottle of Amoretto, because she knew I loved it, but I never had any money. And we'd sneak into movies. . . . She somehow always had money . . . (we were supposed to give it all to the institute when we became Citizens, but I suspect she kept some of it in a secret account). Anyway, she was very generous in spending it on me.

Phases of Displacement of Charisma

"The King Is Come to Live Among His People," Win's spiritual authority began to decline shortly after Pierre's decision to move in with the Citizens at the Nominingue commune, thereby failing to observe the commitment mechanism of "transcendance,"

which Kanter claims insulates the leader from his/her flock and creates a sense of mystery and awe. A series of moves were made that led to Pierre's usurping Win as IAM's leader. One informant believed that Pierre had been plotting a coup all along, but another explained this process as Win's doing: "Win thought she could have more spiritual power by building Pierre up, but it backfired—she was setting him up to depose her! Maybe, deep down she wanted him to take over, maybe she was trying to bribe him to love her more." Former Citizens spoke of how uncomfortable it was living up close to the charismatic duo.

Well, things were going along really nicely, until one day we decided that Win is going to build Pierre a house, and he is going to come and live with us. Now, they'd been getting hokier and hokier as time went on. They were saying that they had a direct link with God and that Pierre was the Second Coming. That's right, they had slowly built up to this. . . . Now, Pierre goes along with this. He acts like he is the Lord Himself when you're in his presence—like he checks out your eyes to make sure you're spiritually OK. I mean, you were afraid to look too deep into his eyes. . . . And when they moved in, that's when things really began to degenerate—when Win became involved in our day-to-day operations. Before that, we'd just had classes with her when she visited, but now she was living there. She would wake up in the morning with a theory and everything would have to be shut down and we'd have to spend the whole day in class. That's fine, we're flexible, but now everything becomes more intense and . . . unpredictable.

Pierre's Four Actualizers. Pierre began to exhibit the first signs of assuming an independent authority. He announced he was to take over and run things, and chose four women from the four colors to be his "handmaidens" or "actualizers." This involved monthly meetings with the blue, red, yellow, and green actualizers, during which his inadequacies as a leader became evident. "We used to walk up the hill together and would feel excited about being with Pierre, but he never actually *said* much. He'd just nod mysteriously and tell us we were doing a fine job and tell us to 'Keep up the Vibe.'"

The Male Vibe. The announcement of the Male Vibe occurred in 1978; shortly after, Pierre moved into the house Win built for him in the Coburg estate. Winifred had been building up his charisma and by this time the yin-yang units understood that "Pierre was in charge, Win was subordinate." The revelation came to Win through Pierre, but she announced that the "Male Vibe" had arrived on Planet Earth. "And the idea was that men were going to be taking over more and more: they were getting more powerful, on the planet, in the commune, in the universe. It was microcosm and macrocosm. At the time I felt she was tired of running the show, and she was trying to get Pierre to take a more active role." This announcement diminished women's power.

And she's been building him up: now she's *his* servant. . . . She's his Handmaiden, and all of a sudden, things start changing balance when they come out with: "Men are superior, and women should find their place as the Servants, the Handmaidens"—oh yeah, you should've seen it. It was *sheer power.* All the men thought, Hey! This is *wonderful!* I mean, why shouldn't they?

Win began to elaborate on a new, spiritual philosophy of sexuality.

And all of a sudden, Win comes out with these theories on women. Woman can be the businesswoman, she can be the farmer's wife, she can be the Geisha girl . . . I can't remember the rest. She broke it down to four groups and we weren't exactly diminished, but a woman could only be this way or that, whereas men were stronger, they would point the direction and women must be the actualizers. I guess it was because Pierre never actually *did* anything—and she was a *big* actualizer.

One informant described Male Vibe's negative effect on the sex-egalitarian work roles in the commune.

It was supposed to be a kind of cosmic energy bearing down on men, and it would be reflected in us [the women] if we *obeyed.* All of a sudden our work routines changed. We had always been strong couples working as teams in our Colors, but now all the women had to get up and feed the animals and do the housework while the men would stay in bed in the Domes [communes] and "meditate"—some of them would stay in bed *all day* because they were "wiped out by the Vibe." And it was always the "Male Vibe" that dictated when we made love.

The Wife-Beating Experiment. Apparently as a direct consequence of the ascension of the Male Vibe, Win and Pierre began to encourage wife beating among the couples. One former battered wife describes this phase, which began in 1979 and "petered out" by 1980.

Some units had severe problems. There was the Red Couple. He was a cute little playboy, about seventeen or eighteen, and she was twenty-five years older (she was an ex-nun). He couldn't stand her and he beat her up all the time! She was walking around with black eyes, and once he even threw her down the stairs and broke her leg! Now, this behavior was not condoned. He used to say she "got on his case" and Win used to reprimand him, especially after he broke her glasses five times and we had to pay for the new ones. . . .

Then there was the Green Couple—they didn't seem to like each other much. She had been one of the earliest leaders and had organized the Madoc school over the summers before he even joined. She was a former Playboy Bunny, made lots of money, was very voluptuous—around twenty-five. He was eighteen or nineteen. Win had put them to work together, and you could tell J. really resented having to share the credit with him. Anyway, he complained she wasn't obeying him properly. They'd go into town and she'd criticize him for buying *Playboy* and she'd want real chocolate, not carob like we were supposed to eat, so he'd criticize her. Well, they went to see Win and she said, "R., you are head of this yin-yang unit and you have to make J. listen, so do *whatever it takes* to make her obey." So, the next time, he dragged her upstairs by her hair into their bedroom and hit her until she was submissive. I couldn't believe it! They were telling us about it and she was sitting there with two black eyes giggling her head off! They seemed to think it was great. . . . And it was like a sign—*whatever it takes* to keep your woman in line! As if God gave the men permission to beat us up! Then *everyone* was trying it. Also, yelling and screaming at each other was considered good.

This informant's defection from the commune was, she claims, motivated by her husband's physical abuse.

The Decline of the Commune

The IAM communes lasted only eight years. The reasons for their decline can be traced to Win and Pierre's loss of charisma, to the recent reorganization of authority patterns (wife beating, unequal sex roles, and a new board of directors) which affected marriages and friendships negatively, and to a financial crisis in 1982. The innovations between 1978 and 1982 might be analyzed as desperate attempts to prop up the crumbling commune.

"God Will Provide." By this time the institute had exhausted the donations of the Citizens of the Universe, and various entrepreneurial strategies had been aborted by revelations and dreams from the top, accompanied by assurances that "God will provide." One informant, a former bank manager who, in tandem with her husband, had been one of the "Four Beasts," expressed her frustration at being responsible for finances and yet having to defer in her rational decisions to the unpredictable spiritual impulses of the charismatic duo.

Now, at this point you have to realize that we were running out of money, and we've been living this way for six years and the money that people brought in, a lot of it has gone into capital, and people were no longer taking our courses. We have become so internalized that we don't have contact with the outside world. We're living on a farm, nobody knows where it is. . . . They've made it into a big secret, nobody's allowed to come there. . . .

And the magazine. . . . We had people who were highly qualified. . . . We would be producing something of very high quality, and all of a sudden, Win would say, "Close it down!" . . . So we would start these massive projects, a lot of energy would go into them and they'd be going well, then all of a sudden, it was, "No. We're not doing this anymore, we're doing *this.*" . . . we'd started a magazine, and a lot of work had gone into it, marketing, writing, layout, setting up the printshop, then . . . "Forget about it!" And because we needed money, we'd start a paint company out in Saskatchewan. A lot of men were working out there. Now, that paint company was really a going concern. We were probably bringing in between two hundred and three hundred thousand a year! And in one day, they closed down the company *in one day!* They had built up enough good will that they could have sold the business, but Win ordered all the men to come back *that day.* They just had to drop it. It was "God will provide." We had people distributing paint all over the country, then one day it was, "Forget it. Close it down." It became nuts. We weren't surviving. We were getting further and further out of touch. And it was difficult to talk to them in practical terms. We would say, "Look, we don't have enough money to cover our taxes. Our taxes are due next month." And they would say, "That's your problem. We look after the higher things." And yet we had no control.

We couldn't tell people to go out and find a job because that was against our philosophy. So the position we held—our responsibility—it just didn't make sense!

Morris's essay supports this view, that a major reason for the decline of IAM was economic. Her survey of what citizens liked least about IAM reveals that, for 45 percent it was the financial problems (i.e., the lack of money for both corporate and personal use). Only 15 percent cited "ineffectualness," meaning the "series of abortive campaigns and projects" (Morris 1986, 98).

Double Couples and the Mega-Nation. In the spring of 1978, Win introduced the concept that IAM's divine mandate was to unite the earth into a "mega-nation," which the "Chosen" would administer the United Nations under the direction of Pierre. This necessitated many citizens leaving the rural communes and finding work in cities, but paying tithes to the institute. These groups were organized into "Double Couples."

We had all been living in seclusion, but suddenly Win decides to set up this experiment of Double Couples, and sends them out into the world to earn money for the institute and to advertise our courses. So, she matched these totally inappropriate couples and *we* ended up with Paul and Jean. We all went to live in Kitchener, and Paul was an electrician, so he immediately got a job and was supporting all of us. I was in charge of money. . . . Anyway, the Double Couples were out for about four or five months. Some sent money back to the Domes. Then Win realized it wasn't working and recalled them all back to Nominingue. . . . [She] had found that the Double Couples were getting corrupted by their freedom. They were starting to get rebellious. So, she decided to train us to be leaders instead.

Win's Radio Transmissions. Extensive radio contact was established between the residential locations and with the Double Couples living outside, and, at this time, Win began to hold forth in lengthy, seemingly interminable—and increasingly incoherent—broadcasts, reputedly lasting up to twelve hours a day. One informant recollects:

She would come on the radio . . . we had radio communication between all the centers to save money. And she [Win] would come on and talk—and her theories did not make sense! Like, she would get lost and forget what she was saying. She could go on for hours, but if you asked me what she had just said, I couldn't tell you. I felt she was, well, going insane. We both felt she was . . . losing it.

In 1984, a ferocious battle between Win and Pierre was broadcast unwittingly over the radio to two residential locations, and embarrassing personal matters like sexual jealousy were publicly aired. At this point, Citizens' repressed doubts began to surface. "I sometimes felt that Win was crazy, mad. It scared me at times. The only way I could cope with it was by convincing myself that I was wrong and she was right" (Morris 1986, 84). They began to see through her transcendance mechanisms.

I was so angry at her; I wanted to kill her. . . . And then I felt bad—because I felt that it must be my mistake. I went over to her and broke down and cried, and I was saying, "I'm so sorry. I was angry at you and I know it's not your fault, and you're beautiful." And I was crying and crying. And Win said, "Don't worry; just be patient." Then she said, "Would you like to see Him [Pierre] now?" And I went to him and looked in his eyes; and it was just beautiful. And he said something totally mysterious like, "You know what's going on, don't you?" So what I'm saying is that when I look back on my own personal relationship with those two people, what I see is really a lot of psychological games that went on. (Morris 1986, 85)

The Displacement. In 1985, Pierre persuaded Win to leave their mansion in Coburg and to move to the Nominigue campus, and assigned a male citizen to accompany her. Win reputedly "sexually abused" her escort, and then attempted to return to Madoc. Pierre overhauled the board of directors at this time, who, by a sweeping majority, voted that Win should resign, not only her leadership but also her citizenship. Morris (1986, 31) writes that on January 20, 1985, Pierre laid charges against Winifred for attempting to break into their common house. These charges were withdrawn by the Crown attorney because the Crown contended that the wife cannot break into her own abode. Shortly after, Pierre was arrested for being "unlawfully in a dwelling house" and was sent to the Kingston

Psychiatric Hospital, but released after a few days. The "local homeowner" who had called the police had complained that Pierre's stated purpose for entering his house was to announce that he was the Second Coming—and that he had refused to leave until the "homeowner" accepted his claim.

Between 1984 and 1985, the citizens began to defect in groups, and former members living in Ottawa and Montreal set up informal "exit counseling" procedures to help their friends, which involved putting them up, contacting their families, helping them find apartments, jobs, and hours of talking things over.

Winifred Barton was admitted to the Royal Ottawa Hospital (psychiatric ward) and Pierre continues to live in the mansion she built for him on the Coburg, Ontario, estate with six Citizens, who (along with six dobermans) act as his bodyguards against potential assassins, for they believe that the premature death of the Second Coming will "plunge the planet into darkness." Recently, at thirty-eight, Pierre remarried, this time to a woman of fifteen, who is one of the children brought into the commune by her mother in 1976.[4]

Conclusion

In describing how their commune failed, all the informants expressed a deep frustration about Win and Pierre's erratic style of leadership. The commune was operating very nicely, they insisted; everyone was happy and perfectly capable of handling financial or other problems, but the charismatic duo was so preoccupied by their spiritual fantasies and conjugal battles that they persisted in tearing things apart. Pierre's usurpation of the leadership was the final blow, for he lacked Barton's gifts as a group facilitator and visionary, and once he stepped out of her shadow, his weakness, passivity, and drug habits were exposed and drove away all but six of his followers. Without being privy to their private relationship, one can only speculate on what really happened between Win and Pierre. Did Pierre take over because he sensed her incipient madness, or did he *drive* her

mad through his ruthless tactics to depose her? Or did Win
self-destructively set herself up to be deposed? [5]

The kind of experimentation with gender and power relationships occurring in IAM fits the "leader's lab" or "charismatic" model (see chap. 1). This is most often found in first
generation, communal NRMs, in which the founder frequently
and unexpectedly changes the basic ground rules governing
sexual behavior and family life. In these cases, the leader tends
to voice extravagant charismatic claims, and appears to be responding to one or more of the following factors: crises or
changes in her/his romantic or family relationships; external
persecution or problems previously encountered in the larger
society; his/her inner creative and spiritual life (i.e., divine revelations or millenarian prophecies).

IAM fits this mode of sexual experimentation because there
appears to be a clear relationship between the emotional ups and
downs occurring in Win's personal life and the experimentation
surrounding gender roles and power relationships that developed among her communards. Each innovation (announced
as divinely inspired) appeared to arise out of the emotional conflicts and power struggle waging between Win and her husband,
Pierre. Thus, in a sense, the ongoing series of sexual experiments
that IAM couples engaged in might be perceived as reflecting or
"acting out" the unfolding drama of the charismatic duo's marital relationship. IAM's extraordinary divagations and ongoing
experimentation in sexuality might be analyzed as examples of
Kanter's "transcendance" mechanisms, which affected the charismatic "love affair" between Winifred Barton and her yin-yang
units. Some of these mechanisms enhanced her charisma; others
diminished it. The mechanisms employed by her messianic
partner, Pierre, eventually led to her displacement. With these
thoughts in mind, we will attempt to fathom women's experience in IAM.

The patterns of feminine conversion in IAM cannot be compared to the other NRMs in our study. There appears to be no
possibility of women choosing to join IAM communes because
of their alternative gender roles. The 200-odd communards

had at first thought they were signing up for a study group, a "world-affirming" type of NRM (Wallis 1985), which through "social implosian" (Bainbridge 1978) unexpectedly transformed into a "world-denying" type, a postmillennial utopian commune. The original "Citizens of the Universe" remained a relatively stable population in their remote country "domes" and did not advertise their unusual family patterns to the outside world. Although "spiritualizing" male-female relationships had begun *before* the communal phase, the other sexual innovations, such as the "Male Vibe" and wife beating, developed *after* the couples had already committed themselves to the communal way of life. Thus, one cannot argue that older women hoping to marry young men, or women who wanted intimate monogamy but no children were motivated to join. IAM women appeared to have no idea what was in store for them.

Some definitive statements can be made, however, about what women got out of the IAM communes, and the social and familial backgrounds of members. Morris found in her demographic survey of former citizens that "a large proportion of respondents had experienced serious disruptions in their family relationships during childhood." Although 80 percent of her sample reported being close with parents and on good terms with siblings before joining, Morris found that 35 percent had experienced the death of a parent before their twentieth birthday, and 35 percent had witnessed marital disruptions, including divorce, unwed mothers, absent fathers, and separation. Morris concludes, "This rate is in sharp contrast to what would be expected for the general Canadian population, in which only 20 percent of ever-married men or women age 18–64 have had a marriage end by death, divorce, or separation." This finding might seem to suggest a "substitute family" theory, but Morris suggests a more complex theory to account for her "disrupted" respondents' reasons for joining. "This situation of group solidarity without individual attachments provided the security and warmth of a new or substitute "family," while guarding against the possibilty of a loss or disruption such as many respondents had experienced in their families of origin" (Morris 1986, 60). Morris argues that the sheer numbers of "family" members afforded a certain security, and quotes one of her informants.

The ideal was bigger than a family. . . . Really, a *tribe.* So you could have that security without that sense of loss. You could ostracize an individual . . . but the tribe would remain intact. . . . Like, I found that my father had been cheating—right before my parents got separated. That really shattered me. . . . So there was not the security there, the meaning. So you're looking for a meaning—in a sense we called it spiritual—but it could have also been a sense of belonging—something to live for.

Morris characterizes the relationships between citizens as "a paradoxical combination of closeness and distance," a closeness based on "tribal" feeling rather than on interpersonal emotional bonds. She argues that this "tribal" feeling was fostered through limiting communication between individuals. This limit was institutionalized through a mechanism of social control called "compartmentalization," which required that "negativity" be squelched before it spread through the community. Any individual having doubts or criticisms was advised to refrain from expressing them, and to sign up for lessons 1, 2, and 3, where they could work them out. Morris concludes, "Overall, then, the issues of community and interpersonal connectedness (both outside and within IAM) seem to have been central to both 'disrupted' and 'non-disrupted' respondents' joining processes (61)."

On the basis of this researcher's small sample, it is clear that IAM members, like many middle-class youth of the 1970s counterculture, were rejecting the "materialistic," "straight" life-style of their parents. One couple I interviewed had already decided to remain childless before joining IAM, and remarked that many of their peers in IAM had felt the same way. The way of life developed in IAM might be seen as a more extreme version of the life-style young, upwardly mobile Canadians were adopting in the late 1970s. Both sets of "Four Beasts," for example, were highly successful in their careers and were living in comfortable, well-equipped homes by their early twenties. They shared finances and work in the home equally, and enjoyed recreation with other young couples. What they had felt lacking (particularly living in Ottawa, which is infamous among young Canadians for its poor night life and its staid atmosphere) was an exciting, fulfilling social life and a sense of adventure and higher meaning. This is exactly what Barton's Institute supplied. Here they met other intelligent, sociable young couples and signed up for courses in which close friendships were forged and the meaning of life was investigated. In the institute they developed more intimate relationships with other couples, which did not threaten the integrity of their marriages, and they enjoyed that feeling of belonging to an elite social club of their peers. In this way they were rejecting the privatism, the boredom, and the domestic isolation that is the lot of many suburban couples, and that John Updike portrays so frighteningly in his novels.

One informant was from the Mennonite community in Winnipeg, but had left her husband for the "freedom" and the "philosophical approach to life" offered by the institute. In retrospect she explained her conversion as an attempt to restore that sense of belonging she had felt as a child growing up Mennonite.

You know, as a Mennonite you really feel you belong, that everyone is together. Then, when I went to univerity, my education opened my mind. I became independent, critical. But that sense of belonging, that security was lost. I think that's why I went into the institute, to fill that gap. Even now, I'm reading a book by Jerry Falwell . . . and part of me is thinking, This is disgusting! But another part is thinking, God, this feels good! There is a powerful appeal in this community he is trying to build in which everyone has the same beliefs. I miss that feeling of *belonging*!

These insights, it might be objected, apply to any communal experience, for all communes, being collective, provide a sense of belonging. In addressing IAM's appeal for women, therefore, we must look at what was unique about this commune and ask, "In what ways did it appeal to young married, childless, middle-class, English Canadian, working women?" Because IAM women had already experienced a taste of Win's frenetic creativity before 1976, they must have realized it was impossible to predict what they would be getting into when they and their husbands became Citizens of the Universe. It appears reasonable, therefore, to propose that it was Win's unpredictability, that sense of adventure she supplied, that attracted them. On the basis of their statements, it seems that the dynamic presence of a female spiritual leader, the responsible posts given to women, and the high value placed on marriage were features that appealed to potential female converts in the early phases of the institute.. In retrospect, however, it appears that IAM women were not so much attracted to a particular model of gender (which in any case kept changing) as to the *process* of experimentation itself. Their faith in Win as a totally self-realized, creative mystagogue sustained them as she guided them through a series of puzzling—and often self-destructive—games that they believed would ultimately enrich their marriages and their spiritual lives.

Experimenting with feminine power was evidently important in the movement's history. Winifred Barton was a strong, dynamic leader, who attracted strong women followers. One informant's husband shared his first impression of the institute as "a place where all these powerful, super-efficient women were running things—it was kind of intimidating." The institute was an environment that supported committed, egalitarian marriages based on teamwork, but in Win's obsessive quest for the religious roots of romantic love, she began to demand from her female citizens that they surrender to their husbands, and adopt the undignified posture of the toiling, servile "handmaiden" who submits to disciplinary blows. Although two wives I interviewed (whose marriages predated joining IAM) insisted that their husbands were far too considerate to take advantage of this situation, some of the "arranged" marriages followed Win's masochistic example. This overt expression of marital discord contributed to the low morale and impressions of chaos felt by members of a declining commune.

While getting to know these secularized yin-yang units, who are now in their early forties and could be described (in the eighties) as "dinks" (double income/no kids), the author was impressed by the care they had taken to preserve the close friendships formed in the commune. At least eight couples continue to gather together for country weekends, to share their problems and exchange the latest news on other former citizens, and to look out for one another's careers and generally to "mother" one another. An annual reunion is organized at one couple's chalet in the Laurentians, which couples from the United States drive up to attend. It appears that out of the demise of the commune some elements of the "spiritual family" have survived.

SIX

Helpmeets in the Messianic Community

*Fully redeemed woman can love and be submissive to fully re-
deemed man, because Christ is truly his head, and his heart
is being restored to woman.*

*We are discovering who truly liberated women are—women
set free to love and trust Him, their husbands, brothers, children and each other. We can gratefully say we were born to
complete man—to help and support him."*
                —Elizabeth's testimony in the Freepaper.

Women in the Messianic Community (formerly known as the
Northeast Kingdom Community Church) define themselves as
the loving "helpmeets" of their husbands and teachers of their
children. Messianic couples live in communal "households" of
six to eight families, and women wear head scarves to denote
their submission to male authority. Men and women have traditional work roles, and are skilled in various crafts, and a strong
emphasis is placed on educating their children in the values and
millenarian expectations of the sect.[1]

The History

The Northeast Kingdom Community Church (renamed the
Messianic Community in 1993) was founded by Elbert Spriggs
(known as Yoneq) in Chattanooga, Tennessee, in 1972. A former
high school teacher and travel tour guide, he joined the Jesus
movement and opened up a health food restaurant called the
Yellow Deli. Its menu stated, "Our specialty is the fruit of the
spirit. Why not ask?" The deli was a success, in commercial and

evangelical terms, so that Spriggs and his wife, Marsha, opened seven more restaurants by 1977. They were soon living communally with a group of young people with whom they bought and renovated old houses. The Spriggses and friends attended services at different churches, but when they arrived one Sunday to find the service canceled because of the Super Bowl, they decided to turn their backs on conventional religion and hold their own worship.

Sensing Chattanooga's declining interest in their message and discouraged by the unwelcome attentions of the twelve professional deprogrammers in Chattanooga between 1978 and 1979, the group sold all its property in Tennessee and moved to Island Pond in Vermont. There they reorganized their communal patterns. From living as "one big business with one set of needs," they established independent communes, or Households. A Household is a group of three to eight families (with a few single adults) who buy and renovate a large Victorian house together and share a communal kitchen and dining room but retain individual bedrooms for couples and their children. The six Households are economically independent, but work together in the Common Sense Store and the printing company and meet as a unit in their Gatherings, which take place on Friday and Saturday at sundown. These meetings combine the old-fashioned revival meeting and a barn dance. The men preach and offer testimonials and women, children, and men dance to Israeli-style folk dances and songs composed by their people, accompanied by handmade Celtic instruments.

The Community identifies itself as the "lost and scattered tribes" of the ancient Jews, regathering as the end of time approaches. For this reason, they adopt Hebrew names and teach their children Hebrew in their alternative school system. They translate "church" in Hebrew as "community" and identify their own as the "pure and spotless bride" of Revelation awaiting the return of the "King" (the Second Coming), whom they call Yahshua. To prepare for His Return, they must "raise up a people," which they explain as increasing their population through reproduction and missionary activity over three generations of purifying maturation before the "Yobel"

will be blown. Their pattern of authority appears to be a gen-
uinely acephalous and collective (but no less charismatic)
phenomenon. Prophecies and revelations, doctrinal and ritual
innovations are abundantly generated and shared by the male
Apostles, Elders, and Teachers during their "Shabat" revival
meetings. Women who are "covered" (as the headscarf denotes)
may pray and prophesy when inspired. Elbert Spriggs is not regarded as their leader but is described as "the first one of our
People to open up his home to his brothers and sisters."[2]

The Community in Island Pond received extensive media
coverage in 1984 because of what they now refer to as "the
Raid." On June 22, ninety Vermont state police officers carrying guns and wearing bullet-proof vests accompanied by fifty
social workers went into twenty bedrooms at 6:30 A.M. and
rounded up 112 children and bused them into Newport. Their
parents (110 adults) insisted on coming along and they were
held in custody while the state requested a seventy-two-hour
blanket detention order for questioning and examining all children. This action was taken in response to the anticult movement's efforts in stirring up official concern for past charges of
child assault, for home schooling "indoctrination," and for failure to report births and deaths. This tension was exacerbated
by a custody battle between an apostate father and his wife,
who remained in the Community with their chidren. The families on trial sang songs in praise of Yahshua during the bus ride,
and on being herded into a large room in Newport to await
their hearing, they engaged in a marathon of Israeli circle
dancing. "The judge loved us, even some of the policemen
were charmed. We could see we had touched their hearts," one
woman who had been there reported. Judge Frank Mahady
ruled against the detention and, one by one, all 112 cases were
dismissed because of insufficient evidence, except for the case
against Elder Wiseman, which was already awaiting trial.

The Community in Barrington Passage, Nova Scotia, also
clashed with local townspeople. Charges of "vigilante" attitudes
among the local business community were brought before the
Barrington municipal council on July 27, 1988, after the Community opened the Old School House restaurant. Efforts were

made to stop building projects and the purchase of more property by the "cult" (*Coastguard* Jan. 1, 1989). (Because members lived communally and worked for free, their prices undercut those of local restaurants.) Ironically, in one of the local newspapers, "there were side-by-side stories which castigated the Cult for beating its children and simultaneously announced that the local school board was going to suspend the long-established custom of caning disobedient pupils" (Poteet 1989, 4).

A series of inflammatory articles appeared in literature issuing from the anticult movement. "Special consultants" and "experts" were interviewed, who related horror stories of children's deaths in purportedly similar religious communes in Michigan and West Virgina, including cases in which two mothers were convicted of involuntary manslaughter resulting from disciplinary beatings (Ewald 1991, 40). *The Cult Observer* (Sept. 1984, 4) cites affidavits of former members, which "tell of systemic, frequent and lengthy beatings of children by parents and church elders with wooden and iron rods and paddles, often drawing blood." A particularly lurid example of anticult propaganda is "Children of the Cult," which compares Island Pond kids to the glassy-eyed aliens in the 1960 movie, *Village of the Damned*.[3]

In 1988, trying to improve relations with the townspeople, the women of the Barrington Community put up the following poster in town advertising a "rap session" at the local library.

FOR WOMEN ONLY
TO ALL WOMEN,

The women of the community at the Old School House in Barrington Passage will be holding an Open Meeting on Tuesday, August 30 from 7 P.M. on.

We would like to warmly invite all of you women to come and break the ice. We will be sharing about who we are, how we live, the way we raise our children, our intentions, our goals, etc. We want to answer all your questions.

From women to women we would like to express our hearts and hear yours.[4]

This meeting was attended by about seventy interested residents, and many men showed up for what had been advertised as a "women only" meeting, and Messianic women responded to cordial questions (*Coast Guard*, Jan. 1, 1989). Ewald (1991) claims that the Community in Island Pond is now on good terms with the townspeople and authorities. This notion was confirmed by an Elder, who said, "The same guy who was threatening to shoot us before the Raid—I'm now workin' for him, renovating his house and he's always invitin' me and the brothers to stay for dinner."

In 1993, the Elders adopted a new name, the Messianic Community, for their growing tribe. There are currently six communities internationally, established in New Zealand, Nova Scotia, Brazil, France, Missouri, and New England. Each group is named by its locality (e.g., the Community in Island Pond, the Community in Boston). Ewald (1991) claims the population in Island Pond is 310, but I counted about sixty adults and as many or more children at their Gatherings, which are supposed to involve every member of their community.

The Community is a particularly striking example of a religious response to family breakdown. Their *Freepaper* is replete with testimonials relating the horrors of modern family life, and exhibits a fierce intolerance for the ambiguity surrounding gender roles, which Aidala (1985) has noted in contemporary youth living in religious communes. The *Freepaper* extends a universal invitation to sinners and sufferers and promises that joining the community will solve all marital and family problems. The following statement appears on the back of every *Freepaper.*

HOW TO REACH US: We used to be desperately lonely, even though most of us had a lot of friends. . . . We were scarred deeply from the effects of mistrust and hurtful relationships. . . . We were lost, scattered, without direction, doing our own thing.

THEN WE HEARD A VOICE THAT SPOKE TO US RIGHT WHERE WE WERE, exposing the emptiness of our lives. This voice matched up fully to the longing of our hearts. . . . It came from a people who had their dirty consciences washed clean. They had a clean slate and an absolutely new life. This new life they eagerly offered to all who wanted it.

WE HATE THE DEATH, WAR, STRIFE, HATRED, MURDER, INJUSTICE, GREED AND SELFISHNESS that is leading the whole world to destruction. . . .

WE ARE A MESSIANIC COMMUNITY AND BY "COMMUNITY" WE DO
NOT MEAN A TOWN OR LOCALITY. . . . "Community" as we use the
term means those who love one another so greatly that they are of one
heart and mind, holding all things as common property, living together, taking their meals together, devoted to one another because
they're devoted to the One who saved them from death and misery.

Although I conducted only three formal interviews with
community women for this study, each time I met a new
member, he or she would freely offer the kind of information I
solicited in the interviews. It appears to be customary for members to greet visitors with a biographical testimonial, which
includes a brief summary of the difficult circumstances or dis-
satisfactions they were experiencing when they first heard of the
community; what their first attraction and their reasons for
joining were; and which concludes with a glowing statement on
how their relationships have improved since "finding love in
the community." Within the first ten minutes of conversation I
would receive a clear picture of their childhood circumstances,
their previous professions, their marital status before and after,
and the problems or emotional dilemmas they had faced in
secular life and in what ways these problems had been resolved
through joining the Community. For this reason, this account
conveys a broader understanding of who joins the community
and why than the formal research methods would indicate.

Gender and Authority

Women wear the head scarf to show their submission to their
husbands and to the Elders, and they are not allowed to preach
in the Gatherings. Paradoxically, members insist that these rules
endow women with greater authority. One of the male leaders
explained:

We believe in reconstructing relations between the sexes. By wearing a
head scarf, the woman is showing she recognizes her rightful place.
The world has been torn apart by the struggle between men and
women. Once she stops fighting for power and stops manipulating and
being greedy, then she is free to become really powerful. Women in

our community have revelations; they can be prophetesses. . . . We *listen* to women who have wisdom. But authority works in a different way through women.

One of the senior women made a similar point.

It says in the Bible that woman must obey her husband. . . . When she puts on the head scarf it's a sign that she has given up the struggle, so then when she speaks to the men they will listen because they know that she speaks from the heart, that she has wisdom and is speaking through revelation. Basically, we're all one working together; we're one body.

Communal Life

The Community in Island Pond numbers about 310 people (including children). There are nine households, which are sets of three to eight families with some single adults who live communally in old restored houses. Each couple occupies a bedroom and their children have an adjacent room. The kitchen and living room is a communal space. Women work together in the kitchen, and in a crafts workshop, where they make quilts, clothing, macramé, soap, and pottery, which they sell in their shops in Burlington and Boston. The men work separately on carpentry projects, restoring antique furniture, building instruments, leather work, and printing leaflets and the *Freepaper* (as well as outside printing jobs). In Island Pond the community owns about eighteen properties, both businesses and "households," or communal residences. They operate a garage, a logging workshop, a shoe store, and cottage industries producing candles, futons, soap, leather goods, and quilts. The community had a beautifully decorated, successful restaurant, the *Common Sense* (which unfortunately burned down on January 5, 1991), where men and women worked side by side. To visit the community is to step back in time, for their houses, furniture, and clothing are nostalgically old-fashioned, and even their printing press is a well-cared-for antique.

Children dress in exactly the same style as the adults. Women and girls wear long hair and part it in the middle; they wear long skirts or pantaloons, pinafores, and head scarves. The men and boys tie their collar-length hair back and wear headbands, jeans, overalls, and T-shirts. All the households congregate on Friday and Saturday evenings at the Gathering. The male leaders take turns preaching, reading from the Bible, and offering testimonials and millenarian predictions, punctuated by "amens" from the assembly.

Women are more prominent in a ritual occasion designed for the religious education of the children and for the community's input into the parents' child-rearing efforts. On Saturday night, after the Gathering, each household celebrates "Communion," in which they drink in turn from the Victory Cup (a very large goblet of homemade wine) and break a loaf of unleavened whole grain bread. An Elder relates and acts out Bible stories for the children's benefit, constantly pausing to test the little ones' knowledge and to encourage their participation. He also delivers a "history" lesson that condenses and syncretizes a patriotic version of American history with legends about the trials of the ancient Jews. This is aimed at reinforcing the children's understanding of the community's self-image as the "lost sheep" of Yahshua, and the "lost and scattered tribes" alert for His Return. The Victory Cup is supposed to evaluate the health of the parent-child relationships in the Household and to promote forgiveness, demonstrate group support, and encourage a fresh start. Women reveal their maternal concerns and interpret their children's statements to the Elder on this occasion. The male leaders praise their efforts and advise the children to show more consideration toward their mothers. One women confessed, "I'm not going to drink from the Victory Cup tonight. An evil spirit entered into me and I stood against my brothers and sisters and caused my little girl to fall and hurt her knee." She received sympathetic noises from the members of her household and a hug from her child. A little boy was prompted to ask whether or not he was eligible to drink, for he had disobeyed his mother and teased his sister. The Elder, after hearing the mother's explanation, judged that the boy was contrite enough and told him Yahshua could see into his heart and wanted him to drink, but to try to be more

A drawing of a Messianic Community bus at a Grateful Dead concert.
Courtesy Parchment Press.

obedient and kind in the future. Having attended two of these
occasions I received the impression that the parents often
deemed themselves unworthy to drink; the children, however,
were only *threatened* by this public chastisement.

Courtship and Marriage[5]

Marriage involves the whole community. Second-generation
members seem to marry young, in their late teens or early
twenties. The "boy," who is usually living in a separate Household, must first ask the "girl's" father for permission to court
his daughter, and then the couple work together every day,
usually for several months. During that time they might turn to
other members of their Household for counseling. They may
separate with no loss of face and remain friends, or they may
wish to marry, but each person in both Households must say
what they feel about the union ("speak their heart"), and the
couple are not ready to marry until everyone has said a "hearty
amen." Married couples entering the Community continue to
live as man and wife, but couples who are not married must live
apart for a year and then wait for a chorus of "hearty amens"
before they can marry (interview with Hannah).

The wedding ceremony might be described as "millennium
in miniature." For a month before the occasion, the bride's
"sisters" take care of her by bathing her every night, combing
her hair, bringing her herbal teas, and watching her diet. "If
she is worried about anything or needs to talk, they are there."
Then, on the wedding day, the women build a bower of
branches and flowers in the woods near the Community and
help her dress. The wedding dress is made of pure, unbleached
linen and must be ironed carefully to remove all the wrinkles.
One sister whose job this was explained the millenarian significance of ironing the dress: "It's hard ironing linen. It's a purification in itself trying to get out all those spots and wrinkles,
but it's got to be perfect because it's for the pure and spotless
bride, like in Revelations." The sisters make a crown of flowers
for the bride and adorn her with their handmade macramé
bracelet and necklace. When she is ready, she sits down in the

"church" (the bower) and her sisters send news to the groom. Then "the King Comes to claim His pure and spotless Bride." The groom is wearing white with a red sash and cloak, which symbolize the blood of Yahshua. The couple are led to a large hall and seated on two "thrones" raised on a platform, and every member of the community offers them a gift in turn. Many of these gifts are poems, songs, or dances composed by the givers, or they might be handmade crafts. Many "revelations" and blessings are bestowed on the couple also, and then a feast and dance follow, which lasts all night. The weddings are occasions for members from other communities to visit, so several double-decker buses are usually parked beside the hall. Outsiders are invited freely to attend also.

There is no question of premarital or extramarital sex being anything but sinful, but, unlike ISKCON or IAM, there appear to be no mechanisms by which the group controls the married couple's intimate life.

Pregnant wives receive close attention from their "sisters," who take them on a daily walk and ply them with raspberry leaf tea. Natural birth at home with MC midwives is preferred, and the sisters will pray to assist the mother during the birth, and "sometimes the way the birth went or the way you carried the child will reveal the name of the child." One sister explained how conceiving and naming a child was a religious process.

We already had three boys and the youngest was six when we came into the community. Before that I thought I never wanted another child. But, after six years our hearts started to tenderize and we had the desire—and I'd always wanted a little girl. So we prayed to Our Father to give us unity and told him we wanted a little girl, and he gave us Hadashah Savav. Her name means "New Encompassing." Apostle Spriggs gave her that name shortly after she was born. He looked at her and saw her gifts and said, "She looks so new and she looks like she could really surround and support a man!" So we found the Hebrew words in the dictionary and named her Hadashah Savav.

Within marriage the wife engages in the traditional work of cooking, cleaning, sewing, and educating the children, but the men are probably much more involved in child care, in teaching their sons carpentry skills, and in the education and moral development of children than are most men in "mainstream" secular families. I observed Messianic women giving orders to their husbands—telling them which jacket to put on their son as they were about to leave for the Gathering. Husbands and wives seemed to cooperate in a harmonious way in handling their children. Also, Sunday is relegated to organized games and projects for children, and I noticed that a single mother and an unmarried man collaborated in organizing the events. The men appear to be as intimately involved in child rearing as the women, which according to the values of the Community appears to enhance rather than diminish their masculine image.

All the couples I interviewed claimed that their marital relationship had improved since joining the community. One French Canadian couple in their fifties said it was because they now saw each other during the day, for the home and the workplace were the same space, and they looked back on how cold and distant their family life had been when he had left every morning for work and the children had left for school. A couple in their late twenties who had lived together before joining said, "Before we had our love for each other, and it was strong, but now we feel the love of the community pouring through our hearts. Before we were kind of cut off, but now we can share our love for Yahshua and each other with *all* our brothers and sisters." One sister described adjusting to Messianic gender roles, in which the wife was expected to obey her husband.

I had a good life before . . . we had a good relationship. But the same purification that goes on in the community goes on between husband and wife. I've had to learn to bear with his faults to see his heart. And he's learned to be a head to me, and that's the order of God, that a man is the head and a woman is the heart. It was hard at first. He was always easy to get along with, we never did butt heads that much, but while he was learning to be a head, it was kinda rough at times. I wouldn't take it well. I had to learn to be submissive to that authority. If I had an opinion I would share it with him and then it would be up to him to make a decision, right or wrong. . . . Now he hears me a lot more. He really listens to my heart and I know he needs me. . . . Because of my submissiveness, he's learned to hear my heart and I trust God to take care of me. I have peace with that—through expressing my heart to my head and then—it's up to him to do what he wants with it. We are one.

New Boundaries Protecting the Family

The new family patterns developing in the Community might be analyzed as an attempt to reconstruct the lineage family while simultaneously preserving the nuclear family. The Household, composed of six to eight nuclear families, consider themselves "one family," all "married to each other." Thus, the boundaries between the different Households are distinct, as between different clans, but the boundaries between nuclear families within the Household are fuzzy. The kitchen, dining room, and living spaces are shared, and the wives work closely together in the domestic realm and in the crafts workshop. Husbands also form a separate work force and have their own prayer meetings. One of the criteria for electing an Elder is that he should not favor his family above the others in the Household.

Families also bond with one another through their children. Although the children have a bedroom adjacent to their parents and maintain a close relationship with them, to a great extent the children's sleeping places, as well as their work and study patterns, are determined by their peer friendships. As a visitor, I found it difficult to keep track of which kids belonged to which parents. Young girls would fight over who could sleep beside the babies to feed them in the night, and a pair of fathers might be engaged in carpentry tasks with a herd of small boys.

The nuclear family receives a high respect and support. Although Household couples describe themselves as "married" to each other, they are strictly monogamous and have their own common belongings and rooms. During one of my weekend visits, I noted that on Sunday mornings it is the custom for the different families of the Household to remain inside their private rooms, sleeping in until noon. The kitchen and living rooms downstairs were deserted, and in our room breakfast had been laid the night before. Lifting up a cloth, my daughter found apple oatmeal squares, a bowl of fruit, and herb tea. It occurred to me that this period had been set aside so that indi-

A drawing of the community circle dancing. Courtesy Parchment Press.

vidual families, after an intense communitarian two-day revival meeting, could relax and reestablish their nuclear bonds.

The Child Abuse Controversy

A fascinating and ironic feature of this communal movement is that their literature presents a mirror image to the anticult propaganda on the "child-beating cult." Each party, the "anticult" and the "cult," is accusing the other, in its own self-serving rhetoric, of abusing children. It becomes clear in perusing the many articles and testimonials criticizing American society that appear in the *Freepaper* that Community members define themselves as the lost, abused and neglected children of their generation. The *Freepaper* features stories and testimonials written by different members—and the women's stories in particular are full of heart-wrenching reminiscences of sexual betrayal, traumatic abortions, cold, career-obsessed parents, and "the ever-gnawing curse we see all around us in every home and on every street corner: loneliness, alienation, division, and the disintegration of basic human relationships" (*Freepaper,* "The Stone" n. d., 4).

In a testimonial entitled "Betrayed," an anonymous member relates "one of the many experiences which led me to mistrust the system"—an illegal abortion. She was wearing her boyfriend's fraternity pin when she got pregnant, and he and his parents chose marriage, but she "didn't want the commitments." The clinic nurse informed her it was "just a blob of tissue" but after a "cold and impersonal" doctor handed her over to a nurse, lying about the term of the pregancy (saying it was two months instead of four months), the nurse panicked and the girl saw "the little baby coming out of me along with blood and water. I began wailing, 'I've been tricked! I was told it was a blob, not a baby!'" The author concludes:

It was not until many years later, when I met Yahshua, that my guilt, shame, and remorse were finally washed away. . . . He delivered me out of that society that rapes its victims . . . that encourages the murder of innocent babies. There was a very small voice of conscience saying, "This isn't right"—but that voice was snuffed out by the sick reasoning and social pressure that directed my life. . . . Now I live in a community where forgiveness rules my life daily.

Another article, "Born to Be Wasted," relates the adventures of a teenage drug addict male prostitute and begins with a brief sketch of his family background.

My life and my conscience started being laid waste probably when I was born. . . . A year later my mom split to California with my sister, leaving us three boys with an alchoholic dad who dropped us off six months later and attempted suicide.

It concludes: "Please, no matter what age you are, you don't need to dwell in a wasteland. Call on the name of YAHSHUA and you won't be disappointed!!!—With a sincere love, TAMIYM."

This story is followed by one with a similar point—called "Freddy Finds Some Trash" about a homeless old drunkard who is horrified to find the mutilated corpse of a baby in a trash can behind an abortion clinic. When the police respond to his urgent call and come to investigate, their response is, "There's no law broken here. It's none of my business"; "Go get a coffee and a donut. See ya later."

Many of the stories are about women who don't know how to be women, who are out of touch with their "conscience" and "gut feeling." The message is that if gender roles could be set straight, if women could find out who they are, men and women would know how to treat one another and their children. A testimonial called "What's Happening" describes a member's sadness when her mother cut off her long hair.

While she was growing up in the fifties and sixties, she wouldn't dare to cut her long, thick, beautiful hair. That was . . . the way she really felt on the inside. Her hair was her glory; I heard her say this countless times. But then the styles changed. . . . She didn't want to be a stick in the mud. So she lopped it all off. Regardless of the sick feeling in her stomach. . . . My dad hit the ceiling and she in turn persuaded him. . . . Maybe that is the reason my dad's voice was silenced. . . . Her voice was silenced—how she felt inside on a gut level.

Another woman, who used to be nicknamed "Crazy Kathy" because she became "the funny girl who cracked the jokes and cried inside," experimented with rock concerts, all-night parties, and drugs, then eventually got married "in hopes of finding a more settled down life" but found instead that "I was married to a stranger. My dream turned into a nightmare. I got pregnant in the midst of a dead-end marriage." When her baby died at birth, Crazy Kathy cried out to God and "a supernatural, wonderful peace came to me." After an intense spiritual search, she found her way to Island Pond, and concludes, "I am no longer known as 'Crazy Cathy.' . . . He [Yahshua] calls me by a new name full of worth, dignity, and purpose. . . . I have come to a place where love endures forever and friendships never die—[signed] Miriam (being completely healed)."

What these stories communicate to the reader is a fierce resentment against the parents of the hippie generation whose permissiveness was interpreted as indifference. The chasm that formed between the values of the youth of the counterculture and their "straight" parents is recollected with pain. "Our parents put virtually no restraint on us. They were too busy making a living to have much time for us. Many of us seemed to be more of a bother to our parents than anything. So, as a result we grew up being disrespectful and disobedient to our parents" (*Freepaper* "Debt of Love," n. p.). An article, "Home Town Girl," signed by "Linda," complains of growing up with parents who "didn't have any set standards of behaviour I needed to follow" and relates the following story.

I came home from school . . . only to find arguing, fist-fighting or dishes being thrown around. There was always strife, bitterness, selfishness and unforgiveness in the air. . . . I allowed much bitterness towards my dad to grow in my heart and it even turned to hatred. At times I would have killed him if I'd had the chance; that's how desperate my heart was. . . . Wasn't it the right thing to do, to follow after my parents' beliefs and their parents' beliefs and their parents? NO! NO!

The *Freepaper* exhibits an intense concern for establishing an orderly society with well-defined rules to counteract the disorder these former inhabitants of the counterculture remember as ruling the homes of their parents. Moreover, they seem to feel the deepest trepidation that the same pattern of teenage rebellion might occur in their own "restored" families. Hence, a strong emphasis is on preserving their cultural values through future generations. For this reason, their children are punished for signs of self-will. The weight of a whole community of adult authorities supports each set of parents in their attempts to discipline their children. One mother noted, "Our children know they must obey. We were in the supermarket the other day and we saw this little boy carrying on having a screaming fit because his mom wouldn't buy him something. Our boys would never do that—they know who's boss."

The Community's alternative religious and social values are carefully instilled in the children, who are insulated from secular influences, as in other sects. Children attend the Community school, read books written by or carefully scrutinized by their teachers, and do not have access to television or go to movies. They do not own commercial fantasy toys, only educational ones, such as blocks, puzzles, and books. One Elder explained that the rationale behind their educational policies was to encourage the development of the child's *imagination* as opposed to his/her *fantasy*.

We don't want them to escape into fantasy worlds, because then they won't be ready to hear the call of Yahshua when He comes. So we don't buy them Ninja Turtles or Barbie dolls or toy guns or dolls. There are lots of babies around and our little girls love holding them and helping to dress and feed them. And our kids play great games— they mix up mud pies or build cities out of pieces of wood. We will need men and women with imagination in the Community. But we want them to stay in touch with reality and not forget who they are and Who Their Father is . . . so they don't "need" new, expensive toys to escape from the world . . . next thing you know, it will be drugs!

This highly disciplined, communal, and religious approach to rearing children might be perceived as threatening by outsiders, for it implies a harsh critique and radical rejection of American "mainstream" permissive approaches to raising children, as exemplified by Dr. Spock. Sensing this challenge, the Island Pond townspeople might have retaliated by accusing them of the very crime the Community itself would consider the most taboo. One of the prime motivating forces behind their culture is to create a society where children will receive love and a caring discipline to inherit the values of their parents.

The Community's Appeal for Women

Many of the women I spoke to described living in difficult or abusive marriages before they joined the community. In some cases their disillusionment with married life appeared to be the chief motivating factor in their seeking out a religious community. Three of them had tried out other religious solutions (Pentacostalism, the Baptist Church, the Jesus Movement, or Billy Graham), but they had finally chosen the intense, communal life of the Northeast Kingdom, where they could "live" their love for Yahshua and for their brothers and sisters daily, not just on Sundays. Others admitted that they joined to *escape* an impossible family situation.

Two women told me their story as we sat at the Friday evening meal, served by teenage girls in long skirts, aprons, and head scarves. The first, "Shoshonah," whose husband used to beat her, said she had collected *Freepapers* and thought about the community for a year, and had finally been moved to abandon her home in a panic when her husband tried to kill her and their two small daughters. She concluded, "So we arrived here scared out of our wits, without any clothes or money, but at least we had our lives, our limbs, and the community loved us and took us in." (I received this story within four minutes of arriving at the Bayview Household and sitting down at their meal.)

Rebecca, in her early thirties from Oregon, had left her husband and children to join the Island Pond Community and was now in the "waiting period" with a bachelor from the Boston Community. She used to be a legal secretary and had been married with two small boys. She had become involved in a Christian right-wing activist group that threw bombs and refused to pay their taxes and were trying to "restore the American Constitution to what it was meant to be." (The name of the organization was withheld). She had been attending both the Baptist and the Pentacostal churches on Sundays, trying to decide which to join. She had already left her husband several times ("He never gave up *anything* for me! He followed his *own* way. I had to take over and run everything because I couldn't respect him."). Her brother and sister had joined the Community and came to visit her, leaving some *Freepapers* behind.

They had changed somehow, their faces were lit up. I read those papers out to my husband every day until finally he said, "Look, I'm really not interested. I really don't want to hear this stuff." Then I realized our paths had divided. I flew out to Island Pond with my kids and the community made us welcome. After three months he came and tried to persuade me to leave. I said, "Come and stay here. You and I could really learn how to love each other here!" He said he wouldn't, and he ended up taking the kids. I *could* have said, "I won't let you take them," but I finally believe that a man must have authority over his kids. That was very hard for me.

And he's not a good father. I went out last summer to see them. It just about broke my heart. He leaves them with different baby-sitters every day! And the younger one is an emotional mess! I feel very sad about it. But I believe it is better to give up my attachments and not fight with him. If I give myself totally to Yahshua, He will look after them for me—for that I pray.

Looking forward to marrying in the Community, Rebecca compared its men with outsiders, explaining why she could surrender to their rule.

> Women are more capable than men, and that's why they can't respect a man who won't submit to God's authority. He's just running around in circles, following his own whims and nothing gets done. So you can't trust him. I like having the men rule over me here because I feel in my heart that they care about me and what's good for me.

One aspect of modern family life that Community patterns address is the problem of single parent families. At least six of the women I met in Island Pond claimed they found single parenting in the outside world "too hard," and joining the Community had relieved them of that burden and improved their children's lives. One woman complained that her previous husband had never taken any responsibility for the children, so that she "felt like a single mother inside." All these women had remarried inside the Community and their children had apparently found strong, concerned stepfathers. An Island Pond Elder informed me that in the case of a single mother joining and not finding a mate, one of the bachelors would volunteer to "stand in" as the children's father. The Community at Barrington Passage has adopted a more radical solution to the problem of single parenthood. Their Elder, Eddie Wiseman, feels it is not good for children to grow up with one parent, so if a couple should separate, there is a strong pressure placed on them to find another mate or to reconcile for the sake of the children.[6]

If one asks why Messianic women have chosen to adopt a meaning system that emphasizes the subordination of women at a time when the mainstream culture defines male domination as oppressive and archaic, the most plausible answer is found in Susan Rose's study (1987) of women's roles in an independent Christian charismatic fellowship in upstate New York. Rose found that although the hierarchical ordering of relationships within the family was explicit in the group's ideology, in practice power relationships were not nearly so rigid. Many of the women who (like NEK women) had been involved in the counterculture of the 1960s, talked about relinquishing their power for their men to assume their "God-appointed" positions of leadership. Thus, although they enthusiastically adopted the "traditional" female role, they simultaneously rejected the "traditional" male role, which limits the husband to acting as the primary breadwinner and protector of the family. They insisted that their husbands must also be "actively and intimately involved in family life and childcare" (Rose 1987, 245). By choosing to live in a utopian commune that endows child rearing with a high value and millenarian significance, women in the community have found an environment in which both sexes cooperate as equal partners in the daily task of raising children.

PART THREE

Sex Unity Groups

SEVEN

Playmates in the Raelian Movement

and the woman, she can be your companion, she can be
your playmate!

—Rael

Women in the Raelian Movement define themselves as the sensual friends and "playmates" of Raelian men, who are themselves encouraged to develop the feminine qualities necessary for the "Age of the Apocalypse." In Quebec, female members of this millenarian, atheistic "UFO cult" tend to be upwardly mobile, Francophone white collar workers from a Catholic working-class background. Their average age is in the early thirties. They reject the institution of marriage, tend to postpone or veto childbearing, are open to expressing their sensuality with other women, and live on an impermanent (but often long-term) basis with the lover of their choice.

The Raelian Movement appears to be one of the rare examples of a NRM that promotes in its members a tolerance for sexual ambiguity and encourages homosexual expression. Angela Aidala (1985) has argued that part of the appeal of religious communes to contemporary youth intolerant of the shifting interpretations of masculine-feminine, is their clear-cut, unambiguous gender roles. The Raelian Movement is not communal in its organization, but it is millenarian, and radical departures from conventional sexuality are also characteristic of noncommunal millenarian groups (Worseley 1976; Balch 1982). Unlike Aidala's religious communes, this NRM deliberately fosters in its members experimental and individualistic approaches to redefining their sexuality. Since Aidala posits a link between the rigid role divisions found in communal NRMs and their tendency to promote sexual inequalities, the Raelians' androgynous anthropology and nontraditional gender roles would seem to promise a fertile environment for cultivating feminine authority.

One of the puzzles confronting this researcher, however, is the surprising *scarcity* of women in leadership positions in the Raelian hierarchy. Mary Farrell Bednarowski (1980) in her study of the roles of women in Shakerism, Christian Science, Spiritualism, and Theosophy, has proposed four characteristics or common factors found in marginal religions that promote female leadership and sexual equality:

1. A godhead that is androgynous or nonanthropomorphic
2. A reinterpretation of the doctrine of the Fall
3. New rules for ordaining clergy
4. A view of marriage that departs from the traditional emphasis on women as homemaker and mother.

The Raelian Movement possesses all four of Bednarowski's characteristics, and yet a study of the 1988 *Raelian Conseil Decisionel* survey on membership reveals that men outnumber women 2:1 and that women in the Structure (the fully committed core group) tend to stay at the lower levels. Of the six levels in the Hierarchy, which represent degrees of responsibility, self-awareness, and proximity to the aliens, women tend to remain in the lowest levels: in level 1 (Assistant Animator), level 2 (Animator), and level 3 (Assistant Guide). Of the fifteen "Priest Guides" (level 4), only four are women, and one of them is a transexual (born male). All three level 5 "Bishop Guides" are men, and Rael, the founder, as "Planetary Guide" represents level 6.

When one considers that, besides fitting snugly into Bednarowski's model of a sex-egalitarian religion, the Raelian literature explicitly deplores the subjugation of women and espouses what Allen (1984) calls the "sex identity" view of gender (i.e., the notion that men and women are essentially the same, hence equal), there appear to be no obstacles in ideology, family patterns, or tradition to prevent charismatic women rising in the hierarchy . . . so, why don't they? This chapter will address this problem as well as the issue of the movement's appeal for young French Canadian women.

The History

The Raelian Movement International was founded by a French racing car driver and journalist, Claude Vorilhon (Rael to his followers) in 1973 as a result of his alleged encounter with space aliens during a walking tour of the Clermont-Ferrand volcanic mountain range in France. These beings, whom Rael describes as small humanoids with pale green skin and almond eyes, entrusted him with the "message." This message concerns our true identity: we were "implanted" on earth by aliens, the "Elohim," who created us from DNA in their laboratories. Rael's mission, as the last of forty prophets (crossbred between Elohim and mortal women) is to warn humankind that since 1945 and Hiroshima, we have entered the "Age of Apocalypse" in which we have the choice of destroying ourselves with nuclear weapons or making the leap into planetary consciousness, which will qualify us to inherit the scientific knowledge of our space forefathers. Science will enable 4 percent of our species in the future to be cloned and travel through space populating virgin planets "in our own image." (Bouchard 1989; *Space Aliens Took Me to Their Planet* 1978).

The movement claims thirty thousand members worldwide, distributed mainly throughout France, Japan, and Quebec, and tries through its books and lectures to unite Christians, Jews, and Muslims in a "de-mythologized" interpretation of scripture as the true history of a space colonization. Denying the existence of God or the soul, Rael (b. 1946) presents as the only hope of immortality a regeneration through science, and to this end members participate in four annual festivals so that the Elohim can fly overhead and register the Raelians' DNA codes on their machines. This initiation ritual, called "the transmission of the cellular plan," promises a kind of immortality through cloning. New initiates sign a contract that permits a mortician to cut out a piece of bone in their forehead (the "third eye") and mail it packed in ice to Rael, who in turn relays it to the Elohim.

Sex Unity Groups

Rael with model of embassy. Courtesy Canadian Raelian Movement.

New initiates are also required to send a letter of apostasy to the church they were baptized in.

The "Raelians" are those who have acknowledged the Elohim as their creators by taking these two steps (initiation and funeral arrangements) and the "Structure" are those volunteers who work for the organization and are committed to the two goals

Female Priest Guide performing transmission of the cellular plan.
Courtesy Canadian Raelian Movement.

of the movement: spreading the message to mankind and building an embassy in Jerusalem by the year 2025 to receive the
Elohim. To this end, Rael sent out letters in October 1991 to the
Israeli government and its international embassies demanding a
plot of land in Jerusalem on which to build the Embassy—and
warning them if they refuse the Elohim might withdraw their
protection of the Jewish people. Although members of the
Structure are committed to making the message available to
those who are "already Raelian but haven't realized it yet," they
are instructed to avoid pressure tactics and evangelizing. Members who attempt to force their ideas or unwelcome sexual attentions on others are expelled from the Structure for seven
years (the time it takes to replace all their body cells).

The Raelians are not communal, but have a strong millenarian
focus in preparing for the descent of the Elohim and the thirty-
nine immortal prophets (Jesus, Buddha, Mohammed, Joseph

Smith, etc.) who, like Rael ("the last of forty prophets"), were born from the union of a mortal woman and an Elohim. Members are encouraged through summer courses to achieve worldly success in their careers, to have better health through avoiding all recreational drugs and stimulants, and to enlarge their ability to experience pleasure, which Rael claims will strengthen their immune system and enhance their intelligence and telepathic abilities. Those who find total self-fulfillment will be immortalized through cloning. Meanwhile, Rael advises Raelians not to marry or exacerbate the planetary overpopulation problem, but to commune with the wonder of the universe by exploring their sexuality with the opposite sex, the same sex, and any other life-forms—even robots and extraterrestrials. To this end, Raelians participate annually in a sensual meditation workshop in a rural setting that features fasting, nudity, and private sensory deprivation/awareness exercises and sexual experimentation, the ultimate goal being to experience the "cosmic orgasm."[1]

Rael's Philosophy of Sexuality

Rael's vision of a perfect society in the future, ruled by the "geniocracy" of intelligent artists and scientists, is based on his revelations. As he phrases it, "The Elohim were starting to speak through my mouth, or rather, to write with my hand." His advice on sexual and other matters he describes as "a code of life, a new way of behaving as a human, that is as an evolved being, and therefore trying in every way to open one's mind to infinity and to place oneself in harmony with it. These great rules dictated by the Elohim, Our Creators, our fathers who are in heaven . . . are all here, expressed in all their integrality" (*Extraterrestrials Took Me to Their Planet* 1986, 122–223).

Rael's recommendations reflect the sexual customs of these space aliens that he observed (and participated in) when they took him to their planet in 1975. As he describes it, the Elohim live on the planet of the Eternals and number ninety thousand quasi-immortal men and women who "can unite themselves freely as they wish, and any form of jealousy is eliminated." They are not allowed to have children, and undergo a small sterilization operation. For these reasons, their relationships are "more fraternal and respectful" than ours, and "the unions among them are marvellously pure and high." To prove his point, Rael then describes his encounter with alien sexual mores in his book, *Extraterrestrials Took Me to Their Planet* (230), as follows.

"Would you like some female companions?" asked the robot. "Come, you will make a choice." . . . I found myself transported in front of the machine used for fabricating the robots. A luminous cube appeared in front of me . . . a magnificent young brunette with wonderfully harmonious proportions appeared in three dimensions within the luminous cube. . . . My robot asked me whether she pleased me. . . . Following my refusal to change anything whatsoever about that magnificent woman, a second woman, blond and heady this time, appeared in the luminous cube. . . . Finally a third young person, more sensual than the first two and red haired this time, appeared in the strange cube. . . . At that moment, a magnificent black woman appeared in the cube, then a very slim Chinese woman, and then a very voluptuous oriental woman. The robot asked me which person I desired to have as a companion.

Because Rael was unable to choose between such magnificent specimens, he retired to his extraterrestial hotel suite with all six biological robots and reports, "There I had the most unforgettable bath I have ever had, in the company of those charming robots, absolutely submissive to my desires. . . . Finally, after a while I went to bed and spent the most extravagant night of my life with my marvelous female companions."

Rael offers some very decisive guidance on some of the ethical dilemmas that confront contemporary women, such as birth control, abortion, and single parenthood. He condones abortion.

If by mishap you have conceived a being without desiring it, use the means which science puts at your disposal: use abortion. Because a being which was not desired at the moment of conception cannot fully blossom because he was not created in harmony. Do not listen to those who try to frighten you by talking about the physical and especially the ethical after-effects which an abortion can cause. (237)

Conceiving a child should be delayed until "the individual is fulfilled" and this can only be achieved through "the fulfillment of your body," which leads to "the blossoming of your mind." In the interim he recommends birth control. He suggests that a kind of eugenics is possible through the psychic control of the parents during the act of conception.

A child cannot be well conceived unless he was truly desired at the moment of conception . . . this moment must therefore be desired so that the first cell, may be made in perfect harmony, the two minds of the parents being conscious and strongly thinking of the being which they are conceiving. This is one of the secrets of the new man. (236)

Rael gives women permission to be unmarried mothers, single mothers, and sexually active single mothers.

To have a child does not necessarily imply being married or even living with a man. If you wish to have a child without living with a man, do as you wish. Fulfill yourself as you wish, without worrying what others think. . . . Don't think you are condemned beacause of this to live alone forever: welcome the men you like and they will serve as masculine models for your child. . . . A change of environment is always positive for a child. (237)

He also gives women permission to dump their children:

Thus, if you gave birth to the child you desired . . . and you no longer desire the child, you will be able to entrust him to society so that he may be brought up in harmony necessary for his fulfillment. . . . If the child becomes a nuisance, however slightly, he realizes it and his fulfillment is affected. (238)

Rael strongly advises against marriage.

You will reject marriage which is only the proclamation of ownership of a person. A man or a woman cannot be the property of anyone else. Any contract can only destroy the harmony existing between two beings. When one feels love, one feels free to love, but when one has signed a contract, one feels like a prisoner, forced to love and sooner or later, each one begins to hate the other. (329)

He even advises against trying to maintain a long-term relationship if there is no "harmony". "You will live with the person of your choice for only as long as you feel good with them. When you no longer get on well together, do not

remain together because your union would become hell" (239).
The rationale behind Rael's version of "free love" resembles
that of Fourier, John Humphrey Noyes, and Rajneesh: he is
concerned that women should not be treated as property and
complains that in society "we still do not recognize women's
right to do with their body as they wish. . . . What is more . . .
if we were to kill someone whom we claim to 'love,' what is
called a 'crime passionel,' we can get off with sometimes five or
six years in prison!" He finds in possessive love the potential
for violence.

The one who truly loves hopes his partner will meet someone who will
give her even more pleasure. . . . The selfish person prefers to keep
"his property." He prefers his companion to be unhappy with him
rather than happy with someone else. And if that happens, he takes his
gun to kill his "loved one." (*Sensual Meditation* 1986, 64)

He criticizes society for endorsing such violence. "This means
we are living in a society which is encouraging its members to
kill those they love and let live those they don't love" (62–64).

Rael's Ideas on Gender

Rael often compares men and women to biological robots
who are programmed to give each other pleasure. He quotes
the Elohim's explanation of gender.

We saw that it was very easy to create a strain of "sexed" robots, each
possessing half a plan so that while "coupling" they would create one
complete plan and so allow the "female" to make a "child." We also
saw, that to incite our robots to reproduce, we needed to render the
act . . . pleasurable . . . by equipping their sexual organs with nerve
endings. (65)

Seeing gender as an artificial construct, Rael emphasizes its fluidity, resulting from different possible combinations of X and Y
chromosomes. This implies that all human beings are essentially
androgynous. In one of the testimonials printed at the end of
Sensual Meditation a horticultural technician takes up Rael's
argument to explain his homosexual orientation.

Maybe you don't realize it, but one is born as a homosexual, just as one is born with green eyes . . . etc . . . that is to say, in one's chromosomes, within the nucleus of an individual's cells, the stack of genes carries the characteristics of each person and determines absolutely . . . everything which makes them original. . . . Even in Paris homosexuals are imprisoned, tortured, harrassed, hemmed in, and forced to live underground in ghettos by this ignorant society . . . and yet one can understand how such characteristics are determined genetically, thanks to the work of our scientists. (143)

This fluid approach to gender is acted out in one of the most hilarious events in the sensual meditation camp. This is a party in which men dress up as women and women dress up as men, an exercise that encourages participants to experiment with different shades of gender and "choose" the mélange of male-female that will best suit them in their everyday life.

Women's Role in the Meetings

The Mouvement Raelian Canadien has found the English-speaking provinces to be unreceptive, thus far, to the Message, but claims to have four thousand members in Quebec. The Montreal Raelians meet on the third Sunday in the month at the Holiday Inn. These meetings begin with a lively half hour of rapturous greetings, then members sit down in the conference room and listen to various announcements and speeches. All participate in a guided meditation, called Harmonization, which involves deep breathing and concentrating on a mental anatomical dissection of the body, arriving at the contemplation of the brain, which engages in a visualization exercise of the planet of the Elohim, to the accompaniment of New Age music.

Women are as active as the men in these meetings. They make announcements, give speeches, caress their boyfriends, and generally behave in an overtly "sensual" fashion. One teenager who is much admired sits through the meetings in a tulle crinoline skirt, tossing her ponytail and licking lollipops. Men usually outnumber the women and few children attend. The style of feminine dress ranges from elegant *Paris Match,* to punk, to (apparently unconscious) parodies of Brigitte Bardot in her St. Tropez heyday. Some male Guides dress in white and wear their hair long, for they believe the hair follicles function as antennae, or telepathic receptors. It is perhaps significant that many of the men I met at the meetings could be described as "effeminate" in their dress and social manner, but I did not meet one woman who was "masculine." All Raelians wear large medallions of the swastika inside the star of David, which they believe is an ancient symbol of the integrity of time and space. Between 200 to 400 people gather at the third Sunday of the month meetings, and even when Rael spoke at the Montreal December 1991 meeting, fewer than 350 Raelians were present.

Sensual overtures appear to be a common recruitment technique. One of my more conspicuously ornamental male students (age nineteen), who attended the 1990 Transmission of the Cellular Plan to write a field report, complained that three different women propositioned him outright or tried to arrange a date; he was shocked because "they were at least forty, and old enough to be my mother!" Another student, an eighteen-year-old Jewish girl, received a pep talk on "free love" from one of the assistant guides she interviewed, followed by a eulogy on her beauty; she confessed the incident so disturbed her that she could not sleep soundly for a week.

One event that illustrates the Raelian disregard for marriage (and for national boundaries) occurred at the 1989 November meeting when two Frenchmen stood up and announced that they were looking for Quebec girls to marry so they could stay in Canada. The group's celebration of sexual adventurism was dramatized in a Guide's announcement in the December 1990 meeting, "Let us congratulate Philador. For one whole year she has been with the same man!" There was a hearty applause. (My student who reported this event commented, "What's the big deal about that? I've had the same girlfriend for three years, and no one ever congratulates me!")[2]

Raelian Women: Who Joins and Why?

I have managed to access three sources of information on female membership in the Raelian Movement. One, the Raelian

Conseil Decisionel released their statistics on Canadian members, which were based on a 1988 questionnaire sent to 1400 subjects, of which 399 were returned. Two, I and seven students from Dawson College passed out a questionnaire at the December 1991 meeting in Montreal and received 30 responses (twelve women and eighteen men) out of 500-odd participants. Three, over four years, I and my students at Dawson College have collected interviews with sixteen Raelians and field notes from participant-observation research at the meetings.

The portrait of a "typical" Raelian woman that emerges from these sources is as follows: she is likely to be in her late twenties or early thirties, from a Catholic and working-class background but upwardly mobile in a white collar job; she has an undergraduate degree or is earning one; and she lives with her boyfriend with no intention of ever marrying. Also, she is likely to be attractive, long-haired, and to wear flamboyant clothing. A comparison of the male and female members in 1988 reveals that twice as many men join as women, and that there are more women in the Structure than among the inactive "Raelians" (see table 4).

The Raelian Survey (which does not distinguish between the sexes) indicates that 59 percent of "membres des structures" are "travailleurs," 24 percent are students, 13 percent were "other," and only 5 percent are "ménagères," or housekeepers. Our Dawson College Survey showed that twenty-eight out of thirty members grew up in families in which the mother was a "housewife." It is clear, however, that Raelian women have rejected this traditional role. The average age of members, according to the Raelian Survey on 399 respondents, was 35, and the median age was 33.9 for those in the structure and 32.3 for Raelians. Our survey (thirty respondents) came up with 28 as the average age for women and 33 for men.

Concerning their sexual "life-styles," or what the Raelian survey terms "le plan sexuel-affectif," 28 percent of Structure members were "celibataire," or living alone and sexually inactive, 8 percent were living in couples ("ou en trio") with "plusieurs rencontres extraco." 13 percent were living alone with many sexual encounters, and 40 percent were sexually ex-

TABLE 4. Sex Ratios in the Raelian Structure
(Canada)

Level	Title	Females	Male
0	Probationer	14	23
1	Assistant Animator	48	52
2	Animator	45	77
3	Assistant Guide	25	34
4	Priest Guide	4	14
5	Bishop Guide	—	3
6	Planetary Guide	—	1

clusive (ou presque) couples. Members outside the Structure were more likely to be celibate, and if in couples, less likely have an "open relationship."

Four of the twelve women in the survey were mothers, and these women were older than the average age—between thirty-five and forty-one. All of them were single mothers and had their children before becoming Raelians. Three of them had children in their teens and twenties and had recently received the transmission of the cellular plan. (The movement administers a test to children of members to ensure they are free from parental conditioning in their decision to join.) Although one Guide informed me that members of the structure did not have children, another assistant guide assured me it was the individual's decision and, to prove it, pointed to a woman assistant guide, who was showing off her new baby at the meeting.

Unfortunately, I did not think to include a question in the survey asking *who* they were living with, but my impression from the meetings is that women and men in the Structure tend to form couples inside the movement.

Of the thirty respondents in the survey, all but one came from a Catholic background. Their parents (or rather their fathers) were described as fruit vendors, farmers, clerks, janitors, etc., and the respondents tended to hold jobs in technologies or in para-scientific professions, such as lab technician, industrial technician, dental assistant, paramedic or male nurse, and security guard for a psychiatric ward. Also, I and my students met a surprising number of strippers, both female and male, in the meetings. At one meeting we noted four male strippers (fully clothed, but they had mentioned their profession during our conversations).

My initial impression of this movement, from observing a great deal of same-sex caressing during the Sunday meetings, is that it attracted a high proportion of "gays" among its following. When I asked an assistant guide to give me an estimate of the number of homosexuals in the Quebec movement, he replied rather coldly, "We don't think in such narrow categories. Some of us are unisexual, some are bisexual, some trisexual, and a few of us are even quadrisexual." When I timidly enquired what the last category might represent, he leaned forward and whispered, "With the Elohim!"

Members exhibit a similar fluidity in their views on sexuality, and this was reflected in our survey. Only two men identified themselves as "bisexual," and one as "homosexual," and all the women ticked the "heterosexual" box, but many wrote comments in the margins objecting to these "rigid" and "misleading" categories. Many of the women I interviewed described experiences in the sensual meditation camp that an outsider would probably categorize as "Lesbian," but that the Raelians would explain as "experimenting with our sensuality."

Portraits of Four Raelian Women

Guylaine is a pretty, slender twenty-four-year-old who studies Spanish and computer programming at the Université de Montréal.[3] She dances at the striptease club Super Sexe for a living, and joined the movement in 1989. She was interviewed by Donald Herman, a Dawson College student.

D. What have you gained from your participation?
G. I have become more conscious, meditating like the way we do has really opened my consciousness. It makes you more aware, it's so different and so real for me. I was never into meditating before. Also, I am more open towards people. I used to be only interested in men, chasing the boys. But now, I see the beauty and sensuality

of women, of all humans. I am not gay, but I've had experiences at the sensual meditation camp I really enjoyed with women, and I don't feel shy about touching my girlfriends anymore.

D. How do you feel about Rael?

G. He has the power of the infinite in his eyes, He is so amazing, so warm. He is the most honest man I know.

D. Have you talked to him personally?

G. Not only was I allowed to talk to him, I was invited to make love with him!

D. Did you?

G. No, he's really not my style

D. What is your style?

G. Someone I can give pleasure to and receive pleasure from

D. Rael wasn't attractive enough?

G. It's not that, it just seems he's not my style.

Sophie is 33 and joined ten years ago and at that time was going through a divorce. She has lived for eight years with one of the most prominent Guides in Quebec. She has worked as a secretary but is currently embarking on a new career as a therapeutic masseuse. This interview was conducted by Jerry Evangelista in 1989.

J. Why did you join the Raelian movement?

S. I believed in extraterrestrials since I was a kid and when I came to see Rael on television ten years ago, I found that it was kind of logical, well, I couldn't say it was logical, but kind of interesting . . . that that same guy had gone to another planet and had met Jesus, Buddha, and all the other prophets. . . . I said, "Wow! That must be interesting," so I went right away to buy the book. . . . I read the books in one night, I was so impressed that someone was thinking like me. . . . My belief was that extraterrestrials were people who were not violent. I also thought they would come to visit us as if we were little mice in a laboratory, just to check where we were but not to bother us, just to have an eye on us.

J. What do you think of Rael?

S. Well, we do respect him a lot because he brought us the message, but he's an ordinary human being like everybody else. He tells us, don't do like people are doing now with Jesus . . . they believe that Jesus showed the way, but everyone kept an eye on his finger . . . and not where he was pointing. They thought the message was less important than he was. Actually, I'm sure the message is more important than Rael because, if he ever dies (hopefully never, but if) the message will still be strong.

J. How is this better than Catholicism?

S. I found that being raised in a Catholic family, in the Catholic religion, some things were stupid. When I asked questions about religion, they would say, "It's a mystery." This would frustrate me very much. And when I read the message, that's where the answers were. In the old days people didn't know very much

J. How did your family feel about your joining?

S. They really thought I was crazy. I was getting divorced at the time when I joined . . . and they did make some threats, not of getting me out of the movement, but of discommunicating [disowning?] me. . . . They were scared because this was new to them and they thought I was being brainwashed. . . . The fact that I was getting divorced . . . was really hard on them too so I guess they laid it all on the Raelian Movement. . . . I see my family often, but we don't talk about it because my mother believes in something—she believes in God. If you don't believe in God, if you don't stay Catholic, you're not a good person anymore.

J. I wanted to ask you about the summer camp—the sensual meditation. What's the purpose of them?

S. We have summer camp for two weeks. You don't have to stay for the whole two weeks, the first five or six days is the sensual meditation seminar that is given every year. This is the meditation technique the extraterrestrials taught Rael when he went on their planet. It's a technique where you can open your mind by opening all your senses. We fast for twenty-four hours and then we start opening our senses. In the next twenty-four hours we don't talk or eat or drink anything but water—we really get inside of ourselves.

J. Are you out of doors?

S. Yes, we're outside, we can move around but we can't talk to anyone, and that's all I'm going to tell you, because if you ever do come to camp I don't want to give you the same scoop. . . . After the twenty-four hours we start eating again, slowly, and the food! Just the smell of it is great after all that fasting.

J. No meat, right?

S. We have rice, bread, vegetables, but no meat.

J. I heard there was a lot of nudity involved. Is that true?

S. Lots of people thought that and still think that.

J. Are people nude during the whole two-week camping trip?

S. That depends on the person. If that person doesn't feel at ease nude, they don't have to be nude, we'll never force anyone and tear his clothes off! We stress the respect of the individual and that means to respect his rhythm, so if he's not ready, that's fine. No one will judge a person because he's dressed or not dressed, we all went through that stage already, so we know what it feels like.

J. Is there any truth behind the rumor that the summer camps turn into one big sex orgy?

S. A lot of people think that, but most of those people never come to see what really happens, if it was like that I would never have joined the movement, because at first I was so shy! When I first joined . . . I would just say "Hi!" to someone and I would blush drastically, I was so shy. I'll tell you frankly, if it had been like that I would never have joined, and it's not like that at all. It's funny the way people interpret things . . . they don't really check or ask questions, they just say what they've heard . . . anyways, that's not what happens at all, it's not like an orgy! We do, after twenty-four hours, have a supper and so on, when you can open up your senses, and if you do find someone appealing, if you feel like going with that person and sharing a beautiful evening or night with him or her; it could even be with another woman, but why not? It's beautiful, you're opening your senses, but you don't have to, it's not an obligation. If someone came to you and asked you, "I'd like to sleep with you," and you don't want to, and that person insists, well, that's not right. That person should not insist if he's really sincere with himself, herself. You're allowed to say no, that's part of the respect, the choice you have. It's never happened to me like that, I've never had anybody come up to me and say, "Hey, baby! I'd like to sleep with you." It's not somebody you've never seen before. He's more likely to just come up and say, "I sincerely like you and I find you pretty." They're not going to say they want to sleep with you right away, because it's *sensuality* that comes out of it, not sexuality. Sensuality is when you eat, drink, or smell something nice, or when you touch something that's soft and it's the same thing with a person.

J. How do you feel when you meditate?

S. It's hard to explain, I feel a sense of joy . . . it's almost like an orgasm, it really is like that for me. But you see, I'm kind of special. We have a Guide in the movement, he's called Nathan, and he's a guy that expresses himself very much and when he meditates, if he has an urge of wanting to yell or cry, he'll do it. I'm sort of like Nathan, if I have an urge to do something, I'll do it, but only if I'm around members,

I won't do it around people who won't understand what I'm feeling. When I'm with Raelians, I let myself go, I cry, scream, or laugh out loud. . . . The meditation is best compared to an orgasm, really. It's a joy so intense inside you, you have to let it out or it will just explode. My boyfriend's reactions are totally different, maybe he'll have tears running down his cheeks . . . from joy not sadness . . . because he feels so good it's like he's floating. That's why we are against drugs also. We can get high without taking drugs and we can remember how we got there and how to come back. We can do this one hundred times a day and we won't be drug addicts. . . . Because it's a special chemical that's natural to the brain. The chemical, when you go into a meditation, will go into the brain and bring happiness and a lot of positive thinking and lots of good feelings, and everything that is positive will permit the connections between your neurons, so you will be more aware and more intelligent. Everything that is negative, like drugs or repressing your sexual drive, feeling guilty and inhibited, will destroy those connections, and you become stupider. That's why meditation is very good.

J. Is that why you are taking massage classes?

S. Yes, it ties in with sensual meditation, but it's also something I wanted to do even when I was a little girl. I wanted to be a nurse, but my mother would discourage me, because she *was* a nurse and knew what was going on in the nursing field. So, I became a secretary like *she* wanted, and I *hated* it! So, that's why I'm taking massage. Most sicknesses are caused by stress, and massage prevents this stress. I don't believe in pills. so I won't give them out—everything will be natural. . . . I finish in April and then I'm going to get into the business of massage. It will be legal, no hanky-panky, because I want it to be professional.

Monte-Marcelline is one of the three woman Priest Guides in Canada. I have included an abridged version of her interview because I found in her an extraordinary example of a highly religious and benevolent woman who wields authority within both the Raelian community and the "sexual minorities" community. As a transsexual, she has achieved a stable and apparently successful family life, which is closer to the traditional model than that of many contemporary women. This woman challenged many of my preconceptions about sex roles and human relationships. She reminded me (because of her charitable activities) of the nineteenth-century Christian women social reformers, and yet her appearance (in tight black leather pants and jacket, long dyed-red hair in a gaudy bow and heavy makeup—as well as her magic acts in nightclubs and involvement in the gay and transvestite demimonde) spoke of Montreal's red-light district: two hitherto incompatible worlds!

Monte-Marcelline's special function as a Priest Guide is to counsel Raelians undergoing sexual problems. She is particularly well qualified for this task, for she did ten years of volunteer work as a counselor for sexual minorities from her home through a telephone hotline. Also, she believes her unique status as a transsexual enables her to see human sexuality from both points of view. This interview was conducted over lunch in my house in December 1990, and what follows is a highly condensed and roughly translated version.

S. Can you tell me about your origins?

M. I was born in Abitibi forty-eight years ago, it is on the north shore of the Saint Lawrence river, and my family settled there in 1830. I was the youngest of four brothers, and my mother had always wanted a daughter, so while she was pregnant she made a pink room for me with pink clothes laid out. When I was born she pretended I was her little girl and dressed me in girl's clothes. Then, when I was four my older sister arrived at the house and she saw me with my bows and lace dress and she said to my mother, "He will be going to school soon, you cannot go on like this." Then she cut my hair and dressed me in pantaloons. So, for a year I was a boy, but then everything changed again because I was almost killed. I was outside playing in the snow and a snow-removal bulldozer was backing up on me. The driver could not see behind, but the little girl next door happened to be looking out of the window and saw the danger and ran outside and climbed up the front of the bulldozer and banged on the window in the driver's face until he stopped. I was inches from the back wheel. My mother was so terrified, she would not let me play outside anymore, and kept me in the kitchen dressed in skirts and aprons, helping her cook. So, the day I went to school I was dressed as a boy, but the children knew something was funny, because they laughed at me and called me "Jeannette."

S. So, did you stay a boy?

M. It was very disorienting to have to change sex all of a sudden as a child, and it caused a total disequilibrium in me, so that between the ages of four to twenty-seven I didn't really live, I vegetated. Then, at twenty-seven, I met my lifelong companion, Jean-Pierre, who loved me for who I was, not for the sex which I happened to be in. There is no need to say that completely changed my life. With him I was able to realize my greatest fantasy: to become a wife and a mother.

S. What kind of employment have you had?

M. All my life I have done volunteer work for people who were desperate. First, I began working when I was fifteen taking care of old people, then I was a comedienne for ten years, and was very unhappy although I made a lot of people laugh. Then I worked as a magician in different cities in Canada and the United States. I became a transvestite at the age of eighteen and felt totally comfortable in my life as a woman. Now I am working with SIDA Montreal for the last year as a counselor, and represent women with AIDS in Quebec. Ten years ago I marched in the first march for sideens [people with SIDA, or AIDS] in Montreal. I have learned a lot working with them. When one has a fatal disease, one learns to live in the present moment. It is the quality of time that is important, not the quantity.

S. What does your counseling involve?

M. Just being there to listen. Sometimes people want advice on how to handle their financial situation, or their lovers or their family. We talk about health problems and a lot about philosophy.

S. Do you tell them about the Message?

M. Never! That is not my role there. But we talk about how to live life and what it all means, and I think what I have learned from being in the movement helps me to have a positive attitude, to enjoy life, and they feel that. Sometimes people will ask, "Why are you always so happy, Marcelline, what is your secret?" If they are persistent I tell them. They may feel guilty about sex, and I help them overcome that. Rael says in his discourses we must become as little children and see everything as a game to amuse ourselves. So long as you treat your fellow beings with respect and don't hurt anyone, there is no such thing as "normal." As he says, "La raison vivre c'est la plaisir!" So, my message to sideens is, "Maybe you will be dead in two hours, maybe two years, maybe ten years. It is not the quantity of your life that matters, it's the quality. So, live now! It's time!" Everyone has the choice to live, now, right here. Why be afraid of dying? We were once sperms and eggs. None of us would want to live backwards and be separated into a sperm and an egg again! But when we think about it, it doesn't frighten us. So why should the future frighten us? Look at the birds, I say. Every day they find something to eat; they fly minute to minute. Do you think they worry?

S. Is your work with SIDA Montreal volunteer work?

M. For a year it was volunteer, but now they have found me a position with a salary, but you know, if I were a millionnaire, I would *pay* to work there!

S. What made you decide to become a transsexual?

M. It was when I was driving home one day with my son and almost had an accident. More than anything I feared being picked up by an ambulance and at the hospital they would discover I was a man under my clothes and put me in the men's ward. I knew from all those years in hospital doing volunteer work how cruel the nursing staff could be to transvestites and homosexuals—I had seen it. I imagined as an old man being stuck in the men's ward and being tormented. . . . So I decided at the age of thirty-two to undergo the operation. I had my doubts, because I wondered about my husband; suppose he were homosexual, he would no longer be attracted to me. Also, what effect would it have on our son? I explained it to Jean-Pierre and he was very understanding; he said it would make no difference, that he loved me for my mind and not for my cock and balls, and so I went in. . . . When I woke up from the operation he was standing there and he was holding a bouquet of roses and he said, "I love you and now I can ask you to be my wife!" I was very touched, but I answered, "If we love each other, what difference will a contract make? I will live with you and love you, but I will never marry!"

So I felt reassured. And my relationship with my husband and son has got better and better. We fight sometimes, but I am always honest with them and it seems to work.

S. Your son you adopted?

M. Yes, when we lived together we wanted a son so we adopted him. My son is now a Raelian—he received the transmission last initiation, and he chose this himself. We sometimes work together in nightclubs giving magic shows.

S. So, how did you become a Raelian?

M. It was through my friend, Lana St.-Cyr, the foremost transvestite in Quebec, who told me about it. He was always talking about flying saucers, and I had no interest in flying saucers, but then I heard Rael speak on the radio and I just felt what he was saying was true.

I stayed up all night reading the Message, and me, I never read books, I find there is too much fantasy, I prefer real life. But this had an enormous impact on me. It was real. Then I played the tape for my brother-in-law, who is an atheist, and he keeled over backward because it was such a shock. He immediately recognized the truth of Rael's message, but it destroyed all his conditioning too fast, so he fainted. I have known many to react that way.

S. What does your work as Priest Guide involve?

M. I spend a lot of time on the phone. I am the counselor for all the Raelians who have problems in love or with sex. I can sympathize with the women, and I know what it feels like to be a man. My ten years on the telephone counseling sexual minorities has prepared me for this. I decided to stay at home with our son, but I wanted to be of service to humanity, so I volunteered for this telephone line, and I would hear every possible kind of story . . . foot fetishes, pedaphiles, kinds of sexuality they haven't named yet, and I learned to respect everyone's search for pleasure and meaning, whatever form it takes. I go to Raelian conferences, weekend workshops, meditations, and I enjoy it. But I also travel to Europe every year to the international conference for transsexuals. There is a priest in Belgium, Pierre Ducette, who started a church for sexual minorities, and we are very involved in political matters, activism, and he was assassinated last year. So, this year I am giving a series of lectures on Suicide and Transsexuals, for I have done a study of why transsexuals often show suicidal tendencies, and will talk about how to help them.

S. You must be away from home a lot!

M. Yes, my husband misses me, but he is very occupied, he works for VIA RAIL, and we have an agreement that we can have pleasure with other people if the other is not around. He trusts me, he knows I love him, and I always use a condom. Often when I travel on the airplane I will meet a man I like and I am always honest and tell them this night is only for pleasure, and I am also a Lesbian, and sometimes I meet a woman who attracts me.

S. It seems you have spent your whole life helping other people.

M. Yes, always I see around me so much suffering, people who need help who need a friend. It is my nature to help, I could not be happy any other way. I don't do it to be "good" or because I feel obliged, I do it because it gives me pleasure. And it is the people who suffer the most who I love most. It is the *viellards*, the old people who most need our love. They have most need of our caresses. There is no merit to being beautiful, and we have many beautiful young men and women in the movement. It is those who suffer the most who become the most beautiful, and the strongest. As Rael says, "All that doesn't kill me will make me stronger."

"Francine," another of the four female Priest Guides and public relations officer for the Canadian movement, might be the prototypical Raelian woman. She was interviewed at her apartment by Dawson students Thi Phuong Thao Nguyen and Tosca Rulli (who were somewhat nonplussed when she answered the door in a bikini). She is thirty-three, from a "very poor" Catholic farming family near Quebec city; she received Rael's message at age twenty, and works as a real estate agent. When questioned about her sexual orientation, she replied, "I'm heterosexual for now, but nothing is constant in the universe. [I] don't know if I might change later on. . . . It's not the sexual habit difference that is the problem, but the lack of respect of another's choice." Her version of Raelian gender roles clearly conforms to the sex unity type.

They are all considered equal—no discriminations, differences, or favoritism—they're all humans. There are more men guides than women but it's not because they are men, it's because women in our society don't have much chance to expand, but we're getting there! When you reach infinity you don't make differences between man and woman.

Reasons Proposed for Women's Minimal Part in Leadership

The rejection of marriage, the de-emphasis on motherhood, and the consensual support for women as *travailleurs* rather than *ménagères*—these values seem to augur power and authority for women. Moreover, Rael preaches a kind of "feminization of millenarianism" that awards the role of world savior to women—and to men who cultivate feminine qualities. Thus, there appear to be no obstacles in ideology, tradition, or sexist attitudes to prevent charismatic women rising in the hierarchy . . . so what is stopping them? The reasons I propose are as follows: (1) A (male) gender bias in the language; (2) The central myth of the movement, which is one of male initiation, the hero's quest for his true father; and (3) Rael's own "sexual life-style."

A Gender Bias in the Language. The Elohim are always referred to as "Our *Fathers* from Space," who created *men* in their own image. The first aliens Rael encountered in 1973 were male, and the great scientists of Genesis who came to earth to "implant" *mankind* are men in the illustrations. The renegade scientists of the Fall, who interbred with mortal women must, presumably, have been males, as were the space alien fathers of the forty prophets (who also happen to be male): "When the Sons of Elohim had intercourse with the daughters of men and had children by them, the Nephelin (mighty men) were on earth, they were the heroes of old, men of renown" (*Let's Welcome Our Fathers from Space,* 1986, 3–4). Although noninclusive language is, perhaps, not sufficient in itself to undermine female leadership (Rajneesh's discourses, for example, are in British Raj prose, and yet he strongly encourages female leadership), the absence of female role models could represent a more serious obstacle to Raelian women.

The Myth of Male Initiation. Rael writes of his visit to the planet of the Elohim, where he had an emotional encounter with an alien called Yahweh, who responds to Rael's question about his origins by addressing him as "tu" rather than "vous," and then proceeds to relate the events leading up to Rael's birth.

After the explosion at Hiroshima we decided that the time had come for us to send a new messenger on Earth. . . . We then selected a woman, as we had done in the time of Jesus. This woman was taken aboard one of our ships and inseminated as we had done with the mother of Jesus. Then she was freed after we had totally erased from her memory all traces of what had happened. (*Let's Welcome Our Fathers from Space* 105)

(Having related this tale, Yahweh turns to Rael, who sees in his eyes "a great emotion and feeling of love" and says to him, "From this moment on you may call me father, because you are my son"—and Rael notes of his half-brother, "Jesus too

Rael's encounter with the Elohim. Courtesy Canadian Raelian Movement.

seemed to be moved by the same feelings. Then I kissed my father and my brother for the very first time.")

It is tempting to use this material to concoct what Jon Wagner (1986) deplores: a "capsule psychobiography" of a religious founder. Rael, who experienced a long and difficult birth in a Vichy clinic, whose mother pretended he was not her child; Rael, who grew up in a small French village as an illegitimate and fatherless child, brought up by his adoring grandmother and aunt; Rael, who heard his biological father was a Jewish refugee; this child grows up and proceeds to create an original religion based on the central myth of the mighty fathers from space descending to claim their sons, who are undergoing the dangerous coming of age. Women in this myth—and in Rael's life on planet earth—appear shadowy and interchangeable, and their loving attentions are taken for granted.

Women are not powerful in this Creation myth. There was no question of "choice" when the Virgin Mary was selected for her "virgin DNA"—not even the opportunity to deliver a "handmaid of the Lord" speech. She and Rael's mother were impregnated as unceremoniously as laboratory animals. There was no "meaningful relationship" between Yahweh and these mortal women; they were not included in the ecstatic family reunion when Rael "kissed my father and brother for the first time." (Although it is tempting to dabble in pop psychology and explore the Oedipal content of Rael's reported conversations with his space father, there is an element of *hubris* involved in the sociologist's attempt to plumb the psychological motivations of a complex and creative genius like Rael—or any religious innovator—for this kind of analysis can reduce or trivialize the religious content of their visions.) Aside from these issues, Raelian mythology speaks to men more than to women.

Rael's Personal Life-style. Rael makes it clear that everyone should choose their *own* sexual life-style, but it appears reasonable to assume that, as in any charismatic community, the leader's intimate relationships are carefully scrutinized by the followers, and provide (perhaps unconsciously) a model for conducting their relationships. Rael was married and a father

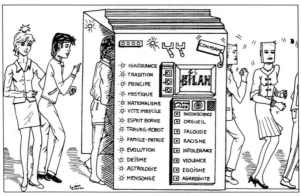

Poster of the Rapture of Extraterrestrials.
Courtesy Canadian Raelian Movement.

when he began his charismatic career in 1973, but he separated in 1987 from his wife (who with his son and daughter has joined his movement). For four years he traveled with his Japanese girlfriend and for the last three years has consorted with a red-haired French Canadian. Although Rael appears to be exclusively heterosexual, he advocates homosexual experimentation and wrote a love song about Lesbian spiders. He eschews the macho image and is often described as "gentle" and "feminine" by his followers. When Rael was grilled in a television interview by an aggressive journalist who asked him outright if he had sex with several different partners every day, Rael replied with self-deprecating humour, "I am forty-four years old. Sometimes it is difficult for me to make love even once a day!" His photographic image, however, resembles that of Hugh Heffner. Photographs of Rael appearing in the movement's magazine, *Apocalypse*, nearly always show him surrounded by young, scantily clad beauties—and they are always different beauties. A film made by Radio Canada *(They're Coming!)* features a scene with Rael surrounded on a Mediterranean terrace by four beauties who, because of their racial diversity and bared left shoulders, might be candidates for the Miss Universe contest. They did not actually peel grapes, but they did offer Rael a bowl of fruit.

While this kind of PR tells us nothing of substance about Rael's private life (except that he seems to enjoy being photographed with beautiful women), and his lack of education concerning gender-specific language can be excused in one who claims to be from another planet, it appears reasonable to assume that women who define themselves as feminists, on first encountering this literature, might be slightly put off by the sexy biological robots, the alien-inseminated, amnesiac virgins, and Rael's bevy of oriental playmates. Outsiders unfamiliar with the feminist dimensions and complexity of his philosophy of sexuality might even dismiss his organization as "sexist" in the same way that journalists, on seeing the swastika and hearing Rael's theory of Jews as descendants of space aliens, have (unjustly) accused him of neo-Nazism. These first impressions might influence the recruitment of women into the movement.

TABLE 5. The Structure of the Raelian Movement International: Division of Members (August 6, 1993)

	Women	Men
Beginners	19	21
Level 1	35	64
Level 2	61	75
Level 3	23	28
Level 4	5	12
Level 5	1	3
Total	144	203

TABLE 6. Division of Members at the Canadian Seminar (July 1993)

Level	Women	Men	Total
Raelians	210	305	515
Structure	135	187	322

These three reasons, therefore—the language, the mythology, and Rael's example—appear to be deep-seated and unconscious barriers to women's claiming authority in the Structure—at least during the present phase. In a movement so committed to experimentation and individualism, however, it is not unlikely that the situation might change. One of the four women Priest Guides of Canada has recently been appointed to head the Raelian Movement in the United States, which has begun to respond positively to the Message, and the Korean leader is also female. Recent membership surveys, moreover, indicate that women's authority and presence in the movement are increasing (see tables 5 and 6).

The Raelians' patterns of authority suggest that "equality" is not a good enough place to start for women aspiring to religious leadership. After all, leaders in charismatic communities must exhibit special (as opposed to equal) qualities. Two NRMs that favor feminine leadership, the Brahmakumaris (Babb, 1986) and the Rajneesh, espouse a view of gender that Rosemary Reuther (1983) has labeled "radical romantic feminism"—the view that women possess unique spiritual qualities superior to those of men.

The Raelian Movement's Appeal for Women

The conspicuous numbers of strippers and transvestites and highly expressive homosexuals among the congregation might suggest that this movement is particularly attractive to people who define themselves as sexually marginal. To support this hunch, it should be noted that I observed three transvestites and one transsexual at the December 1988 Raelian Disco Dance. For the sexually "deviant" living in a Catholic culture where they are treated as sinners, the appeal of a community where their sexual experimentation, creativity, and exhibitionism are interpreted as charismatic, as signs of belonging to the elite, the sensuallly awake who will achieve salvation when the UFOs descend—is a phenomenon not difficult to understand.

It could be argued from the interview data that one of the movement's attractions for women is its holistic approach to sexuality. This is not the only, nor indeed the main, attraction. Alain Bouchard's unpublished research and the Dawson College Survey both indicate that, for men and women alike, the initial appeal of this movement appears to lie in Rael's theory of humanity's origins. The notion that extraterrestrial scientists created us reconciles our reverence for science and our need to feel protected by superior beings.

The second strong reason for joining seems to be that the Message represents a rejection of Catholicism, and it provides a substitute: a modern, "scientific" atheistic religion, which nevertheless parallels the doctrines, rituals, and clergy of the Catholic Church. Part of "deconditioning" from Catholicism for Raelians is to adopt a more positive view of the body, and to celebrate their sexuality, linking it to a more general appreciation of the senses. In the Raelian worldview, human sexuality is aligned with the sacred cosmos and functions as a technique of telepathic communication (with the Elohim) and consciousness expansion (with the whole universe). For working-class Catholic women in Quebec, this religion offers a way out of the miasma of guilt and secrecy surrounding their sexuality, a miasma that clings more closely to woman as the "temptress" traditionally identified with nature and the body (Clarke and Richardson 1986). For the Raelians, there is no "double standard," for the women seem to be as active in choosing their partners in sensuality as the men, and also free to refuse overtures from male leaders without suffering loss of status, as the interview with the striptease dancer indicates.

One woman's testimonial printed in *Sensual Meditation* (1986, 146) states: "When I discovered Sensual Meditation at twenty four years of age, I had my first orgasm. . . . I express one wish, and that is for every woman to be able to discover this, especially as I have learned that 70% of women have never experienced an orgasm." Another woman, an assistant guide from El Salvador, wrote in her questionnaire that her family had taught her that "sex was a sin," and on joining the Raelians she had come to feel "less guilty."

Besides noting in members an experimental approach toward their sexuality, I also observed in several members the assumption that the human body (with a bit of medical assistance) is highly malleable. Plastic surgery, bodybuilding, and bleached hair lend a sort of (nordic) Venice Beach glamour to the Montreal meetings. One of the assistant guides must go to hospital three times a week for kidney dialysis, and one of the Animators (a former Catholic priest) has had a face-lift and hair implant since joining the movement. Not only one's sexual orientation but also one's gender is regarded as a matter of choice.

It is perhaps significant that the most charismatic woman in the Canadian movement is a transsexual. No mere woman could choose to refashion her sexual life-style in such an impressive act of faith in science. In an age critical of the ecological problems caused by science, in a religion that exalts the individual's power of choice, she is a living testimony to the magic of scientists and the shamanic power and mobility resulting from an experimental approach to sexuality.

EIGHT

Secret Shamans in the Institute for the Development of the Harmonious Human Being

Woman is a great, white, open grave!
—E. J. Gold

In E. J. Gold's view, the "Being" is an utterly alien, incalculable creature who has existed for eons on other planets. Human sexual identity is a superficial crust to be shed or exploited during "The Work." By cultivating an inner detachment from their bodies and sexual/social identity, Gold's students seek to tap hidden sources of occult power that will increase their creativity and entrepreneurialism in their daily lives.

The History

The Institute for the Development of the Harmonious Human Being (IDHHB) is the permanent and underground name for the spiritual movement surrounding Eugene Jeffrey Gold, who resides in Grass Valley, California. Gold is the son of the late science fiction writer and editor of *Galaxy* magazine, Horace L. Gold, and he was born in New York City about 1940. During his protean career, Gold has changed his title from "al Washi," the Sufi master, to "Mother Beast" to "Mr. G." to "Just Jeff," and is currently referred to by his disciples as "E. J." Gold has concocted, directed, and debriefed a series of "spiritual schools" in the United States and Canada since 1968, which have opened under different names in different cities. These "schools" try out an eclectic range of traditions, from Sufism to Gurdjieff work, from Ethiopian martial arts to astronaut training, from natural childbirth to Tibetan Buddhism. Gold will dress up and retitle himself to tour the new centers, appearing in blackface as an Ethiopian warrior during the *Wushalo!* martial arts phase, or sporting a fez and fake mustache to speak to the "work groups" as "Mr. G."

Gold declares his mission is, "The education of the Universe, one idiot at a time" and his teaching method is to administer "shocks" to his students to break down their social conditioning and mechanical patterns, in the tradition of Zen and Sufi masters who awaken disciples by what Gold's disciples refer to as "the quick way of head-bashing and ego-squashing." Underlying all Gold's short-lived "schools" is a core philosophy of reincarnation, spiritual evolution, and a quest for the shamanic powers of mobility and ecological adaptabilty—and a brashly American celebration of "snake-oil salesmen" entrepreneurial skills.

IDDHB eschatology and techniques appear to be influenced by George Gurdjieff and by L. Ron Hubbard, and the courses are designed to excavate the powerful Being buried beneath false conditioning and mechanical habits. The Being tends to repeat the same life over and over with the same boring obsessions, unless it is de-automatized by conscious "Work." "Work" provides an environment within which "Being can grow" and achieve a Zen-like awareness in the present and cultivate the "abilities of Being." These include the ability to die fearlessly, to stay awake in between lives, and to choose one's next body, but also the detachment to play the social roles given to one in this lifetime with the gusto, humor and flexibility of a mime artist. The ephemeral nature of Gold's short-lived cults, or "outer schools," designed with built-in obsolescence in mind, can be best understood as a ritual enactment of Gold's eschatology, offering Gold students practice in "staying awake in between lives." In Gold's view, each day is a dizzying carousel of death and rebirth experiences in which we drift in and out of the "transit state." It would seem, therefore, that his techniques aim at cultivating a shamanic ability to travel through in-between states that is applicable to changing social roles, job mobility, and life crises as well as to physical death.[1]

Gold's Philosophy of Sexuality

When I first began to research this group in 1973, as a graduate student under the direction of Fred Bird at Concordia University, I received the distinct impression that men and women were treated as equals in every aspect of "The Work." I spent much time at the *Shakti!* center—Wednesday evenings and all day Sunday—and after being told sternly several times (while socializing) to "stop chattering in the landing field!" and (when smiling) to "drop the mask!" I began to realize it was not considered "cool" for us, the students, to exert what we were accustomed to considering our feminine or masculine charm.

The four core-group members instructed us to "erase personal history" on entering the center. For the Sunday meditations in motion, called Moonwalk, and the Nine Obligatories, we dressed in loose, unisex white linen tops and pants. We would begin by standing in a circle and perform the ritual called "Dropping the Mask"; we would inhale deeply, place the hands over the face, pull down slowly, causing the cheeks to sag in an unsightly fashion, and then suddenly drop the arms letting out a sharp "pooh!" of air. It was understood that the face should maintain its expressionless expression for the next two hours of dancing. It was also customary to speak in a level, neutral, almost metallic tone like a machine, so that even our voices were genderless.

E. J. Gold's idiosyncratic version of Creation dramatizes the sex unity view of gender, and appears in his picaresque novel modeled on Gurdjieff's *Beelzebub's Tales to His Grandson.*

"Anyway," The Lord added, "I was going to tell you about My good friend Yerginkenambelh and what happened to him the last time he went to Earth just before the big catastrophe which took the continent of Atlantis. . . .

"He had known something like that would happen to him when they processed him out of the vats in the life-storage systems storage hold of the interspace ship 'The Interval,' within which he was jour-

neying on a mission to save the men on Earth, if at all possible; but
they neglected to brief him on the situation, so that he had to "wing"
it by ear with only a few hours to spare; and so, as soon as they could
arrange for it, and there was no time for him or anyone to do anything
else, he force-tractor-beamed two human beings from the continent of
Atlantis, and of course, you know the rest of the story, how not one
single individual human being survived anywhere during that un-
foreseen catastrophe—except the two human beings which My friend
Corbie managed to save and take aboard his ship. . . .

It wasn't until later that Corbie realized what a terrible mistake he
had made; and then it dawned on him only slowly. Human beings
tend to all look so much alike, that the mistake was understandable,
from my point of view, and Corbie, you'll remember, had just been
jerked out of the storage vat—no time to research before the catastrophe occurred.

"Reproduce?" asked one of the human specimens. . . .

"But I don't understand," muttered the other human; where are
the women?

"Beg pardon?" Corbie politely inquired . . .

"Oh, shit." said the first human. "We're both male. Didn't you
know that?"

"Goddam," said the first human again, "We're the last two
humans in the entire Galaxy, and you didn't check it out first?"

"I understand your concern, but what's the problem?" Corbie
asked innocently. . . . "One of you could easily be altered to
female . . . our ship's surgeon could duplicate a human female very
easily . . . you would be up and around within hours, and ready to
begin procreation within a few days time!"

"Like hell I would!" he roared at Corbie, "You aren't getting me
to be a female!"

"Me either!" the other Atlantean shouted. "You change me into
a dame and I'll kill myself!"

"He won't hafta," screamed the other one. "If you make me live
with him the rest of my life and ball with him and like that, I'll kill
him for you!"

"And so," concluded the Lord, "that's the story . . . that's what
they did; and you know the rest of it . . . how the entire race of
man living on the Earth presently is descended from those survivors
of the catastrophe of Atlantis . . . and so. . . ."

"Lord," interrupted Phaniel, "you never said which one was
changed."

"Oh . . . I don't know which one it was," the Lord admitted. "I asked Corbie the same thing, but to him all humans look alike."(*The Creation Story Verbatim: As Told by the Archangel Gabriel*, 15–16)

The Divine Indifference of the Creator toward His creation seems to be the moral of this tale—hence we're on our own. If the ship's surgeon can "duplicate a female in a few hours" and even God Himself can't tell the difference, then gender must be no more than a superficial and temporary state. The main thrust of Gold's absurd tale is didactic—it is deliberately designed to baffle, shock, and "gross out" the reader, and to make mincemeat out of any latent Christian conditioning. By this "Crazy Wisdom" method, Gold is trying to awaken the "Being" who is usually "snoring away" beneath its layers of false identity.

E. J. Gold rarely advises his disciples on how to conduct sexual relationships, or how to handle their family problems. He stated in the 1984 workshop in New York that as long as the Machine's attention is on conflict—marriage, money problems, etc.—it can't be on the Essential Self. Therefore, as long as we allow the machine to have its conflicts and to refrain from resolving them, it has no energy left over for the Work. The appropriate strategy when faced with divorce, desertion, or other family problems, therefore, was to maintain an inner detachment, or nonidentification with one's social role or emotional state.

In a more recent publication, Gold examines the conditions of the working partnership of the machine and the essential self and finds a parallel in the relationship between woman and man. He presents almost a caricature of the romantic, unliberated woman who "wants nothing but man's complete, utter, totally nonwandering attention . . . placed entirely upon herself." To this end, he insists, "she will do absolutely anything, no matter how degrading or debased or self-effacing to her own interests. . . ." Man's deepest need, however, represents a serious conflict of interest: "He wants his attention to be free to wander wherever it will go. He wants to be distracted and amused . . . scattered and fickle" (*The Human Biological Machine as a Transformational Apparatus* 1986, 82–83).

Newcomers who have the temerity to ask Gold's advice on sexual matters do so at their own risk. One young man was told: "Of course you have trouble with sex. How can a two-year-old with the understanding of a rubber duck understand what's happening with sex?"

In a manner like the tradition of Gestalt therapy and Erhard Seminars Training, ritual obscenities and earthy language are often used as shock tactics to "peel away" layers of false identity. Although female leaders currently dominate the core group and are highly respected, Gold and his male leaders often deliberately insult or "gross out" young female initiates to "snap" them out of their social conditioning as pretty women. This was explained as an ancient Sufi teaching device called the "Way of Malmud" and offered the new student an excuse to reject the spiritual master, thus testing his/her serious intent and ability to recognize a "real" master. Aside from its spiritual purpose, it allows much leeway for unconventiomal sexual behavior. Gold once described how he was sitting in a restaurant with a wealthy dowager he had just persuaded to write a generous check toward the "Work" when the impulse moved him to begin drooling into his food and to utter crude, unintelligent comments; this so repelled the dowager that she retracted her donation. On another occasion in Montreal, April 1983, Gold was speaking to a group of local students, and responded to an attractive girl's question about "the meaning of enlightenment" with a leer and a proposition: "Come to my bed at five o'clock tomorrow morning, honey, and I'll show you what enlightenment is!"

An example of the "Way of Malmud" was witnessed by one of my informants in the early days of *Shakti!* in Montreal when the Wednesday night "White Room Training" began to shift from traditional meditations and sensory awareness exercises to "ordinary" secular activities. The aim was to retain the meditative state while interacting in an everyday environment.

We were developing the weirdest relationship with the people at the center. . . . Dan gave me the creeps sometimes. . . . He was like a precocious child . . . he would ramble on in a philosophical vein and I couldn't follow him. I was worried about Lena because she was developing an infatuation for him. He knew it too, and kept pulling weird trips on her. We were used to coming in and listening to sounds, or breathing or chanting mantras, then all of a sudden they started giving us things to do like . . . washing the floor. One evening Dan suggested we all go out to the movies. . . . We first dropped in at a brasserie for a beer, and I remember sitting there feeling strange and wondering if this was an esoteric exercise and was I doing it correctly, or were we just relaxing over a beer? I kept attaching occult significance to the remarks Al and Dan were making about the hockey game on TV. In the cinema I felt that Lena, who sat between me and Dan, was very tense. When we got home she told me that Dan had moved his hand incredibly slowly along the back of her seat until it rested lightly on her shoulder, and the other hand had reached, millimeter by millimeter, until it brushed her knee. He left both hands there during the whole film, but they were just barely touching her and they tickled like spiders. This made her really nervous and she couldn't decide whether Dan was terribly shy and repressed, or if this was a "paying attention" exercise to make her see beyond physical attraction. She seemed to hope it was the first, but I suspected that Dan had a sadistic streak and was just teasing her.[2]

Women in the Leadership

The leadership in the IDHHB seemed to be composed more or less equally of both sexes; beautiful women appeared to have no advantage over older, plainer women; indeed, they would be teased and harrassed until they shed their posturing and vanity. My impression of Gold's long-term female disciples is that they all seemed to develop a social manner that could be described as tough, detached, efficient, and ruthless. Men behaved this way too, but it was more striking in the women. I think this was their idea of how to achieve Gurdjieff's "objective thinking." I noticed that when they conducted an exercise for new students, their eyes were unfocused, they would speak in a cold, neutral, tone, but when Gold came to Montreal, watching them responding to his joking banter around the kitchen table, I was surprised at how animated their faces were. One core-group woman interviewed noted that the younger leaders of the far-flung Canadian centers tended to "act cold and constipated because they're trying too hard," but that once she joined the IDHHB community in Crestline, she found "the people there were more warm and natural."

The first director of the Montreal *Shakti!* center, in 1973, was "Lucilla," a waitress and barmaid by profession. My informant "Ilona," who worked under her, described her as "a tough broad, kind of like Janis Joplin ten years from now, who gave the guys at the center a real hard time." When Ilona first contacted the group, however, she received a very different impression of Lucilla's role.

Dan led us down the stairs at the back of the shop into a room with a long table and chairs. He told us to sit and wait in silence, and it must have been fifteen minutes before he returned with a woman. He guided her to the seat at the head of the table, followed by a man carrying books and pencils. Dan introduced us to Lucilla and Al. They asked why we were there, and we talked a bit about ourselves. They seemed to have a protective attitude towards Lucilla, who didn't say anything but just sat there with a stunned, sleepy expression on her face. She was overweight, with pouches under her eyes and tangled hair, and I wondered if she were a poor deaf mute or a drug addict—or a mental case they had picked up on the street and were rehabilitating. Al handed out exercise books and pencils. "Lucilla here is going to tell you a story with her hands. Listen very carefully, and when she pauses, you must write down what she has just said. Ready? OK, Lucilla!" Her hands floated slowly upwards and her fingers formed a series of very precise gestures. She kept the same deadpan expression on her face, so there was something mediumistic about it. When she paused, I had to think up a story . . . by the end I fancied I was able to "read" her hands. "Now, each of you read through your stories," said Dan.

We stumbled through our garbled stories and expected to be told if we had got it right or not. Instead, the three just stared at us for such a long time we felt cowed.[3]

It appears that Lucilla was using the "ancient Sufi practice" where the spiritual master comes disguised as a humble outcast.

A male leader who presented an unusual role model for the students and is a good example of the group's inconoclastic attitudes toward sexuality is Tyrell. Tyrell was described by a couple from Montreal (who met him in the "Nazi Concentration Camp" staged by Gold in Crestline in December 1973) as "obnoxious! He's a Hell's Angel . . . or he used to be and still looks like it . . . he's a loudmouth, wears greasy black leather and chains. He's fat and rides a motorbike." Another informant explained Tyrell's history.

One day E. J. walked into a bikers bar in L.A., and just sat there and talked to them all night and in the morning a whole bunch of them followed him up to Crestline, and he got them into the Work. Tyrell was a writer for the Forum section of *Penthouse,* and he was going to give up writing, but Gold told him that people who bought *Penthouse* for sexual highs were really looking for spiritual highs, but didn't know it yet—that sex was the closest they'd come to touching Spirit. So, he advised Tyrell to go on writing pornography, but to inject hidden teachings in his column—spiritual clues that might help the readers find the Path. So, apparently if you read this stuff in *Penthouse* about masturbating in your Mixmaster, it might just contain one of Tyrell's secret mystical messages![4]

Gold encourages leaders in his core group to use their initia-tive in devising new teaching methods and exercises. The most interesting and powerful leader who temporarily "feminized" Gold's religion by introducing ritual and sexual innovations re-flecting her interests, was E. J.'s wife, Cybele Gold. This phase of the movement (between 1974 and 1978) is the most inter-esting for our purposes because, under her tutelage, the group developed radically alternative and highly elaborated sexual-spiritual practices, which are described in the two books she coauthored with her husband, *Joyous Childbirth* (1976) and *Be-yond Sex* (1978).

Cybele Gold's Story

Cybele Gold was married to E. J. for almost a decade, and together they formed a charismatic duo. The Golds would dress up for photographs posed as gurus from different tra-ditions. *Shakti!* magazine in 1973 features a photograph of "al Washi" and "Mataji," Sufi masters, dressed in white robes and turbans and posing in front of a Disneyland mosque. Cybele began shaving off her eyebrows to imitate her husband (I have not succeeded in discovering the spiritual significance of this autoplastic ritual, but it seems to enhance the scary, hypnotic quality of the human gaze). Memos sent from the institute bore her signature and current title: "Th.D." for the Institute of Thanatology, "Mme. Harkounian" for the Gurdjieff phase, etc.). Following in her husband's entrepreneurial footsteps, she chose as her spiritual name, Cybele, the ancient fertility goddess of Asia Minor. By creating a "spiritual school" out of natural childbirth in which her expertise outweighed her husband's, Cybele became a "master" in her own right. Her charismatic career began with a highly unconventional courtship.

Cybele met her spiritual master and future husband in Los Angeles in 1964, in a side street off Hollywood Boulevard at the Psychedelic Supermarket. She describes the occasion in the preface to *Autobiography of a Sufi* (1977). She entered his tiny stall stacked with essential oils, candles, and incense and, as she was browsing, Mr. Gold emerged from behind a curtain with a box of vials and proceeded to place them in a glass case. On finishing the task, he looked at Cybele and suddenly asked, "Well, are you willing to get to work this lifetime?" She replied without hesitation, "Boy, am I *ever* ready!" Cybele remembers, "How familiar he felt to me!" and describes her first impression of him.

His hair was all frizzed out as if he had stuck his finger in an electric socket. . . . His eyes were just open pools of tranquillity. The certainty and childish playful innocence . . . was a joyful surprise for me. But, he was greasy looking and smelled of sweat. Since I was not used to associating with human grizzly bears, I thought it would be okay to study with him . . . as long I could do it at a distance. (vii)

Cybele attended the Thursday night classes on Cosmo Street in Hollywood for three years; during that time Gold had moved to an estate in the mountains of Crestline, California, and had invited her to join their work group there. She was hesitant, but one evening during the Cosmo class, experienced hallucinations of Gold's voice, and "a definite feeling that if I waited . . . it would be much harder or impossible later on." She packed her bag, got her dog, and drove to Crestline in the middle of the night. When she arrived, a "nervous wreck," "I saw Mr. Gold standing on the last step next to the study house with his arms wide open, just as I had pictured him." She concludes the preface: "The following day, the Cosmo Street meeting house was closed, with no forwarding address." She describes an intense, arduous regime at the Crestline Institute ("working, cleaning, doing seated meditations, moving exercises, group readings, and group study periods") and working under Mr. Gold as "the hardest most grueling task you could take on in this lifetime. . . . He was a determined and ruthless fanatic about the work" (xxii).

She describes the first stages of their courtship, which involved a charisma-building relationship and paranormal phenomena: "Mr. Gold asked me if I would like to come up to his room and talk for a while, if I was feeling like having some company." She said she was feeling tired and declined, but when she lay down, "I noticed something out of the corner of my eye . . . a hole seemed to be opening in space. . . . I saw a large, beautiful, brownish-grey snake with featherlike glistening scales in a crisp diamond pattern slithered out of the hole and circled around the room at a height of about five feet." Terrified by this apparition, Cybele ran upstairs and banged on Gold's door. He greeted her with, "What's the matter, serpent got your tongue?" They talked all night and she felt she was "reviewing past experiences of this and other lives."

Shortly after this experience (which might be interpreted within the context of shamanism, kundalini yoga, or Freudian psychology), Cybele began to receive flashes of a past life experience, and these happened to support Gold's close identification with the great Russian mystic, Gurdjieff. She entered an altered state of consciousness while engaged in circle dancing: ". . . our arms melted into a pair of tubular arms encircling the group," an "aura of yellowish white light glowed around the circle," and "My perception increased to where I was occupying every point existing in that space, and simultaneously experiencing every viewpoint's impression of what was occurring at that time." When Mr. Gold asked what was happening, she told him to "stay away from me," because "I wasn't sure who he was or who I was." Then she described her hallucination: "I told him that it was June of 1921, of course, and that we were near Paris. I could see Mr. Gold dimly . . . he had the familiar shaven head and the same piercing but kindly eyes—but his body seemed shorter and thinner. Later she interprets the experience as the memory of "another time in which I had left the school before I could accomplish my work there. That memory had come back for me to look at and to remember where I had left off last time" (xxx–xxxii).

As Gold's wife, Cybele played the role of the perfect disciple who protected and enhanced the master's charisma. In Montreal, at the August 1973 workshop I attended, she gave a speech to the assembled students in which she blasted them for not knowing how to recognize a master and for wasting his valuable time. She also took over the administration of the institute to leave Gold more space for creativity.

In the early 1970s, the Golds had three children, and Cybele developed a strong interest in natural childbirth and set up a course on "Conscious Birth." I received a poster in 1975 sent from the IDHHB, illustrated with photographs of the Gold's first baby, Gabriel.

CENTER FOR CONSCIOUS BIRTH

WE ARE WILLING TO TRAIN:
THOSE PEOPLE WHO ARE INTERESTED IN HAVING A BEAUTIFUL AND CALM EXPERIENCE OF CHIDLBIRTH AND ARE WILLING TO WORK TO CREATE THE CONDITIONS UNDER WHICH THAT CAN OCCUR.

FREE CLASSES IN PREPARING NATURAL CHILDBIRTH WILL BE GIVEN EVERY WEDNESDAY EVENING AT 6:45 P.M. BY CYBELE GOLD, AUTHOR OF "THE MANUAL FOR NATURAL CHILDBIRTH AT HOME" AT PLUMMER PARK, 7377 SANTA MONICA BLVD. THE MOST IMPORTANT FEATURE OF THE CLASS IS A FULL, SIMULATED LABOR & DELIVERY WITH AN INSTRUCTOR CHECKOUT. NO DONATION IS REQUIRED, BUT SINCERITY OF BOTH MOTHER AND COACH IS!

From all accounts, most of the women attending the course were not pregnant, and the emphasis was on learning how to give birth to your soul. Pregnant outsiders, expecting to find a New Age prenatal class, were, to their surprise, invited to join in "The Work." The 1975 course in Los Angeles resembled a shamanic ordeal of initiation and culminated in the simulated birth experience of all participants, who reported reliving their births and deaths in former existences and traveling on weird astral planes. While Cybele was teaching women how to give birth, E. J. had set up the Institute of Thanotology in which he instructed men in the art of dying.

Cybele approaches conceiving a child as a magical act, and describes the "conscious conception" of their second child in *Joyous Childbirth* (1977, 13).

We got the "call" to go upstairs and "bring him in," so we did. . . . We ourselves determined the moment of conception through various combinations of mental, psychic and physical maneuvers. Before conception we expanded to include the space of the universe. All the inner space seems at that time like a suspension of jello, but very electric and sticky. There is a sensation of hot wetness . . . and an elastic feeling to the sides, but in back there is nothing but the void. The forms of both of us kept mingling and swirling. . . . Suddenly . . . we could see a small light coming toward us . . . then the small compressed form of light entered into the active/passive body. . . . There was a hole in front of us and we knew it was our universe. We . . . passed through the hole . . . and I felt we had "passed ourselves going the other way" if you know what I mean. . . . Afterward we looked at each other and I said, "Well, we've landed another one!"

Gold (ever the teacher) responds to his wife's triumphant announcement with a technical question: Which nostril were you breathing through at the moment of conception?

Cybele cowrote *Joyous Childbirth* (1976) with E. J. Gold and this opus appears at first sight to be another New Age handbook on natural childbirth, but in the preface Cybele states her real intention: to assist a being to "come through childbirth completely intact, with its eternal memory and meditation unbroken and interrupted . . . maintaining its full spiritual identity throughout the birth process."

Cybele adapts Leboyer to Gold's ideas. Leboyer's controlled, soothing environment and close physical contact of mother and child after birth was designed to promote their mutual emotional welfare and bonding, but Cybele relies on it to avoid "shocks" to the "Being," which might cause it to forget its divine nature and to identify with its human form.

The ritual preparations of the expectant mother resemble the shaman's apprenticeship.

Centering Meditation: The mother pronounces "I AM" a hundred times a day, imagining a corresponding vibration in her solar plexus, the aim being to develop the "attention," or will, in the solar plexus.
Getting in Touch with Baby: The mother's will is focused on the "I AM," or will, of the baby, to establish psychic contact. During the birth, the mother must act as a spirit guide to the baby's soul. This will not only help the delivery, but will help the Being maintain its spiritual identity to avoid "massive memory Blackout."
The Mask: The face is relaxed and wiped clean of expression, the "Wearer" of this impassive mask is, like the African tribesman, identifying with the mythic ancestor, who in the IDHHB is the "Being"—ancient, formless, and immortal (hence beyond the pain of childbirth).
The Confront: Mother and father sit two feet apart and maintain eye contact without physical or emotional responses. The underlying message here is that they are two timeless "Beings," floating free in space, disassociated from their temporary planetary role as expectant parents.
Solarization: The mother imagines her uterus is the source of all life and as she exhales, imagines the life force radiating, filling the universe with light and love.

The usual prenatal exercises are also outlined, only Cybele chooses titles that imbue them with mystical significance; perineum clenching, for example, is called Tantric Exercise. These exercises are presented as a kind of apprentice's hard training leading to the shamanic ordeal of birth. They also prepare the mother for the out-of-body experience of "Tunnel Vision." This phenomenon is described in prenatal books as a moment of distorted sensory perception during the final stage of expulsion in birth, but Cybele equates it with the shaman's magical power of flight.

Your vision changes radically . . . sound perceptions will take on a distant quality. Your eyes may change colour. Mine are brown, but during pushing they change to bright green. You may be able to combine all perceptions into one . . . see/hear/smell/feel/know/remember, etc. Everything happening for miles around all at once.(*Joyous Childbirth,* 1976, 123)

These rituals were practiced by the community of students surrounding the Golds in the mid-to-late 1970s in Grass Valley, and they describe their "conscious birth experiences" in a chapter of testimonials. Natural childbirth was a public and communal event, involving family, fellow disciples, and E. J. Gold. The birth was filmed or videotaped, and everyone present was cautioned to maintain silence, to avoid "shocks" to the baby's "Being." The husband coached his wife in her spiritual work by "holding the Confront" with her, and as soon as the baby was born, he would solemnly read out the *Address to Being.*

This is the planet Earth in the Solar System Ors of the galaxy Milky Way. You have just been reborn into a human body. The time and day are _____ , the location of this room is in _____, in the state of _____, in the country of _____. My human name is _____, and I will act as your planetary father. This is your planetary mother. Her human name is _____. We will be taking responsibility for the development of your psyche and body until the maturation of that body.

Those present must not refer to the sex of the newborn baby, lest "Being" should identify with its new body and forget its spiritual nature. Gold would welcome each newborn into his spiritual community. In one account, he kneels beside a freshly-born infant, gazes into its eyes and says, "Welcome back, old friend. Ready to get to work?" There are references in IDHHB literature to ancient spiritual schools, implying that Gold's contemporary group is the reincarnated congregation, carrying on its "work." Thus, the birth becomes a formal initiation in which the baby is admitted as a student into Gold's spiritual school.

Objective Sex Workshops

In 1978, the Golds published *Beyond Sex,* the results of their research into "the theory and methods of sex yoga." The back cover informs prospective readers that this work will enable them to "regain the wonderful, enlightening experience of sex while allowing its essential spiritual qualities to bring us into higher states of consciousness." The book begins with a long, spooky "sutra" titled "Journey Through the Great Mother."

Apparently inspired by the *Tibetan Book of the Dead,* this prose poem describes the soul's journey through different astral realms conceived as a tunnel leading to the womb of all life, in which the Mother and Her Consort are encountered. Next, a section called "Tantraspace" instructs the couple in breathing and visualization and telepathy exercises, to unite their astral bodies and achieve identification with the Cosmic Couple. What follows is a series of testimonials written by students in the Objective Sex workshop. Far from being erotic, these descriptions (1978, 86–91) sound like William James dabbling in science fiction.

Second Couple: Almost immediately upon entering MetaSpace we started taking on different bodies. Then we got a lot of mental chatter and visual phenomena. . . . The next memory is of moving straight up toward a latticework of white lines on a black background.

Seventh Couple: Flying sensations at first. . . . Got into a space where everything was airless . . . mental programs kept interfering.

Eighth Couple: Far off we heard a woman's voice calling us and we thought it might be the coach. Forms began to appear . . . the court of a king. . . . Then a rapid swirl through stars and galaxies towards some distant goal. Blacked out . . . and remember nothing more until returning to BodySpace.

The theoretical section explains how "Objective Sex" is just one possible "intentional stress factor" designed to "replace the automatic habits of Essence with conscious habits," to bring the body, mind, and emotions into "usable form." At this point, the authors assure us, "one is ready to begin Real Work."

The practical section featuring "Beginning Exercises" could be described as a series of humorous skits that satirize standard American sexual mores. Like many of Gold's techniques, their purpose is to disassociate the "personality" from the essential, inner man, to create a distance between the "programmed" habit-ridden culturally conditioned and sexualized self and the Real Self, who is conceived of as immortal and formless. These skits mock the ethos of romantic love and deliberately engage participants in the ritual breaking of societal taboos, as conveyed by the following examples.

Tom Jones: Go to a restaurant . . . and quietly create a conversation as
if you were engaged in wild lovemaking, but just sit quietly and eat
your food as you carry on this conversation. . . .

> "Oooooh, that's good. Oh, do it again."
> "Yeah, baby, wow."
> "Grunt, groan, uhhhh."

(For example, you might read Zap Comics.)

Cosmic Couple: Seated opposite your partner, imagine each other to be
the other half of the Cosmic Couple. Describe aloud your partner's
cosmic qualities. . . .

> "You have a blue body. Your eyes are very large.
> "You have four heads . . . I can see ripples of lightning over your
> eyebrows."

The advanced exercises focus on techniques of "bypassing
orgasm." The Golds outline a model of the three barriers, or
"points of climax," to achieving "objective sex," which, if suc-
cessfully resisted, will strengthen the will and enable the couple
to receive the "tantric effect." The first temptation to climax is
in the Moving Center, owing to the "survival mechanism"
allied to the reproductive urge. The second point is a "protective mechanism in the nervous system," and the third is "a
result of the psyche's resistance to effort." Thus, this exercise is
to develop the willpower of a powerful shaman so that Essence
can be extracted from the obscuring embrace of Psyche, a condition necessary before "Being" can change or grow. The
Golds' spiritual approach to sex obviously warrants comparison
with Taoism, tantra, and John Humphrey Noyes, but, unlike
these traditions, it does not focus on semen retention and male
sexuality, but treats men and women as equal and undifferentiated adepts.

Conclusion

The sex and childbirth workshops in the IDHHB provided
an opportunity for members to act out or dramatize their belief
in reincarnation. For participants in the Conscious Birth Workshops, the central mystery being enacted was not birth, but rebirth. Cybele's rituals were designed to reinforce the spiritual

identity of family members, and the newborn babies were welcomed by the parents to Planet Earth with the same cautious
respect one might extend to a visiting Martian. For the
IDHHB mother, childbirth becomes a shaman's initiatory
ordeal. She shows off her mettle as a "Being" and her relationship with the unborn child resembles that of the shaman with
his helping spirit. She undergoes a sort of ritual dismember-
ment through the disassociation exercises to render her imper-
vious to pain and approaches the moment of expulsion as if it
were a dress rehearsal for her death.

These exercises speak of a dichotomy between the soul and
the body. Cybele's analgesic method depends on breathing and
eye contact to disassociate the inner self from the body. The
"Being," in Gold's neo-gnostic view, is an alien sexless entity
only temporarily inhabiting a human form, and the photograph
of Cybele and E. J. demonstrating the Confront exercise eloquently conveys this notion. E. J. is bald, and they both have
shaven eyebrows that lend an eerie, masklike quality to their
fleshy faces, as they stare coolly—like rival sorcerers—into each
other's eyes.

After the Golds' marriage dissolved, and Cybele left the institute, marriage and family life were no longer emphasized. E. J.
currently lives with five of his female students, who have organized an alternative, cooperative day care for their toddlers,
where "Being can grow." Although a few long-term couples are
in the movement, my impression from attending the July 1984
workshop in New York City was that there were many divorced
people among Gold's students. It struck me as significant that
despite the idealized portraits of their marriage that appeared in
IDHHB literature of the 1970s, equating their relationship with
the dance between Psyche and Essence, their divorce did not
tarnish Gold's charisma. Their marriage was explained by one
informant as just another obsolete role-playing exercise played
out within the context of the master-disciple relationship.

Cybele? Oh, Cybele never was *really* his wife. Cybele just thought
she was, she *wanted* to be his wife—she needed to play that role—and
E. J. let her *think* she was his wife, because he always lets the student
act out what we want to be, or who we think we are—and then if we

fall on our faces, that gives us the opportunity to wake up and learn. Cybele was taking it all too seriously, so he let her go ahead and fall on her face, but she couldn't accept the lesson he was offering her, so she left. E. J. let her know he'd be ready to work with her next time 'round.

The ritualization of sex and childbirth in the IDHHB might be interpreted from a sociological perspective as deriving from the anxiety and trepidation about the fragmentation and impermanence of today's urban family. The determination to maintain a warrior's impassivity and shaman's detachment amid sexual intercourse and labor contractions might well be motivated by the fear of getting "stuck" in the limited and powerless role of wife and mother—who is very likely today to be abandoned by her mate. To survive in an insecure and changing world, the ability to shift roles and maintain an inner identity independent from those roles is useful, if not vital, to the contemporary American woman's survival and self-esteem. If viewed from this angle, both the "conscious birth" and the "objective sex" rituals of the IDHHB appear to express the central dilemma of the modern woman who fears the risks and loss of social mobility that marriage and motherhood often entails. When Gold's secret female Sufis "Hold the Confront" with their mates or "Drop the Mask" before dancing, they seem to be telling their spouses, the world, and themselves "I am not really a woman, this is just one of many masks. My *real* self is utterly alien and free; a Being with infinite powers."

PART FOUR

Paradigms or Parodies?

NINE

Spiritual Solutions to Problems Besetting the Family

The interpretation that follows—that the unorthodox patterns of sexuality developing in new religions are responses to social change—echoes the ideas presented by historians Lawrence Foster (1981) and Louis Kern (1981). These authors have argued that the "sexual experiments" found in nineteenth-century utopian communes represented religious solutions to the decline of the lineage family in the antebellum period, and to the rise of the nuclear family, with its unique set of problems.

Chapter 1 reviewed Glendon's analysis of the problems confronting contemporary women as a result of social and family change. She demonstrates in a compelling fashion that the characteristics of the "new family" do indeed constitute a source of threat to women's traditional roles within the family. The next step, therefore is to attempt to analyze NRM gender roles as "spiritual solutions" to this threat. Having explored the surprising diversity of sex roles available to women in new religions, one begins to notice that the seven groups in this study share common features, and demonstrate concern over the same abuses and problems:

1. Each group rejects the courting phase in favor of arranged marriage or instant intimacy

2. Each group emphasizes one (or at the most two) role(s) for their women, which are defined as sacred, and other roles are rejected as profane

3. Each group rejects the model of the child-centered family by providing cooperative day care, and by either delaying parenthood, shortening its term (ISKCON), or by rejecting parenthood altogether.

These three features bear a clear relationship to the three main problems confronting contemporary women who are attempting to cope with the difficult, ambiguous family relationships described by Glendon. Many of these new models of marriage and parenting are explicitly presented in the groups' literature as superior to secular forms, or as healing, restorative panaceas to the widespread abuses of love (this theme is conspicuous in the *Freepaper* of the Messianic Community). For these reasons, it seems appropriate to analyse NRM gender roles as offering a variety of ingenious "spiritual solutions" to the high divorce rate, the unjust burden of work and responsibility borne by working mothers, and the attenuating bond between parents and their children.

Solutions to Divorce

In response to the problem of impermanency in marriage, each group emphasizes the invisible spiritual bond between the couple and their higher allegiance to God/Moon/Krishna/Bhagwan/Yahshua.

In ISKCON there is no divorce, at least not according to the "Vedic" ideal, and the wife must remain faithful to her husband even throughout her "widowhood." Even though a "widow" can never speak to her *sannyasin* husband again, the ties of karma that link them are still strong, for "whatever spiritual advances he will make she will share." It is understood, however, that the marriage is to be of limited duration, occupying only one or two of the four *ashramas* in the individual's life. Glendon observes that in the previous centuries marriages were dissolved by death about as often as they are now by divorce. Thus, she surmises with irony, divorce may be merely a functional substitute for death. ISKCON marriages could be decribed as shortened by the symbolic death of *sannyasa*.

Divorce was also out of the question in the Institute of Applied Metaphysics, for they believed their yin-yang weddings represented the reunion of two halves of the same soul separated for eons. So was widowhood, for Barton declared that her "citizens" were immortal. In this respect, IAM marriages resemble the lineage family, but in their emphasis on cultivating an intense, therapeutically oriented, and sexually satisfying companionship between husband and wife, they appear to be a variation of the new family. The seniority of the wives might be seen as an exaggerated consequence of the modern trend for career women to marry late in life, and for men to choose wives as partners in work and recreation rather than for their youth, beauty, and fertility, as was the custom in the lineage family.

The modern trend toward intense, companionate, inherently unstable marriages was exaggerated in the Rajneesh communes, which might be seen as offering an extreme example—indeed a parody—of this trend in marriage. Male-female relationships for the Rajneeshee are intense, companionate, and unstable to a point where monogamy has become impracticable. The interchangeability of marriage partners through divorce, which Glendon describes in the new family, has been speeded up in the Rajneesh communes to such a degree that not only do *sannyasins* enter a relationship with reduced expectations concerning its durability but also seem to view a one-night stand as a superior form of communication. As one swami boasted, "Our relationships are so intense that in three months we can work through a love affair that otherwise might have taken three years!" Rajneesh was quoted as recommending short-lived relationships: "Bhagwan says a honeymoon normally lasts three months. If you're intelligent it will last three weeks. If you're *very* intelligent you can see through all the games and get it over with in three days!"

Nevertheless, the Rajneesh do resemble the other groups in emphasizing the eternal quality of male-female relationships, but instead of viewing marriage as lasting beyond the grave, they find flashes of eternity in their love affairs and seek a sense of timelessness through sexual ecstasy. Another strategy to cope with the emotional pain resulting from the end of a love affair is to turn to the doctrine of reincarnation, which offers a certain solace. I heard several *sannyasins* express the notion that, although the relationship was over, they sensed it was a carryover or continuation of something to be "worked out" from a past life. "I don't see her very often, but somehow I feel we are deeply connected, that we will be together again, although probably not in this lifetime. Sometimes I would have this sense that we'd been Japanese lovers long ago." One swami, who was hurt that his lover not only abruptly dumped him but also refused to engage in a postmortem analysis of the relationship, found solace in imagining future reincarnations that he conceptualized as an unending round of T-groups involving her and all his past lovers.

OK, so she says she's being "honest with herself" and "true to her own feelings" by ignoring me, but I still feel some very intense energy for her which has to be worked through . . . probably in another lifetime we'll have to go through it all again . . . at some point (it might be a thousand years) . . . we're going to have to talk!

Although in the Rajneesh movement the problem of marital instability has been solved through *speeding up* of marriage, divorce, and remarriage, the Unification Church has solved the problem by *slowing marriage down*. The average Unificationist must wait six to eight years before beginning a companionate, sexually consummated marriage. The church does not recognize divorce unless one of the partners leaves the movement. Reverend Moon has gone far beyond the relative permanence of "till death do us part," and has created an eternal marriage, which continues on in the Spirit World.

In the belief system of each group, the religious drive to unite with God or the spiritual master is expressed through union with one's partner. Human love must be modeled on—and is secondary to—love of God or guru.

We both love God more than we love each other and that's the way it should be to create the Perfect Family. (Moonie couple)

Swami Prabhupada is my guru, but my husband is following him also, so there is no contradiction. I guess you could say my husband is my *shiksha* guru, or my instructing guru. (Krishna Mother).

If marriage led to perfect happiness, then no one would ever need Bhagwan! (Rajneesh therapist)

Each new religious community has rejected that highly stressful and essentially contractual process of "dating," which is a major American rite of passage for adolescents (a phase of life that NRMs tend to ignore or bypass). Courting is essentially a transitional relationship and often an ambiguous one. As a transition between noninvolvement and intimacy, it is fraught with potential humiliation and danger. The two solutions adopted by our groups are to dispense with it altogether or to treat it as an intrinsically enjoyable ritual.

Arranged marriages on the advice of the spiritual master are the norm for first-generation Unificationists and Krishna devotees. When second-generation members reach their teens in these groups, the parents often choose their spouses. At the other end of the spectrum is the instant intimacy and pantagamous sexual experimentation cultivated in Rajneesh therapy groups and Raelian Sensual Meditation camps, a process that also avoids the need for two individuals to negotiate a series of contracts. The couples are formed in response to the therapist's suggestions, or to the authority of the body and its arbitrary sensual impulses—what Christopher Lasch (1977) would probably view as narcissistic self-absorption. These radical patterns imply a harsh critique of mainstream, secular styles of courtship, in which gender confusion, poor communication, lack of supervision, and conflicting interests have led to highly publicized abuses, such as the transmission of AIDS, unwanted pregnancies, and date rape (not to mention the minor agonies of telephone protocol, the first kiss, etc.).

Glendon links marital instability to the individual's increased power of choice: "In close personal relationships today, impermanency, fluidity, and interchangeability are mainly the result not of death, but of the exercise of choice" (Glendon 1985, 32).

It is interesting to compare Rajneeshees' and Moonies' views of the role of choice in love. In the UC, members have no choice as to whom they will work with, live with, or marry.

Personal preferences for people are considered trivial and even sinful. This idea was eloquently expressed in the following interview.

Q. Do you have any close friendships within the movement?
A. Yes, but I didn't choose my friends. I don't say I like Charles here and am going to hang around with him. This is very much not the way we do things here. This is why some people say the Moonies talk a whole different language. We talk about brothers and sisters. Well, again, we didn't choose our brother and sister. In our physical family you may or may not like them but you still love them. Love does not depend on liking. Love is something more profound, less tangible. So I can say, yes, I do like some people more than others. I can enjoy on a superficial and personal level the company of one person more than another. But I do not encourage that in myself. I would have to pray to actually understand what God sees in you that I don't see in you.

The Rajneesh movement holds the opposite view: choice is the essence of love. Rajneesh compares the sibling relationship with the lover relationship and claims that marriage is a cowardly attempt to turn one's lover into one's sister to feel safe.

Love is a changing relationship, it is not stable. Hence marriage came into existence. . . . Marriage is the death of love . . . strictly speaking society tried to protect you from love. . . . There are two kinds of relationships. One is stable with your father, mother, sister . . . the other is a love affair, which is fragile, and the relationship with the master is almost the same kind of phenomenon. Marriage is to avoid fear of change. (*The Rajneesh Bible* 1986, 22)

The Unificationists achieve their "Perfect Families" by eliminating the individual's power of choice. In this respect they resemble traditional societies. That their marriage partner is believed to be chosen by God working through Reverend Moon means there is no question of "correcting" the choice.

The Rajneeshee choose their lovers, but because staying with the same partner would of necessity limit their power of choice, life becomes a series of choices—a continual romance—and courting becomes an end in itself. The adolescent stage of premarital sexual experimentation is held on to just as in the Unification Church it is eschewed as an abomination.

It could be argued that new religious women are seeking to avoid accountability in their love life. They are relieved of the anxiety and burden of choosing their mate. In the NRMs that encourage the power of choice (as in the Raelian or Rajneesh movements), women and men do not have to *live* with that choice.

Solutions to the Loosening of the Parent-Child Bond

The parent-child relationship in these groups might be viewed as a response to the recent attenuation of family bonds in the larger society. Glendon asserts that demographic surveys have revealed that parents today spend less time with their children than their great-grandparents did, and that children leave home at a younger age. One can argue that these communes are reversing this trend by establishing close, intimate "spiritual families" that are an attempt to recreate an environment for growing children like the old extended families. The child's attachment to its biological parents, however, appears to be weaker than what would generally be considered "normal" in the American family (although not the British upper class) in communes such as ISKCON and the IDHHB, which provide socialized child care, and it is very weak indeed in the Rajneesh and Raelian movements.

When the IDHHB father reads out the "Address to Being" to his newborn baby, this ritual conveys a sense of his ambivalence and uncertainty toward assuming the burdens and attachments of a parent. Although three societies in our study (IAM, the Raelians, and the Rajneeshee) have gone to one extreme in dealing with this ambivalence by eliminating parenthood altogether, in other communities the parent-child bond is taken very seriously. ISKCON mothers breast-feed for years and are the child's primary caretaker for the first five years if a boy and eight years if a girl. Then the child is sent to a *gurukula*, a

TABLE 7. The Unificationist
Four-Position Foundation

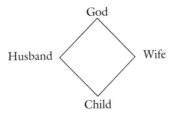

boarding school based on the Vedic system, where the teacher becomes its guru. Parents see their children on weekends and holidays. The father-child relationship is modeled on the *guru-chela* one, and the father's responsibility lies in training his progeny in the strict discipline and antimaterialistic values of Krishna Consciousness.

In ISKCON the relative importance of the parent-child and the couple bond is the reverse of that in the Rajneesh and Raelian movements. Parenthood is of far greater importance than marriage, for bearing and raising children in Krishna Consciousness is the main rationale of marriage. ISKCON women always live with their children, but often not with their husbands. A father who has taken the vow of *sanyassa* still sees his children but not his wife.

The Unification Church appears to offer a balance between the two relationships. The "four-position foundation," which is the emblem of the church, suggests an equilibrium and an interplay between marriage and parenthood. See table 7.

The "vertical axis relationship," which each Unificationist has with Reverend Moon (who is both God and father), is considered the basis for forging strong and durable marriages. In return for devotion and obedience to "Father," each member is "blessed" with a God-chosen spouse, and (ideally) enters married life with shared values and a selfless attitude. The ties between generations appear to have greater weight than the conjugal relationship. For example, one "Blessed Couple" I interviewed, who had just begun living together, were surprised to find that they often fought. The wife was Japanese and the husband British, and they explained the fighting phenomenon as "ancestral differences" —his British ancestors quarreling with her Japanese ones. Their means of solving the problem was to kneel in prayer together and ask God to reconcile their warring and tormented ancestors in the Spirit World.

The Messianic Community families also seem to have found a happy mean between the demands of marriage and the demands of parenthood by encouraging the fathers to participate in child care and domestic life. Both communities seem to have achieved a harmony and a wholeness between marriage and parenthood through turning child rearing into a collective activity.

Many of these groups concur with Peter Berger (1974) in analyzing the vulnerability of the nuclear family as resulting from its isolation, or its privatism. They have sought to solve this problem by embedding the nuclear family firmly in the "spiritual family," or whole community. The Messianic Community is an example of this approach. Children live with their parents, but the whole community is involved in raising children. Parents enjoy some degree of autonomy in deciding how to handle their children, but parents and children must conform to the group's strict standards of behavior, and the elders are available for support and counseling. The Saturday night Gathering ends with a children's ritual involving testimonials, confessions, and a Bible lesson. This combination of communal involvement in child rearing and a hierarchical priesthood to back parental authority seems to be particularly attractive to single mothers.

Although women do not preach or hold authoritative positions in these "traditional" communities, the group supports their priestly authority over their own children. Mothers in some of these communes resemble the examples of feminine piety of the nineteenth century, in which women held a priesthood in the home and were valued for teaching their children to pray, to sing devotional songs, to "be good," and to observe the community's taboos and rules of purity.

Solutions to "Woman's Triple Burden"

In none of these communitities are women expected to bear the triple (or even quadruple) burden of parenting, bread-winning, and housekeeping . . . and sometimes sexy, attractive wife. This seems be the strenuous and frustrating lot for many contemporary American women, who often express their resentment about the "Superwoman Syndrome" in popular women's magazines (*Cosmopolitan*, June 1986). Women's role and function is simplified and specialized in each community. In ISKCON and the NEK, she sticks to mothering and "wifing" and does not hold jobs in the world outside the sect, and is not expected to look glamorous, thin, or sexy. Women in these communities cover their heads, wear long skirts, and renounce makeup. In the Rajneesh and Raelian movements, she is expected to maintain her sexual attractiveness as "lover" and "playmate" by staying slender and wearing makeup and revealing clothes, but she is relieved of the burdens of having children, cleaning a house, and caring for a husband. In the Institute of Applied Metaphysics the "wife" is expected to become the intimate companion and work partner of her husband. Motherhood is rejected, and her sexual desirability is defined as a *spiritual* phenomenon resulting from the yin-yang interaction—and therefore her age and declining physical attractiveness is (at least in theory) irrelevant. IDHHB women, in identifying with their "essence" rather than their bodies or social roles, are busy cultivating the "abilities of Being," which empower them to cope with making the swift, giddying, daily transitions between the roles of wife, lover, mother, entrepreneur, and housekeeper—and this is perhaps the most "relevant" response of all among our religious minorities, in the sense of providing a useful paradigm for many secular women who must acquire the skill of a quick-change artist and the detachment of a mime just to get through the day.

New Religious Responses to Contemporary Issues

Each century has its own set of dilemmas. In the biographies of Shaker founder Ann Lee and the Oneidan leader, John Humphrey Noyes, childbed fever and infant mortality were common tragedies, driving Lee to advocate celibacy and Noyes to practice, and then to preach, coitus reservatus. Masturbation, alcoholism, syphilis, prostitution, miscegenation, and the decline of paternal authority were some of the pressing concerns reflected in the writings of nineteenth-century doctors, social reformers, and religious innovators. Today, we are more likely to worry about individuals who do not masturbate, and send them to sex therapists; the cure for syphilis has been found; and giving birth is no longer a life-threatening activity. Instead modern sociologists of the family, social workers, feminist writers, and theologians tend to focus on the painful or controversial issues of child abuse, sexual harrassment, AIDS, wife beating, male violence, Lesbian motherhood, abortion, and birth technology—issues highly magnified in the media. Charismatic "cult leaders" seem just as likely as their Victorian ancestors to interpret current forms of social deviance as "Signs of the Last Days," or "Birth Pangs of a New Order." Like Joseph Smith and Ann Lee, today's prophets are impressively decisive in their moral stances regarding these problems—whether they advocate sterilization, mechanical wombs, and obligatory AIDS testing (as does Rajneesh) or they condemn homosexuality and abortion (as does Reverend Moon).

The founders and followers of new religions are eloquent in expressing their concern over the fate of the modern family, and many of them perpetuate the myth of a stable, static family found in some past golden age. Reverend Moon and Swami Prabhupada portray modern American family life as a nightmarish hell of child neglect, child abuse, rape, adultery, sensual indulgence, and general moral chaos. Contrasting with these nightmares are their idealized images of "traditional" family life in ancient Korean or Vedic societies. Each NRM in this study is offering its own panacea to the perceived suffering and abuse of members of the modern family, and one of their main strategies is to reconstruct the role of woman by educating her in the spiritual qualities associated with her gender (or her genderlessness), and by teaching her her rightful place in the universe.

New religious responses to current debates centering in sexuality and family life are at once varied and extreme. The collection of new religious policies toward wife beating, corporal punishment, and sexual abuse of children might be seen to represent extreme, varied, and provocative "spiritual solutions" that almost parody secular responses to these forms of social deviance:

Child Beating. Rael advocates spanking children who interfere with the grown-ups' enjoyment of life, but makes it clear at what age this must cease.

The little being who is still nothing but the "larva" of a man must, in its infancy, be accustomed to respect the liberty and tranquility of others. Since he is too young to understand and to reason, corporal punishment should be sternly applied by the person who brings up the child, so that he suffers when he makes others suffer, or when he disturbs them by lacking respect. The corporal punishment should only be applied for very young children, and then gradually as the child reasons and comprehends, should disappear progressively, and eventually, completely disappear. From the age of seven, corporal punishment should be very exceptional, and from the age of fourteen, it should never be applied. (*The Message Given to Me by Extraterrestrials* 1986, 228–29)

One of the Teachers from the Messianic Community explained as follows the biblical authority that formed the basis of the community's disciplinary practices, but strongly denied that there was any truth in the accusations of cruelty and systematic, "ritual" beatings.

We never did do what the journalists accused us of doing—we never beat our children in a ritualistic, systematic fashion. We generally left it up to the individual parents to decide how and when to discipline their own children. Yes, we do believe in disciplining our children, the way it says in Timothy II—with a thin rod, but we don't believe in being cruel, we love them very much as you can see. Tell me, look at our kids—do they look abused and neglected? We discipline them because we care about them and want them to learn respect and obedience.

Cybele Gold of the IDHHB represents the opposite school of thought and cautions parents against inflicting their "negative vibrations" on the "pure Being" that happens to inhabit their child's body.

Now that you have had your baby . . . what are you going to do to help your new friend develop a usable psyche? You may suddenly find yourself reacting in a negative way, as a result of your own state, to the child's manifestations. If you wish to really do something for your child, we can offer some advice.

[Don't] freak out at the child for not behaving like an adult or a well-trained animal. Do you really think it's going to be beneficial to the child's development and increase his or her ability to handle life to have the person closest to his or her inner world manifest these stupidly shocking and negative reactions? How are you going to fix the programming already implanted? You can't without special techniques and they can only be applied much later in life. . . .

From your baby's point of view you are like a god. . . . Help produce a conscious being, not a "walking source of negative vibrations" as is the usual product of contemporary human parents. As you observe the growth of your child's psyche you will see yourself reflected, duplicated, existing in that child's form. Will you be happy about this or not? Act as consciously as you can in all things, be in essence as much as possible, and do *real* things with your child. Above all, be *authentic* in your relationship. (*Joyous Childbirth* 1977, 187–90)

Lines Between the Generations. Sexual abuse of children, particularly in incestuous relations, is obliquely addressed through the various experiments with reorganizing lines between adults and chidren. In the communes that emphasize woman's role as mother and procreatrix, such as ISKCON and the Messianic Community, girls in their early teens are considered adults ready for marriage, and parents have much input into the choice of a husband. Messianic girls marry boys of their peer group; teenaged ISKCON girls might be engaged for years to a man at least a decade older. All these communities have strict taboos governing premarital sex, which (presumably) encompass the taboo against incest or child abuse.

The Unificationist Church insists that only women over twenty-eight are mature enough to enter into a sexually consummated marriage, for their version of the Fall as a primal act of child abuse between the thirteen-year-old Eve and the fortyish Satan was the origin of all evil, suffering, and subsequent abuses of love.

The communes that reject childbearing and the role of parent, and perceive women as lovers or companion-wives, attempt to erase or soften the line between generations. In IAM and the Rajneesh communes, ageist attitudes toward mature women were consciously undermined, and sexual liaisons between women in their forties and fifties and men in their twenties and thirties were considered normal and even encouraged. The notion of the child-within-the-adult is explored in both communes. IAM workshops stimulated childhood memories, and members relived or playacted experiences remembered from childhood. Gold students during the *Shakti!* phase held a workshop in which they all wore diapers and bonnets and played in a giant playpen (Palmer 1974).

The charismatic image of many of these founders includes a childlike aspect. Winifred Barton's books contain many photographs from her infancy and tales of her earliest years, so that one receives a strong, sentimental impression of Winifred as a tiny, curious, tot in a frilly dress. Stories of Rajneesh as a willful, rebellious boy in India, and his pranks and dangerous antics, are related in Joshi's official biography, *The Awakened One* (1977). E. J. Gold, surrounded by doting female students, plays the role of the unpredictable enfant terrible. The followers of these "Crazy Wisdom gurus" often have a store of anecdotes about the outrageous, childish behavior of their leaders: Winifred pulling down her pants and peeing into a pot in front of her students, or Rajneesh gleefully driving one of his ninety-three Rolls Royces into a ditch, or E. J. Gold staging a tantrum and smearing his wife with strawberry tarts. In contrast, leaders such as Reverend Moon are always dignified and responsible, and stories about him emphasize the extraordinary degree of his suffering, rather than his joie de vivre or playfulness. One such story concerns his flight to South Korea where he hid in the attic of a farming family's cottage in the countryside. In the middle of the night the family awoke to find water pouring through their ceiling. Baffled, because it was not raining outside, they climbed up into the attic to find that Reverend Moon had wept so profusely in his nightlong compassion for mankind's suffering that his tears had inundated the house (personal communication).

Rajneesh disciples in particular seem to enjoy the notion that they (the adults) are really all *kids* together, playfully inhabiting adult bodies. Real kids, however, are currently banished from the Poona ashram, and were segregated into their own small "Kid's Commune" in Rajneeshpuram. The children's commune in Rajneeshpuram was modeled on the adults', with kids living collectively in trailers, "worshiping" in adult jobs four hours in the morning, going to school only in the afternoons, and spending the evening in the Kid's discotheque. Children were fed in the cafeteria, and their laundry and cleaning was seen to by rotating "worshiping" adults. Otherwise they were left to their own devices to settle their own quarrels and were encouraged to experiment sexually with each other. For major crises, like leaving Rajneeshpurma, they received the therapists' attentions in "kids groups." Strict rules prohibiting sexual relationships between children (defined as below eighteen) and adults were observed by Rajneeshpuram residents. This situation was explained in legal rather than moral terms by a swami, who noted the leaders were aware a scandal of this nature could become a pretext for further attacks from secular authorities on the commune.

The *Rajneesh Times* featured a section called "Kid's Corner," which explained the commune's philosophy of child rearing, described the activities of Rajneeshpuram's sixty-odd children, and contained interviews with both parents and children that deny the differences or age barriers between adults and children. "Interviews with Adults" (June 26, 1985) contains these statements from mothers.

"Everybody is a child. Some people just aren't as old as others."
"Like every other friend, she is my buddy. Friends are my friends, I don't care what age they are."
"My daughter is my best friend. Kids are little big people."
"Grown-ups are really just kids. Some kids are just a little older than others."

I received the impression during my many visits to the Grada Rajneesh center that the *sannyasins* disliked having kids around because it made them feel old. Swamis and Mas would roll on the floor, throw cushions at each other, tickle tummies, and jump on each other's backs and spontaneously burst into tears, but when I brought my two toddlers to the center and they behaved in a similar "childish" fashion, I was sharply reprimanded. "Can't you control your kids?" the director asked. My (probably not unbiased) opinion was that my children *were* fairly well behaved, especially when compared with the adults, but that having them around irritated the *sannyasins* because they began to identify with their repressive parents and were reminded of their age. This impression, that *sannyasins* were *being* kids instead of *having* them, was reinforced by a conversation with a friend who lived in the country with his girlfriend. He was complaining that rural life was dull and lonely since the Rajneesh therapist was no longer holding workshops locally.

We used to do all these fun, creative things, like sit in a circle and put our bare feet under a parachute and the "crocodile" would crouch under the parachute and grab our toes. Or we used to take off all our clothes and sit lined up like a train, and we'd chant "choo-choo!" and the therapist would tell us about the scenery we were passing— it was really innocent and refreshing and there was a real community going on.

My spontaneous response was to comment that my kids insisted that I participate in similar activities all day, every day, so that the prospect of these workshops held very little appeal for me. I suggested, at the risk of sounding sanctimonious, that perhaps he was compensating for the absence of children in his life.

It could be argued that these groups are responding to the decline of the cult of youth. American society is unique in creating an extra stage of life, sandwiched between childhood and adulthood, called "youth." Because baby boomers, products of this cult in the sixties, are hitting their forties, and young adults, owing to the recession, are forced to shoulder more adult responsibilities, the carefree, rebellious and experimental phase of "youth" might become a thing of the past. The Rajneesh and Raelians are determined to hang onto this phase well into late middle age; the Messianic Community and ISKCON appear to be disciplining their children into a premature (and preternaturally solemn) adulthood.

Lines between the Sexes. Because all these communities are experimenting with the boundaries of gender, and their major concern is to clean up and clarify those boundaries, they tend to be egregiously intolerant of homosexuality—an orientation that "messes up" or undermines their attempts to keep those boundaries unfuzzy. Rael, however, is an exception to this pattern. Perhaps because his organization is not communal, and thus social control is less of an issue, he advocates bisexual experimentation as necessary for making an informed choice.

It is quite simple: each individual has the right to do with their body as he or she sees fit. . . . Each person must live [a] harmonious sex life according to their tastes and natural tendencies. . . . The aggression aimed at homosexuals is a form of racism. It usually comes from people who lead a miserable sex life and, being jealous, cannot tolerate that others could blossom while living something different. . . . Amongst the Raelian guides there are male and female homosexuals, there are heterosexuals, and bisexuals. All of whom are blossoming because they are conscious of being loved for what they are . . . in a fraternal communion of thoughts that no other religion was able to give them. (*Let's Welcome Our Fathers from Space* 1987, 79–80)

Other spiritual founders condemn homosexuality as opposed to God's will or against nature. Reverend Moon calls it "the most unnatural kind of love" and demands in a rhetorical fashion, "At the time of creation did Adam have other men to love? Then it is in the Principle that woman must love a man and a man must love a woman. Homosexuality is unnatural, against God's law of creation" (*Master Speaks* 4:5).

Bhagwan Shree Rajneesh is surprisingly judgmental toward homosexuals considering his positive views on women and uninhibited sexual expression. In *The Darshan Diaries* series he grudgingly admits to a newly initiated gay disciple that homosexuality can also be a valid path to superconsciousness. However, since the advent of AIDS, his statements about homosexuality are unequivocally negative. He explains AIDS as "the ultimate development of homosexuality" and warns homosexuals that "you have gone so far away from nature that there is no way back. You have broken all the bridges behind you: that is the disease AIDS" (*Rajneesh Times* August 16, 1985).

Homosexuals—because they were perverted—created the disease AIDS. Heterosexuality creates life for your children and a divine life for you. Homosexuality is absolutely barren. It does not create anything. (*Rajneesh Times International* March 1, 1988)

A 1991 issue of the Messianic Community's publication, *Freepaper: Back to the Garden* features a member's testimonial denouncing homosexuals.

OK, so I'm homophobic. . . . To me this is loathsome, shameful, extremely disgusting. . . . If homophobic is having a hatred for homosexuality, I guess I'm homophobic. I also hate the sin of murder. I have heard many times, "I am a woman trapped inside a man's body." This is ridiculous. Why would God introduce such confusion into the human race? Now we see in the USA that gays are demanding family status. Fine. Let them go and make their own families. Of course this is biologically impossible. Cannot nature itself teach us what is right and healthy? Homosexuals refer to their partners as "my significant other." What is significant about someone who participates and shares in a sin that makes you worthy of death? *You shall not lie with a male as one lies with a female; it is an abomination. (Leviticus 18:22)*

Wife beating. A survey of new religious views on wife beating reveals a tremendous concern for establishing the boundaries between husband and wife, and the balance of power deemed appropriate in marriage. IAM's charismatic duo officially condoned wife beating as a means of reminding the woman of her "rightful place" in the universe. For ISKCON householders, however, beating their wives would be regarded as a sign of attachment or impurity. Lovers in the Rajneesh therapy groups occasionally beat each other, for the therapists encouraged them not to "repress" their anger and frustration, but to express it through ritual combat, and in practice this sometimes resulted in outbursts of physical violence. Although Rajneesh women might be considered spiritually and structurally superior to men, they were still physically weaker, so that the swamis often got the upper hand in these debacles. In the commune also, lovers would occasionally batter each other, to the delight of their fellow communards, who would intercede if the fighting became too violent. One woman who was the target of her former lover's jealous rage in a therapy group seemed to gain increased respect from her fellows.

A question was included on the issue of wife beating in the interviews conducted over the summer of 1985, and there were some surprising responses.

Question. What should a woman do when her husband, who is a good man in many respects and whom she loves, keeps hitting her?

Rajneesh woman. He must feel a lot of *energy* for her. He has to let out that anger—she could bring him to Dynamic [meditation], and then he'd get in touch with the love he is repressing underneath.

Krishna mother. Perhaps she should stop cooking so much meat for her husband. It gives him *rajas* and bad karma. Our husbands do not beat their wives—it would show too much attachment to them.

Unificationist. There is really not much she can do but pray to God or leave him. He sounds like he is "Cained out" and this kind of violence and abuse of love in liberal families which get started on the basis of sexual attraction is getting more and more common today!

"Patriarchal" versus "Feminist" Groups?

As the preceding statements on wife beating indicate, new religions tend to reflect their host society's intense concern over the issue of power and authority in male-female relationships. The groups in our study experiment in various directions, by awarding authority to women, by laying down rules by which decisions can be shared, or by avoiding marital conflict altogether by telling woman she must "obey" her husband. The Rajneesh represent one extreme in promoting female leaders; the Messianic Community adopts the opposite stance by refusing women the opportunity to preach. IAM appears to be attempting a compromise by defining marriage as complementary teamwork, and in the group's later phases engaging in a "flip-flop" style of experimentation in which every possibility (even wife beating) was tried out.

The issue of feminine power versus authority is subtle, and it would be misleading—and far too simple—to relegate the groups in our study to the polar categories of "feminist" versus "patriarchal," or to assume that women in explicitly male-dominated NRMs necessarily have less "say" or find less satisfaction in their social and family relationships than women do in "liberal" or explicitly "feminist" organizations.

First, these data challenge some of the assumptions about the relationship between new religious communalism and sexual equality. The temptation to lump groups that are "totalistic," that have a charismatic leadership, and are based on some ancient, mythic, or foreign tradition, all together in the category marked Neo-Patriarchy, and to mix up groups that are "contractual," nontraditional, and antimarriage or antiparenthood into a polar category marked "liberal," "matriarchal," or "feminist" must be resisted if we are to understand the NRMs in our study. Bromley and Busching (1988) have identified a central point of structural tension found in modern society resulting from two conflicting and yet integrally related forms of social relations, the contractual and the covenantal.

Contractual social relations are those in which individuals co-ordinate their behaviour through pledging themselves to specific reciprocal activity without pledging themselves to another's well-being. Covenantal social relations are those in which individuals coordinate behaviour by pledging themselves to one another's well being without pledging specific reciprocal activity. Thus contracts are articulated through a logic of calculative involvement and individual interest; covenants are articulated through a logic of moral involvement and unity.

Robbins and Bromley (1991, 7) associate patriarchal NRMs with *covenantal* forms of social relations, and feminist or sex-egalitarian NRMs with *contractual* forms.

Some of these experiments have moved in a covenantal direction, such as groups emphasizing communally regulated sexuality or creating patriarchal communities with very traditional conceptions of gender roles. Other groups, such as feminist spirituality groups, seek to em-power women for equalitarian participation in the modern/contractual social order.

They note, however, that, paradoxically, "the formal ine-quality and expected submissiveness of women in traditionalist and ideologically patriarchal communities may afford women greater power in interpersonal relations than does the 'liberated' milieu of 'sexual freedom'" (Robbins and Bromley 1992, 13).

Aidala (1985, 297) posits a link between authoritarian religious communes and the subordination of women. Our groups, how-ever, challenge this assumption because of the overwhelming evidence of the instability, the ephemeral and self-consciously experimental nature of their institutions. The balance of power between the sexes can shift dramatically within a commune's short life span—as it did in IAM and the IDHHB. Sexual mores can also swing from one extreme to another, as Wallis (1982) has shown in his study of the Children of God. Furthermore, there is always the problem of distinguishing between rhetoric and reality. Utopian "perfect marriages" might appear to be im-pressively neat and aesthetically congruent with the sacred cosmos when described in the group's literature; but the field researcher often finds while interacting with members that human relationships, even in "totalistic" societies, are complex, fuzzy, and full of surprises.

Aidala has compared religious to secular communes, and notes that secular communes exhibit the same intense concern over gender issues, but they tend to take an experimental and individualistic approach toward resolving gender ambiguities. The NRMs in this study are definitely religious, and their mar-riages certainly possess the qualities of clarity and authoritative-ness that she describes. Yet, somehow, the "closer up" one moves to examine their patterns of sexuality, the more experi-mental and flexible they appear to be. If Aidala's religious com-munes are anything like ours, her characterization tends to oversimplify the situation. She describes them as "ideologically rigid" and offering a single model of the "right" relationship between the sexes. One might point out that a close scrutiny of the history of the Children of God, the early Mormon Church, the Oneidan community, and other radical departures from conventional marriage suggests that her portrait does not do justice to the dynamic and experimental nature of these communities' endeavors to restructure relations between the sexes. Religious communes' "rigid role divisions," if observed over time, often manifest a surprising flexibility and may undergo radical transformations. New revelations can alter the "ideologically absolute" systemic explanations of the "true" nature of man and woman, and within the short history of a charismatic cult, the balance of power between the sexes can shift dramatically.

There appears to be the widespread expectation that religion-at-the-margins will follow the same rules of behavior as American mainline religion, and that nonconventional spiritual groups will conveniently arrange themselves to the right or to the left of the "lines" that Wuthnow (1989) refers to in *The Restructuring of American Religion*. Wuthnow observes this process as follows: "By the early 1980's, the lines separating religious conservatives from religious liberals had come to be drawn with a wide brush." He claims that churches were ignoring their doctrinal and denominational differences and realigning their allegiances around issues such as abortion, ordination of women, and homosexuality. The impassioned ongoing debate over these issues he explains as "symbolic warfare; a war that was about symbols and was waged with symbols" (Wuthnow 1989, 107).

Charismatic founders and oriental gurus in the West do not necessarily conform to this pattern, as they appear to feel equally alienated from Christian Liberals and from the Moral Majority. They stand aloof from the fray and refuse to declare their allegiances—right or left—and indeed, why should they? Thus, we find paradoxes, like Rajneesh denouncing homosexuality as "against nature" and yet sanctioning abortion and encouraging women in leadership roles. We find Rael encouraging homosexual expression, writing love songs to Lesbian spiders, exhorting men to develop feminine qualities, and yet . . . indulging in high tech, extraterrestrial pornography! E. J. Gold promotes feminine leadership, and expounds views of the "Being" as alien and sexless—and yet he and his male directors practice a kind of ritual-istic "gross out" (we in the nineties would term it "sexual har-rassment") to awaken women out of their "sleep"—and one of his core members writes the "Forum" column (pornographic testimonials) for *Penthouse* magazine, in the effort to turn it into a secret "spiritual school"! This behavior scrambles our cultural categories of right, left, feminist, patriarchal, and suggests an-other form of postmodernism.

Attempts to divide NRMs into those that support the femi-nist cause and those whose female adherents have "copped out," or betrayed the cause of sisterhood, are similarly "ker-flummoxed" by the information provided by our informants. The question of women's power in unconventional religions cannot be ignored, but some of our informants seemed to be seeking—and finding—freedom and authority within the most explicitly patriarchal organizations; other women described ex-periences of what certainly *sounded* like sexist exploitation and abuse in groups that officially espouse a radical romantic femi-nism. A new angle on this enigma is found in Rita M. Gross's study (1987) of women and men's participation in ritual life among the Australian aborigines. After observing that men have a secret ritual life that is closed to women, she avoids facile explanations involving "patriarchy" but promises "a different interpretation of the relationship between men's sacred life and the exclusion of women might emerge," which she explains as follows.

Men's avoidance of women is only part of the total picture. It is one element of an ambiguous, ambivalent reaction to an incredible potent and significant presence. Therefore, the exclusion of women is part of a typical avoidance-attraction pattern relating to that which is per-ceived as sacred and should not be interpreted as indicating religious irrelevance or lack of value. Insofar as the term "sacred" is relevant, there is every reason to use it in interpreting men's ritual responses to women. (51)

Whether the women interviewed for this study chose to join a group that awarded them with spiritual leadership, or whether they converted to a commune that insisted on their function as housekeeper and procreatrix, my argument is that what they all appear to be seeking is a *safe and sacred environment* where they can explore their sexual identity and/or pursue their relationships with men. Strictly segregated societies that foster gender-based work roles and dress codes (and often tend to stress the subordination of women) seem to be particularly successful in conjuring up an aura of mystery, charm, and taboo around the opposite sex. Kanter's observations on the charisma of "transcendance" and its dependence on distance and insulation might also be applied to sex segregation. The head-covered women in ISKCON and in MC Households appear to enjoy a sense of collective, feminine mystery and charisma in relation to the men, which can only be generated by forming a secret, separate sisterhood.

Although new "spiritualized" sex roles in communes appear to offer solutions to very different problems and traumas resulting from the fragmented social relationships and constant danger of "facelessness" encountered in the larger society, what seems to draw these women is not so much the alternative "sexual life-styles" but the "New Eves," or role models of womanhood. Buried in the heart of each role is a jewel-like portrait of woman's spiritual identity. This model is women's key to understanding—or at least testing—who they are, how to conduct their relationships with men, and what their expectations about female-male relationships should be. These portraits of a New Eve allay their anxieties about the place and value of sexual desire, and how to control their fertility within the context of their spiritual path.

Many different levels and modes of experimentation are possible for women who investigate, try out, or join new religions. These groups offer pathways of exploration into a mystical life bordered by clearly defined rules of feminine behavior. Women choosing to live in "neo-patriarchal" communities like the Northeast Kingdom and ISKCON have, from a feminist perspective, given up the adult, responsible role, and renounced the range of interesting choices available to contemporary women. They apparently prefer to take a backseat in religious leadership, in family decision making, in government and economic enterprise. In return, they receive the protection and rule of their husbands and male leaders. One might ask, what are the consolations of perpetual obedience and passivity?

From their statements and my experiences participating in women's work and rituals, it is possible to glimpse a quaint and archaic beauty in societies based on patriarchy (despite the recent sinister connotations of the word). In turning their backs on feminism and the challenge and torment of adult life, these women dwell in a carefree, innocent environment where their religious imagination has free rein. They have found a modern equivalent to the cloister, where the emphasis is on cultivating an inner, spiritual life, nourished by daily rituals and insulated from mundane distractions like gas bills, job security, and television. Wives and mothers in ISKCON, the Messianic Community, and the Unification Church cannot test or express their feminine power through flirtation, adorning their bodies, or creative leadership (as they might in the Rajneesh and Raelian movements); however, a deep respect and mystery is associated with traditional feminine functions and work. Baking bread becomes an aesthetic, sensual, and richly symbolic activity in the Messianic Community. Pregnancy and birth elevates a woman to a high spiritual status in these communities. Women working, chanting, and dancing together, segregated from the male members, develop a collective pride, a "feminine mystique" and a sisterhood that they feel more than adequately compensates for inequality.

Perhaps the main advantage these women enjoy is living in communities that reinforce the integrity of the family. NEK wives do not have to worry about attractive secretaries in their husband's workplace, or drug dealers in their children's school yard. They do not have to struggle and agonize to keep their family together. The community shoulders most of the burdens of child care, but women receive far more praise and moral support for playing the role of "mother" than do most women in secular society—where mothering often involves complex feats of juggling.

"Lovers" and "playmates" attracted to the message of Rajneesh or Rael are encouraged to explore their sexual impulses and feelings within therapy groups with men equally vulnerable, open, and insecure. They can dominate men and boss them around, pick them up and discard them, express their spirituality in ritual, and "network" with their sisters in building new institutions. These women have chosen an environment where they are educated to perceive themselves as independent, mobile, and strong—characteristics traditionally ascribed to men. Artificial distinctions between the sexes are consciously undermined, so that women in these movements can cultivate close, equal, and therapeutic friendships with men in which sexual attraction is no longer an obstacle to communication. Part of the attraction of these new, spiritual roles for women appears to reside in the authoritative voices of those who have created them, for women are listening for authentic voices to tell them who they are and what they might become. The authority of "charismatic leaders" on matters of sexuality contrasts strongly with the rather "wishy-washy" stances of mere priestly authorities. Bibby (1987, 164), for example, comments on the minimal influence that the different churches in Canada can exert on their members' sexual life-styles.

When it comes to sexuality, the country's religious groups are frequently both ignored and stripped of any unique claim to authority by the committed and uncommitted alike. In the case of most Protestants and Jews, the tendency towards selective interpretations of sexual norms might in part reflect organizational structures. Official hierarchies seldom have authority over individual conscience.

If Bibby is correct in saying that orthodox religions are ineffective in their traditional function as protectors of the family unit, the appeal of new religious authority figures who receive divine revelations about the place of sexuality in the cosmos begins to "make sense."

Objections to the Social Change Hypothesis

It would be grossly misleading to assert that *all* women joining alternative spiritual communities are motivated by a search of love and family. Nor could it be said that this need necessarily outweighs the "purer," essentially religious motivations. At least three of our informants described strong conversion experiences resulting from reading the founder's ideas, and even reported their dismay on encountering the first followers of the master they so admired, or complained of feeling out of place when they first joined the commune. Because conversion experiences tend to be complex and varied, and open to reinterpretation during different phases of involvement, it would be going too far to claim that IAM women became Citizens of the Universe to find younger husbands, or that ISKCON women recite the four vows to eventually have babies, or that women "surrender" to Rajneesh as a means of access to an abundance of lovers. These assertions would caricature my argument. What I am claiming is that there is ample evidence in the interviews that women on first encountering the group were moved by the leader's theology of love. They were impressed by the glimpses they received of harmonious relations between the sexes on their first visits to the center, and they often admired the female leaders in the local core group. What inspired them about the leader's philosophy of sexuality was its implicit theodicy of love, which "made sense" of their romantic disappointments or family tragedies in the past, and provided new guidelines for building better relationships in the future.

　　Certainly, this study is not intended to trivialize women's religious quests by claiming that *women* who join strange religions are searching for emotional satisfaction and better relationships, but *men* are more likely to be driven by the purest ideological or spiritual considerations. If there are any differences between masculine and feminine conversions, these might reside in the language used to relate their experiences. Davidman (1987), for example, has convincingly demonstrated that men and women *construct their experiences* of joining a religious community in different fashions; women tend to emphasize social themes above overtly religious themes. This finding corroborates the theories of Gilligan and Chodorow, "who present women's experience of self to be more intimately connected with their relationships with others, in contrast to men, who have a more independent or disconnected sense of self" (Davidman 1987).

Rather than insisting that women join NRMs to pursue particular *kinds* of relationships, it might be more accurate to suggest that they join to find a hidden, sacred *meaning* or *spiritual dimension* to their interpersonal relationships—a dimension that appears to be lacking in secular, contractual relationships. It is, after all, possible to be a "perfect" Unificationist "wife" for three whole years without seeing one's husband. A Krishna "mother" might be a celibate, childless wife living in separate rooms from her celibate husband who is involved in active service in the temple. These women appear to be "tuning in" to the sacred core or spiritual identity imbedded in the clear-cut feminine roles they have chosen to inhabit.

Foster (1981), Kern (1981), and Hansen (1981) all managed to arrive at their versions of the "social change hypothesis" through perusing historical documents. Similar conclusion have been reached in this study, but through meeting, observing, and interviewing living women. These two sources of religious testimony are more than a century apart, but both indicate an intense preoccupation with social disorder. Both sources express a determination to create a more orderly society based on divine authority and reflecting the sacred cosmos. Foster (1981, 245) writes of his research into Mormons, Shakers, and Oneidans as follows: "Reading through the myriad letters, diaries, and other accounts of these communal experimenters, I . . . have been impressed by their intense concern with social disorder. . . . I have been struck . . . by the acute sensitivity of these men and women to the anguish of their transitional age."

Many of the interviews quoted in the preceding chapters evoke impressions akin to Foster's; they reflect the intense anxiety felt by the informants who are trying to build satisfying love relationships with men, to find meaningful work, and to create secure environments for their children. Recurring themes throughout these interviews are the intolerance for the perceived chaos in social relations, the sadness in witnessing family dissolutions, and the frustrations in trying to juggle traditional domestic roles with the modern roles of career woman and sexual aggressor. Many informants expressed a sense of hopelessness regarding male-female relationships in the modern world, and also a sense of relief at having discovered a haven of love and sanity. Women participating in new religious "sexual innovations," therefore, seem to be using communal structures and voices of authority for their own, individual ends—and often in a self-consciously experimental fashion. In their quest for order and meaning they join new religions where they might undergo a self-imposed rite of passage into a new identity—a liminal experience that conveys an enlarged and "spiritualized" sense of their sexuality.

TEN

Social Experimentation and Sexual Innovations

Scholars in communal studies and the microsociology of NRMs have often emphasized the experimental nature of the sexual innovations found in unconventional religions. Wagner (1986, 172), for example, characterizes utopian communities as "laboratories for experimental institutions that even traditional societies in their astonishing diversity have not encompassed." Robbins and Bromley (1992, 1) note that NRMs are significant as laboratories of social experimentation, and point out the different senses in which their patterns might be perceived as "experimental." The seven new religions described in this study are striking examples of this phenomenon. Having examined the range of their experimentation in the previous chapters, some concluding statements might be made about their different markets and areas of sexual experimentation and, hopefully, new insights might be gained into the origins and function of sexual experiments in nonconventional religion. Finally, the difficult issue will be raised about what relation or relevance (if any) do these alternative patterns of sexuality have to the changes in family life and gender roles occurring in the larger society.

Three Modes of Experimentation

New religious sexual innovations can be observed as taking place on at least three different levels: on the individual level, on the communal/collective level, and within the charismatic relationship between the spiritual master and disciple

Forums for Individualistic Experimentation. Many young people embark on an investigation of the new religions in an "experimental" mood, in the sense that the group provides them with an opportunity to "try out" new concepts of gender and new modes of relating to the opposite sex. Strauss (1979) notes that individuals participating in NRMs have often explicitly stated in interviews that they conceive of themselves as engaged in an experimental reconstruction of self. Several of my informants described "conversion careers" of moving through a series of NRMs, assuming different feminine identities, and experimenting with various sexual life-styles. Most informants emphasized the element of choice, that deciding *which* experiment to participate in was important, and for specific personal reasons.

A comparison of sex ratios indicates that some movements hold a stronger appeal for women than others. The Unification movement in Britain and America has a sex ratio of 2:1 in favor of men (Barker 1985, 206). James Grace (1985, 104) postulates that "the opening up of leadership positions for men might explain why there are considerably more male than female members in the movement," and he claims the ratio is 64 percent to 36 percent.

Of ISKCON, Johnson states that "in most regular temples men outnumber the women by about two to one" (Johnson 1976, 46). Rochford (1985, 46–47) discovered that more than one-half the members joined before their twenty-first birthday, and only one-fifth are unmarried, which suggests that the sex ratio at this phase of the movement was 3:2, for it is very rare to find unmarried females (aside from the *brahmacarinis*) in the movement. The Children of God also attracts more men than women, for Wallis (1979) states that among the single members men outnumber women by about 2:1.

Unlike the NRMs that are male-dominated, both numerically and structurally, the Rajneesh movement attracts more female than male adherents, although the predominance of women is not so marked as in other NRMs, such as the Brahmakumaris (Babb 1984), Wicca, and the Spiritualist churches (Haywood 1983).

Contributing to the argument that women select NRMs that serve their particular needs is evidence that different age sets are represented in different movements, as are specific classes of women. Most women attending Spiritualist séances and churches are in late middle age to elderly (Haywood 1983), but the mean age of women in the Rajneesh movement was between thirty-one and thirty-five (Braun 1984; Carter 1987), and studies have consistently portrayed disciples as highly educated professionals (Wallis 1986). ISKCON appeals to girls in their late teens or early twenties and most recruits are white and upper-middle class. Judah found that 85 percent of devotees were twenty-five or younger, and only 3 percent were over thirty (Judah 1974, 111). The average age of Unificationists today is in the mid-to-late twenties. Barker states, "The average age has remained fairly constantly around 23 years. In 1976 nearly 80 percent of the British membership was aged between 19 and 30; in 1978 the average (mean) age of full-time Moonies in both Britain and America was 26." Women in the Ansaaru Allah Community are recruited from the middle to lower-middle classes and are exclusively black (Philips 1988). Single mothers appear to find the Messianic Community attractive, whereas nearly all the Rajneesh and Raelian women interviewed had postponed or rejected childbearing for a career and had lived out of wedlock with a number of men before joining the movement. These data challenge prevailing notions that "cult women" are the passive victims of the ineluctable forces of charisma and "brainwashing," who will submit to whatever excesses emanate from the leader's dark libido.

Neotraditional, Collective Experimentation. The prophets and leaders in these communes present their idealized visions of marriage as ancient, natural, or divinely ordained, and would probably object to hearing their sacred institutions labeled "experiments." Neotraditional family patterns do not *look like* experiments. They appear static and predictable, being based on foreign traditions, neoprimitive reconstructions of colonial America. Nonetheless, they are intentional communities that

often bear little resemblance to cultures they imitate, and represent radical alternatives to the liberal, secular models of family
life in the mainstream.

Robbins and Bromley (1992, 3) have stressed the cooperative
"trial and error process of experimentation aimed at solving
collective problems of living," which they see occurring in intentional communities. Certainly, a close study of nineteenth-
century "spiritual families" (Mormon polygamy, the Oneidans'
"complex marriage") suggests that these patterns are not static,
but are constantly adapting to new internal needs and external
pressures. The Messianic Community, for example, has evolved
marriage rituals and alternative child care patterns through the
collective "revelations" of its elders, which are then tried out
and adapted by the whole community.

The initiate might intented to "try out" these "traditional"
roles, but once having joined the group all individual experimentation stops. The group's family patterns are held to be
absolute and divinely ordained, and thus the community is
unreponsive to criticism. The individual is "tried out" by the
group; his or her ability to adapt to well-established rules and
roles is what is on trial. These experiments are attractive to
those seeking community or a stable environment in which to
raise children. They promise an alternative to what is perceived
as the contemporary situation of confusion and chaos. These
communities reject the privatism of the nuclear family and
appear to be attempting to effect a reconciliation between, and
mutual reinforcement of, the extended family and the nuclear
family.

Charismatic Experimentation. The "Leader's Lab." A survey
of religious communes, past and present, seems to indicate that
those exhibiting the most extreme, deviant, and ephemeral patterns of sexuality have developed these under the direction of a
charismatic founder-leader, originating from his/her creative
imagination. Therefore, one of the most obvious and yet convincing explanations of strange sexual practices among a
prophet's flock is what I shall call the "leader's laboratory" hypothesis. A key notion in this hypothesis is that revelations
about new, spiritualized gender roles constitute *charismatic dis-*

plays that test the loyalty of followers. An intense degree of commitment must already be established for members of this "market" to accept radical alterations in their sexual ethics based on their leader's prophetic utterances. Foster (1981, 150) pursues this argument to account for Joseph Smith's authorization of plural marriage, and Wallis (1982) explains the dramatic divagations in Moses David's apocalyptic prophecies and fluctuating guidance about sexual mores as an example of "resistance"—a leader's deliberate strategy intended to undermine the "institution builders," who are seeking some form of "tenure of office."

Another key element is found in biographies of charismatic leaders. Historians of America's nineteenth-century utopias have focused on the romantic disappointments or tragedies in the lives of founders, and have interpreted their innovations in sexuality among their flock as attempts to heal their *own* psychic wounds. Thus, according to Campion (1984), Ann Lee's revelation of Adam and Eve's sexual encounter in Eden, which explained the origin of sin, resulted from her *personal* quest to make sense out of the suffering she felt when four children died in birth or infancy. Her advocation of celibacy as a "sexual solution to the problem of death" (Hansen 1981) just happened to resonate with the social problems of her time, and thus held a relevance for many of her contemporaries. Eventually the Shaker way of life became a workable "spiritual solution" for an age in which childbed fever and infant mortality were real dangers (Foster 1981; Kern 1981; Campion 1984). Other scholars have chosen to dwell on the founder's sexual proclivities, or what they perceive as symptoms of psychopathology. Kern (1981, 142–43), for example, notes of Joseph Smith: "Polygamy . . . allowed Joseph to play his psychologically satisfying dual role of confidence man-prophet and victim of persecution . . . a satisfactory integration of the contradictory elements of a paranoiac personality."

The danger inherent in this approach is that it can easily degenerate into what Wagner (1985) terms "capsule psychobiographies." Nevertheless, a value-free application of the "Leader's Lab" hypothesis does appear to be relevant (and in some cases unavoidable) when trying to make sense of the relation between charisma and sexual innovations.

TABLE 8. Three Markets of NRM Sexual Experimentation

Individualistic	Charismatic	Collective
Rajneesh/Osho	IAM	Messianic Community
Raelians	Unification Church	Unification Church
IDHHB	COG/The Family	ISKCON
Arica	Love Israel	Divine Light Mission
est	Happy Health Holy	

I propose that our seven NRMs correspond to these types; see table 8. Some of these NRMs might represent a combination of two types, or might be undergoing transformation from one type to another. Several other well-known NRMs fit under these types.

Spiritual Signposts to Sexual Certainty

It is understandable that new religious models of sex identity might exert an aesthetic and emotional appeal for young people suffering from "decidophobia" when confronted with society's baffling range of sexual orientations in the "choice explosion" (*Globe and Mail* Jan. 25, 1991). The founders who propose these models are offering strategical responses to what they portray as the vicious battle of the sexes waging beyond the walls of their utopias. These responses might be seen as extreme versions, even parodies, of journalists' advice to the modern urban women. After reading popular magazines deploring the staggering divorce rates, describing women's frustrating quest for "intimacy," and applauding new feminist lawyers' challenges to rapists, violent husbands, and child abusers, these extreme solutions begin to appear almost reasonable.

The *sex polarity* groups are saying, "So what if men and women aren't getting along. They're not supposed to be together in the first place!" If men are so prone to exploiting and beating up women, they argue, why not separate the sexes into two, distinct societies? Little girls protected in the women's *ashram* would no longer be available to incestuous advances from male relatives, and women working with other women would be free from sexist discrimination and sexual harassment. These groups tend to regard the American family as a perilous battleground, and the working place as a slave market where women are bought, sold, and ruthlessly exploited. Members of ISKCON appear to think rape is rampant in secular society, and that mothers habitually abort their unborn infants and abandon their lawful husbands to become prostitutes. For Rajneesh, however, *monogamy* is the ultimate claustrophobic nightmare. As he sees it, the ownership of the father over his wife and children turns the marriage bed into a coffin where conjugal love is comparable to necrophilia. For sex polarity groups the sole solution is to acknowledge the inequality of the sexes and restore man (or woman) to his/her rightful place as ruler—in the commune and within the couple. Sex polarity groups often diagnose society's problems as arising from a blurring of the margins between male and female—from women trying to act like men, or from men trying to be women. Rajneesh (1987) finds the feminist movement "ugly" because in his view, it is "women trying to imitate men." What Mary Douglas (1964) calls "pollution fears" appears to flourish in these communities. The Rajneesh try to keep the boundaries between male and female clear by obligatory AIDS testing, by expelling homosexuals from their community, and by advising monogamous couples not to "cling" or their "energy" will get "stuck." ISKCON segregates the sexes, and a strict code of purity is maintained in diet, dress, and washing and in sexual identity. Married men are warned that if they get "too attached" to their wives, they might come back in the body of a woman (!). Child rearing is relegated to one sex or the other—to swamis in the Rajneesh communes and to women in the other communes. All these strategies for achieving harmony between the sexes emphasize the inequality of, and the difference between, man and woman, and establish rules for keeping the margins tidy.

Only the *sex complementarity* groups still insist, "It is absolutely *tragic* that men and women can't manage to live happily ever after. Marriage is not only lifelong, it is eternal! We are willing to make any personal sacrifices necessary to preserve *our* marriages!" These groups tend to deplore threats to the nuclear family. Spinsters, bachelors, or divorced people are pitied as lonely and unfulfilled, and sex outside the bonds of matrimony is considered wicked and destructive. Sacrifice and cooperation is valued over individuality and freedom. The solution to the world's suffering is to restore "true relations" between the sexes, and this is often done by placing marriage within a sacred and millenarian context. The impermanence and fragility of secular marriages today are "solved" by religious notions of marriage as timeless and eternal—so that even if there is a startling discrepancy between the IAM spouses' ages, even if Unificationist husbands and wives are separated for years, they are nevertheless guaranteed to live "happily ever after" (eschatologically speaking). The cooperation of both parents in raising their children is important in these communities, so much so in the Northeast Kingdom in Barrington Passage that if a couple should separate, the children are given to another, *united* family until one of the parents can attract another spouse and win his/her children back (personal communication). Sex complementarity groups emphasize the differences—physical, emotional, and spiritual—between men and women. Although sexual equality is questionable in these groups (man is the "head" and woman the "heart" in the Northeast Kingdom and the Unification Church), though woman often lacks spiritual authority, she often possesses, in compensation, considerable power, for without her, man cannot attain salvation.

The *sex unity* response, however, demands: "What's so tragic about marriages breaking up? All this sexual antagonism and poor communication results from *false expectations* about the opposite sex. Gender is an illusion. We are all independent individuals, essentially androgynous or asexual." Unrealistic expectations attached to gender are blamed on early social conditioning, sex stereotyping, and attitudes of guilt and repression toward sexuality learned from parents, teachers, and orthodox religious authorities. The current high rate of divorce is not perceived as problematic, for the individual is all alone on the spiritual path anyhow; emotional entanglements provide (at best) a temporary therapeutic or didactic function. Even the spiritual master is only a passing guidepost or teacher. Sex unity groups tend to deny or understate the obvious physical differences between men and women. IDHHB members' *real* self is not their bodies or the accompanying social identity, but the immortal "Being" that temporarily inhabits the body. Raelians, however, insist the "self" is *only* the body, for there is no soul—but from their point of view the body is infinitely malleable through science, and can be rendered immortal through cloning.

Women do not need permanent male partners in the "sex unity" groups, because they are seen as endowed with the same intellectual and spiritual qualities as men, and are therefore considered complete, independent beings. Either sex is considered able to rear children, and children are perceived to be independent beings with minds and rights and spiritual paths, not to be treated as the property of their parents. These groups accept homosexuality because we are all androgynous anyway, but they tend to exhibit pollution fears about the parent-child relationship. They worry about parents "repressing," "owning," or "laying their trips on" their child, and conversely, they are concerned that the child might drain the mother—inhibit her freedom or stunt the spiritual development of adults trying to meditate. For these reasons, sex unity groups tend to advocate socialized day care.

A strong concern underlying each of these types is the need to discern a new clarity, integrity, and purity in male-female relationships. Whether the group practices marriage, celibacy, or "free love"; whether it conceives of the sexes as eternally separate, interdependent, or indistinguishable, the couple is treated as a microcosm of the social body. Moreover, the idea of gender is expressed consistently throughout every area and aspect of group life. These notions of sex identity are not altogether unfamiliar, for the same models of gender can be found in the larger society, although their clarity and religious aspects are obscured.

One could argue that the main problem with our pluralistic and secular models of gender is that different models seem to apply to different spheres of life. A day in the life of a secretary, for example, illustrates these underlying dissonances. The secretary will demand *sex unity* in the workplace and in her paycheck, but during her lunch break prefers *sex polarity* in the YMCA aerobics class and locker room. Later, on meeting her lover after work, she might secretly yearn for *sex complementarity* over a romantic dinner. People in our fragmented, complex society must cope with conflicting concepts of gender roles as they move from one sphere of life to the next. Expectations of men and women's appropriate behavior vary greatly as the individual travels from the public to the private, from the domestic to the recreational, from the voluntary to the economic realm—sometimes all in one day! There are bound to be embarrassments and disjunctures in a woman's experience and self-image as a sexual being. A clear example of this conflict is the recent concern over sexual harassment in the workplace, which might be analyzed as a conflict between *sex complementarity* and *sex unity.* Women dress to enhance their beauty to pursue their careers, and yet . . . when a man responds by making a sexual overture, he has transgressed the code of sex unity in the workplace!

This kind of conflict and ambiguity surrounding male-female interactions appears to be absent in new religions. Sometimes their clarity and consistency is achieved by limiting women's range of roles, but even in groups that award women prominent positions in work, ritual, and family life, the same ideals of sexuality prevail in all spheres. New religious women are constantly reminded of who they essentially are, and are relieved of the anxiety generated by a dissonance between their families', their male friends', and their bosses' conflicting expectations of who they should be.

Areas of Experimentation

A phenomenon observed during this investigation is that many groups experiment in letting each sex "take turns running the show," or they "flip-flop" in their policies for awarding leadership posts. Two outstanding examples of this behavior are the Institute of Applied Metaphysics and the Rajneesh movement.

Trading Authority. The authority awarded to men versus women fluctuated dramatically throughout IAM's communal phase. In the early days of the institute, women were conspicuous in leadership positions. One husband of a former "Beast" commented, "When I first started going to the classes in Ottawa I got this impression the show was run by these strong women—women seemed to be the main organizers." Once the yin-yang units were formed, authority was equalized, for husband and wife were viewed as equal, indispensable halves of a whole person, and took part in ritual and work life as a team. The authority of the wives began to plummet as Pierre proceeded to wax in charisma and depose Win, and they became the subordinate to and (in some instances) abused by their husbands. IAM is an extreme case of this kind of experimentation, but even the apparently rigidly patriarchal NEK will make slight adjustments in their gender roles in response to new, millenarian revelations. For example, NEK women put aside their head coverings for a month in the spring of 1991 in response to a revelation received by the Elders in Boston (field notes of April 1991 visit to Island Pond).

A similar mood of experimentation can be found in the history of the Rajneesh movement. During the 1981–85 communal phase in Rajneeshpuram, women were conspicuous in leadership positions. One swami I interviewed explained this phenomenon as follows: "Bhagwan thinks that we should give the women a chance and let them see how it feels to be the boss for a change." At the time, I interpreted his statement as a condescending and grudging acknowledgment of what I felt was a just and refreshing regime. However, the swami turned out to be right; it *was* all an experiment, for in October 1985, disillusioned with "Sheela's fascist gang," Rajneeshpuram and the Montreal center began to appoint male leaders. This experiment was abandoned after the group settled back in Poona, and women took over the reins again.

Trading Gender. Role-playing exercises that permit members to play-act the opposite sex are an interesting feature found in the four therapeutically oriented groups in this study. The Raelians hold a transvetite banquet and dance to round off the sensual meditation camp, and as one member put it, "We show the opposite sex what we don't like about the way they treat us!" She described the "men" pinching the bottoms of the "women," and the "women" turning down dance invitations, commenting: "Someone did that to me, and I realized how *humiliating* it is to have a woman say 'No!' when you ask her to dance." The Rajneesh also hold a "sexual fantasies" party at the end of their Tantra Workshops in Poona, and my informant described how one man dressed as a prostitute, another as Lolita, and one woman came as a flasher. The IDHHB also practice gender switching in their workshops. When I participated in the role-playing exercise "daysnap" I had to vocally assume the personalities of "Helpful Herbie," then "Doubtful Danny," then "Angry Andy"—all in one Sunday morning (Palmer 1976). Another example is found in Luke Rhinehart's ethnographic study of an est weekend. He reports the third day of the Erhard Seminars Training involves a role-playing exercise that "offers the opportunity for all the trainees to make asses of themselves." Rhinehart (1976, 150–51) writes, "In two of the most difficult roles, women are asked to play the role of a loud, stupid, blustering drunk, and men are asked to play a "cute" ten-year-old girl reciting a silly flirtatious poem about herself: the women being asked to be aggressively masculine, the men pertly feminine." Rhinehart describes the discomfiture of the trainees as follows.

"Gimmee a WHISKEY!" shout twenty-five women in unison in front of the audience, and then, addressing an imaginary piano player in the imaginary western bar, "PLAY ME A TUNE ON THAT THERE PEEANNY, BROKEN NOSE!". . . Lillian, a pretty dark-haired woman is more wooden than a puppet. . . . "Oh, no" whispers Lillian, when she realizes she has been singled out to perform alone. . . ."

". . . Okay men, your turn . . ." and twenty-five men are soon on the platform reciting in high-pitched voices how they have:

> Ten little fingers, Ten little toes,
> long wavy hair and a turned up nose
> Big brown eyes and a cute little figure,
> Stay away boys, 'til I get bigger!

One of the men. Terry, "who looks like he might be a linebacker for the Pittsburgh Steelers, has trouble wriggling his hips. . . ." The trainer singles him out and explains what seems to be Werner Erhard's philosophy of sex identity: "Every man has a little girl in him somewhere, and if he's got a barrier to expressing it he's got an area of stuckness. Every heterosexual has a homosexual element in him, and every homosexual has a repressed heterosexual inside (Rhinehart 1976, 153).

Each NRM has its rationale for these exercises. The aim of est is to facilitate a detachment from the external "fake" self, the goal being "let us introduce you to your Real Self." For IDHHB members, the daysnap exercise permits the participant to distinguish between "Personality" and "Essence." The Raelians and Rajneeshee seem to be more relationship-oriented, and concerned with helping the sexes understand and empathize with each other. Underlying the techniques offered in all these workshops, however, is a message about the participants' sexual identity: that conventional sex roles are an artificial construct, that everyone has bit of male and female in him/her, and that we will be able to play the gender game with more gusto, flair, and "empowerment" if we stop identifying with our sex-stereotyped social roles.

The Larger Social Significance

Various explanations have been offered to account for new religious experimentation: the *series,* the *festivals of misrule,* and the *rites of passage* hypothesis.

The "Series," or Paradigm, Hypothesis. The individuals who embark on these spiritual-sexual adventures must be studied within a historical context, living (as they do) in a rapidly changing era. Warren Lewis (1982, 191) writes, "New religions in the history of the American people have served at least one particular function: they have allowed the nation to explore, work out, and relieve deep cultural needs . . . to solve within the laboratories of those new religions some more general cultural problem."

As argued in the preceding chapter, new religious marriages function as laboratories of sexual experimentation in that they obviously represent radical departures from the mainstream model of the nuclear family. Given the current situation of do-it-yourself marriage contracts, and the ongoing debate over gender issues, it makes sense that we find in NRMs extreme versions of (and, as Foster [1981] pointed out, even "parodies" of) the pluralistic and multifaceted approaches to sexuality and family existing in the late twentieth century.

From this perspective, some of the groups in our study might also be analyzed as a *series* (a closed class of equivalent items directed to some solution of a cultural problem), to the extent that they "constitute a response to the same structural conditions" (Robbins and Bromley 1992, 3). The Raelian movement, for example, might be interpreted as a response to several sources of tension in the Quebec working-class culture: the underlying resentment against the power and hegemony of the Catholic Church, the decline of rural communities as youth migrate to the cities, the dramatic fall in the birthrate, and the newfound independence of women in the urban job market. The Institute of Applied Metaphysics, however, expresses different cultural tensions representative of the middle class in English Canada: the isolation of the upwardly mobile, childless couple, the handicap of "ageism," and declining beauty confronted by women in the job and marriage markets.

The "Festivals of Misrule" Hypothesis. Some of the more excessive sexual innovations described above might appear more comprehensible (at least from a sociological perspective) when compared with the "festival of misrule." Wuthnow (1976), in *The Consciousness Reformation,* has compared the ritualized nonconventional behavior in weekend encounter marathons or in rock festivals to the medieval "festival of misrule." He argues that, paradoxically, societies create these occasions to safeguard the sanctity of the very taboos they violate, and afford a safety valve mechanism for antinomian impulses. In this way, he claims, society sets the temporal and spatial bounds within which deviant behavior can occur. One could argue that new religious movements serve a similar social function in that they create arenas or testing grounds for adopting various solutions to contemporary moral ambiguity. It seems fairly obvious that est training seminars (Rhinehart 1976; Tipton 1982), Rajneesh therapy groups (Palmer and Bird 1992), and Raelian sensual meditation camps could all be considered modern versions of the "festival of misrule" in that they simultaneously challenge and reaffirm normative sexual behavior. What is less obvious is that a similar analysis might be applied to the highly structured, neopatriarchal, neoprimitive patterns of sexuality found in "totalistic" NRMs. Medieval festivals of misrule contrasted with the stable, highly regulated feudal system within which they took place; contemporary spiritual groups are responding to a social environment that is unstable, pluralistic, and rapidly changing. From this perspective, one could argue that the Northeast Kingdom and the Unification Church fulfill a similar function, but it would be more appropriate to call them "festivals of alternate rule." Aidala (1985) has noted the intolerance of contemporary youth to the moral ambiguity and changing concepts of male and female. In looking at feminine conversion to the Northeast Kingdom or ISKCON, one might speculate that women who secretly yearn to be "covered" by strong, God-fearing men—an embarrassing and unfashionable sentiment for those dwelling in a postfeminist age—can (if only temporarily) "live out" their fantasies and rediscover the delights and drawbacks of presiding over the domestic role in "old-fashioned" patriarchal societies.

Wuthnow (1976, 209–10) notes "the purpose of the festival of misrule is to innoculate. But the danger is it may infect instead." In failing to keep their members, despite the initial appeal of their alternative sexual ethics, NRMs might be "infecting" society with incongruous fragments of new, "spiritualized" approaches to sexuality. In this way, their effect might be like other ritualized expressions of deviance, or to the commercialized packaging of nonconventional behavior, such as sensitivity training workshops and rock concerts. Wuthnow notes that, though encounter groups "drain off" some of the energy that might be invested in more permanent attempts to form a community, they also infuse communitarian and expressive ideals into other areas of life. Similarly, religious communes are resented for diverting and absorbing the emotional energies of the young, and yet those who filter in and out of their spiritual/sexual innovations at lower levels of commitment may provide the conduits for influencing the larger society at a future date.

Robbins and Bromley (1992, 4) state a similar point, that whether the NRM achieves organizational longevity, and whether its experiments can be said to "succeed" or "fail," it may contribute to "a subterranean cultural tradition, a cultural resource pool for mobilizing protest. Specific social innovations might eventually become part of the cultural 'tool kit' upon which other groups may draw." Thus, even if a cult fails to influence its host society, through the indirect route of eclecticism and syncretism within the cultic milieu, its homespun traditions might influence future generations.

The "Rite of Passage" Hypothesis. "No one . . . has grasped the extent to which the phenomena of the cult experience, to be understood properly, must be seen in the context of states of transition—particularly the transition from adolescence to young adulthood." This assertion was made by Gordon Melton and Robert Moore (1982, 46) who debunk the "brainwashing" myth and argue that the extraordinary personality changes observed in "cult members" that so alarms parents and tends to be interpreted as a pathological state by deprogrammers seeking clients, is, in fact, a *normal* feature of the liminal state. The same point, that new spiritual and communal groups fulfill a social and psychological function equivalent to primitive rites of passage, has been made by Raymond Prince (1974) and Saul Levine (1984). These psychologists argue that these self-imposed rites of passage arise out of a *lacuna* in our society that, on one hand cultivates a "cult of youth"—that extended, ambiguous stage of life between childhood and maturity—and yet has set individuals adrift as the role of public ritual has declined in the wake of secularization. Melton and Moore (1982, 50) note: "Instead of having one's change in situation acknowledged clearly and publicly, with social support and with knowledgeable ritual elders to usher one through the limbo of a transition state, in modern culture one is all too often left to one's own devices, having to seek out social support and 'ritual elders' wherever they may be found."

Levine (1984, 23) interviewed more than four hundred "radical departers" in "radical groups" and noted the profound personality changes they experienced while involved with the group, and yet, paradoxically, the relatively short duration of their commitment—usually less than two years. He concludes, therefore, that "radical groups" are a modern substitute for puberty rituals. Youthful participants "give up the usual adolescent struggle to form an independent self and instead participate with relief in a flawless group self." Rejecting the interpretation of this intense, collective experience as pathological or coercive, Levine nevertheless observes that his radical departers are "not quite whole," and attempts to explain the liminal phase of cult involvement in psychological terms. He notes his impressions of radical departers; their beatific faces and gushes of joy are merely a *performance*—"a case of bad acting." Their "spurious air fails to convince" and leads parents to the mistaken impression their chidren have become brainwashed zombies. He argues they have chosen to store the painful emotions associated with growth and separation temporarily in the unconscious, while they go through the psychological adjustment necessary to deal with them later on. Meanwhile, their commitment to the group is "a rehearsal for separation, practice for the real task of growing up." Levine's insectlike description of this rehearsal (26) calls to mind Prince's metaphor of "cocoon work."

While the departers appear to be passively frozen into their narrow mold of commitment, they are actively rehearsing for their coming out. . . . Now the young people are ready to come out of rehearsal and try the painful thrust to adulthood for real. . . . They are now psychologically fortified to deal with conflict.

The unconventional, even bizarre, nature of some new religious sexual behavior is made more comprehensible if one focuses on the liminal aspects of these groups. Melton (1982) and Prince (1974) refer to Turner's description of the undifferentiated *communitas* created by those who submit to the authority of the ritual elders. These elders often mete out arbitrary punishment or seemingly irrational tasks. The function of these ordeals, many of which are erotic in nature, might be analyzed in various ways. Prince argues that through ordeals "the initiate's ego with its childish concepts and emotional sets is reduced to a kind of primal ego-plasm by terror at the hands of masqueraders . . ." so that "the adult identity can be imprinted like a seal in wax." Foster (1981, 9) has argued that sexual innovations in communes enhance that "sense of communitas and fellow feeling," and adds that "in no area of life are such direct personal relations, free of all institutional constraints, more powerfully expressed than in sexual communion." Challenging the historians who dismiss utopian movements as pathological, Foster emphasizes their healing, restorative side as "the birth pangs of a new order, both within the individual prophet-founders . . . and within the new society which they attempt to create."

Levine's analysis seems to imply that the 10 percent (or less) who remain in radical groups do *not* grow up, but are somehow stunted, psychologically speaking. Yet, one might object, many charismatic religions *do* survive and mature into socially respectable churches. What about the first generation of Mormons, for example, who crossed the prairies in covered wagons, bore many children, and built their own log cabins? Were these committed pioneers left in an arrested stage of emotional development? One must be cautious in applying the "rite of passage hypothesis" to every case of conversion to an unconventional religion, but when applied to the phenomenon of the hordes of young defectors and apostates from cults in the contemporary social situation, this hypothesis does succeed in making sense out of what otherwise might be regarded as a mysterious outbreak of abortive, pathological, or inauthentic religious conversions.

"The temporality of membership should alter dramatically the way in which unconventional religious movements are perceived," noted Wright (1988, 163). It is difficult to access hard data on defection rates in NRMs, for often the groups themselves do not keep records or are unwilling to advertise their failures. Even so, ample evidence suggests that defection rates in NRMs tend to be high.

Sociologists have consistently maintained that NRMs exhibit high rates of defection and that the average length of membership is less than two years (Judah 1976; Ofshe 1976; Skonovd 1983; Wright 1988). Studies of ISKCON and the Unification Church have shown that roughly 80 percent of members leave after two years (Barker 1984: Bird and Reimer 1982). Levine's estimates (1984) of fifteen different "radical groups" are even higher—90 percent in less than two years. Although no studies of voluntary exiting from the IDHHB, the NEK, and the Rajneesh have been published, these NRMs also exhibit high rates of spontaneous defection. E. J. Gold's ritual "turn offs" and "gross outs" drive his disciples away in droves. The members of the Messianic Community refer wistfully to "brothers" and "sisters" who have left the community. Rajneesh defections are more difficult to determine. Although there have been some well-publicized apostasy (Milne 1986), all the former communards I encountered who currently "live in the marketplace" still claim they feel the "heart connection" with Osho.

This suggests that far more young women than are currently members have tried out these radically alternative approaches to sexuality, which range from functioning as a sexless robot to wearing the veil or head scarves to denote their subordination to men; through communing with aliens by "quadrasexual" awareness, or, maybe living as a yin-yang unit, to releasing their "sexual energy" in a Rajneesh Tantra workshop. In trying out these alternative ethics, if only for a few months or years, new religious participants are finding an arena for the symbolic and ritual expression of their own half-formulated and conflicting notions of sexuality, and its place in the divine cosmos.

But how does comparing the "cult experience" with the liminal state help us understand *women's* partial and intermittent participation in new religious movements—as opposed to men's? I would argue that it provides us with a framework for understanding *why* women's roles in NRMs are so "quaint," so stylized, so apparently "rigid," and why they are so attractive and yet . . . only temporarily satisfying. If one regards NRMs as sacred, secluded ritual spaces, their leaders as ritual elders, their sexual innovations as initiation ordeals, and their "spiritualized" gender roles as ritual masks, it seems plausible to suggest that women inhabiting these alternative roles are engaging in a kind of feminine "cocoon work."

None of the theorists quoted above address whether these ritual processes are different for men than they are for women, an oversight that apparently also exists in anthropological literature where "discussions of female initiation ceremonies are fewer by far [than of male] and often their function is clear: a severe suppression of female sexuality and symbolic expression of female inferiority (Myerkoff 1982, 123). An exception is found in Lincoln (1981, 101), who argues that Van Gennep's rite de passage model is based on a study of male initiations, and proposes a trope of insect metamorphosis as more descriptive of women's initiations. Lincoln (1981) suggests female rites of passage follow a tripartite structure of enclosure, magnification, and emergence, and that these dramas celebrate woman's new reproductive function and invest sacred power in her body, which ensures the future of her society. Women's roles in NRMs, which tend to be far more stylized and confining than the roles of men (Aidala 1985, 311), might be analyzed within this framework. For the collective, woman's body is often a symbol of the commune—the maternal womb whence the "New Man" will emerge. The Lamb eloquently expresses this notion.

We are the caterpillar that crawled around on the ground alongside the snake in America. . . . We metamorphosed step by step into a perfect being. We wore all kinds of African attire . . . like bones in our ears. . . . The destination of the caterpillar was that he would be painted by the hand of the Artist of the Universe. . . . So we walked around cloaked in our cocoon (the veil, Jallaabiyah) awaiting the great day when we would unfold the cocoon and come forth in our beauty as a nation. (*Nubian Village Bulletin* 1992, Ed.1, 15)

Women living in communes experience the "enclosure" of a stiff, cocoonlike group identity, and, on emerging from it, give birth to a new feminine identity, which is frequently better suited to living in the larger society. In studying the progress of Ansaar apostates, for example, it might be argued they retreat behind the veil to undergo racial deconditioning and psychological metamorphosis, until they are ready to expand beyond the boundaries of the sect; and they emerge perhaps better equipped to cope with the problems of being an Afro-American woman in a white society.

Those scholars cited above have all insisted that rites of passage are a dire necessity for youth in our pluralistic society, particularly as the coming of age in America involves confronting so many complex and depressingly insoluble problems. One of the most overwhelming dilemmas, they point out, is the daunting prospect of choosing one's sexual orientation and code of sexual ethics. Prince (1974, 271) writes: "What is it to be a man or a woman, a father or a mother? Educated side by side and equipped for identical roles in the same universities, how can male and female find difference and sexual identity?" He notes the pessimism of contemporary youth at the prospect of adopting their parents' way of life, which they seem to feel is "a blueprint for disaster." Given this situation, is it not reasonable to suggest that at least *some* women are turning to spiritual groups and adopting their ritualized, clear-cut feminine roles as a dress rehearsal for their eventual "coming out" as a woman? It might be argued that contemporary woman's coming of age is even more problematic than contemporary man's, for it not only requires the initiation into obsolete "traditional" female roles but also requires a second initiation into what was until very recently an exclusively male society—the public realm of career and job market. Glendon (1985) deplores women's "role overload" in the "New Family." For women facing pluralistic and open sets of possibilities, their gender identities must be "accomplished" (McGuire 1992) and sexual relationships "negotiated" (Rose 1987).

NRMs, therefore, provide a close substitute to the traditional rites of passage and an opportunity to enter the liminal state. From this perspective, at least one of their valuable functions is to *facilitate the difficult metamorphosis from girlhood to womanhood*. The tentative and improvisational nature of this process cannot be overemphasized, for there *is* no coherent, well-established role model of "modern woman"—that multifaceted, ever-adapting creature who must compete with men in the job market while she makes hard decisions about juggling the rest of her "triple burden" of motherhood and marriage. Today's female adolescents seem to be facing what Toffler (1972) called "future shock," Ellwood (1974) labels "overchoice," and Stephen Waldman (1992) describes as "choice explosion." Waldman sees this abundance of choice as threatening to our mental health: "From an insecure sense of self, you then spiral towards . . . multiphrenia, in which the beseiged, populated self frantically flails about trying to take advantage of the sea of choices." If this is more than a journalistic fancy, and indeed an experience that many contemporary people face, one begins to understand why the simple, clear-cut roles created in NRMs might appear as alluring, protective cocoons to young women with egos as wobbly as caterpillars. Their cocoonlike function might account for the stiff, masklike, or stylized quality of some of these new spiritual roles.

The rite of passage hypothesis suggests that the "success" of the communal experience does not have to be measured by its longevity, nor do "cult escapees" necessarily warrant the pity and attentions of "exit counselors." The individual's involvement in communitarian groups can be interpreted as a sort of self-imposed rite of passage that allows him or her to experience different modes of self-other relating, and to assume various sexual identities. In this way, our female spiritual seekers gain a temporary distance from their culture and its bewildering mixed messages, and can construct the "endoskeleton" of their internalized culture or meaning system.

Sexual Innovations and the Liminal Period

Some of the more singular features of NRM sex roles—their ideological rigidity, their surrealism or postmodernist qualities—can be better understood within the framework of Turner's thoughts on the liminal period. Turner (1968) outlines Van Gennep's three stages, and expands upon the second. The first "separation" stage involves a symbolic death of the novice to his/her former sociocultural state, and the third stage of "reaggregation" involves rejoining the community. The second "liminal" period is found to be the most central to the ritual process. Described as a "social limbo" of ritual time and space, the liminal period has three major components: the communication of *sacra*, the encouragement of *ludic recombination*, and the fostering of *communitas*.

The communication of *sacra* can be observed in the instruction female novices receive in new religious narratives, creation myths, and iconography of female saints or deities. Besides these exhibitions, there are ritual actions, stylized postures and greetings, and community dances that reflect sacred models of sex identity.

Some of the more outrageous sexual innovations found in these groups begin to make sense if considered *ludic recombination*. NRM courting rituals—the Rajneesh "tantric" exercises, the Raelian transvestite balls, the IDHHB "objective sex" workshops, the "Moonie" Matchings and mass marriages— might strike the outsider as extreme versions, even parodies, of "mainstream" American courting rituals, and many of them imply harsh critiques of the poorly organized and minimally supervised "dating game" practiced in secular society. These playful recombinations of American cultural traits resemble the "unusual, even bizarre and monstrous configurations . . . masks, images, contraptions, costumes . . ." found in traditional rites of passage. The clear-cut, spiritually based gender roles outlined in new religious literature invite participation in *communitas*, the "direct, spontaneous and egalitarian mode of social relationship, as against hierarchical relationships among occupants of structural status-roles" (Turner 1968, 202).

A recurring theme in interviews was woman's hope of rebuilding better relationships with men based on the mutual recognition of each other's essential spiritual status, which outweighed the sexual element. One Krishna Conscious "widow" noted, "When I talk to my godbrothers and godsisters, there's a special understanding. We all know we are spirit-souls and have lived on this earth in many different bodies for hundreds of thousands of years. We know our godbrothers respect us and would never treat us as instruments of sense gratification."

What these women appear to be describing is the experience of *communitas,* a generic bond outside the limits of social structure, a transient condition that liberates them from conformity to general norms and opens a space for experimentation.

I would argue that the deceptively conservative roles of "wife" or "mother" present opportunities for self-reconstruction that is no less radical than that observed in "feminist" groups. I would also argue that some of these "traditional" roles, on closer examination, appear no less deviant than those found in "free love" NRMs, and their stiff, stylized quality suggests that the women who inhabit them are not embracing a permanent life-style, but trying on a modern version of the ritual mask. "Wives" in the Ansaars, ISKCON, Unification Church, and CUT might dress up and play the role with gusto, but in most cases are not permitted to live with, sleep with, clean up after, or cook for their "husbands."

Whether the group espouses sex unity, complementarity, or polarity, a common thread running through their rhetoric is the notion of the androgyne. Women and men, whether they practice monogamy, celibacy, or "free love," set aside their individuality and strive to build a collective identity, to experience "communion" (Kanter 1972) with the opposite sex, and to merge into an undifferentiated whole. Rejecting hierarchical relationships and social status, initiates embrace the symbolism of totality, the presexuality of childhood innocence or the perfection of androgyny. New religions function as protective microsocieties where women can recapture a sense of innocence, and slowly recapitulate the stages of their sexual/social development in a new cultural setting. These "traditional" women, therefore, also seek "empowerment," though of another kind. As Gross observes (1986), societies that segregate the sexes through gender-based work roles and dress codes seem to be particularly successful in conjuring up an aura of mystery, charm, and taboo around the opposite sex. For this reason, the phenomenon of modern women choosing to inhabit the stylized roles in NRMs might be better understood *not* as a rejection of pluralism and contemporary experi-

mentation (Aidala 1985), nor as a lifelong choice to opt for traditional family values faced with gender uncertainty in the
larger society (Davidman 1991), but as the ancient and familiar
search for the powerful religious and social epiphanies available
within the ritual passage.

Conclusion

This study has endeavored to prove that one of the significant cultural contributions of NRMs is their provision of a
modern equivalent to the feminine rites of passage found in traditional societies, which allow women to engage in an intensive
process of self-reconstruction. Although utopian sexual innovations have usually been interpreted as collective rites of passage
(Foster 1981), or as "commitment mechanisms" (Kanter 1972)
designed to bind members to the whole community to become
the hierophants or parents of the next generation, evidence
shows that most members eventually reject the authority of
their ad hoc "ritual elders" and appear to use these rites of passage for individual ends. It is argued that the significance of our
apostates' erotic/ascetic ordeals, whether in retrospect they
found them to be repressive or empowering, resides in their
ritual aspects. Thus, although NRMs are not indistinguishable
from traditional rites of passage, but might be seen as near sub-
stitutes, the experiences of their women—though it might not
be authentically "liminal"—at least it is "liminoid."

Our data suggest that the innovations in sex roles and sexual
mores presently developing in NRMs, far from representing a
conservative reaction against "mainstream" experimentation
and feminism, might more accurately be characterized as offering even *more* extreme, intensified, and diverse versions of the
ongoing experimentation already occurring outside these
utopias. The highly organized and strictly supervised group experiments occurring in NRMs appeal to prospective members
as safe havens in which they might engage in more radical
forms of experimentation than are possible in the secular
sphere. Our informants appeared to be responding not so
much to gender ambiguity per se (Aidala 1985, 287), but to the

disorganized and haphazard ways in which "sexual experiments" were being conducted in the larger society.

To conclude this study, I would like to suggest that an important avenue of investigation for researchers in the future would be to learn what female apostates from spiritual communes fostering radically alternative sex roles keep and what they leave behind. How are their current romantic lives or family patterns influenced by the sexual mores they internalized while living in spiritual communities? In other words, to what extent (if to any extent at all) are new religious ethics influencing our dominant culture? This would be a difficult undertaking—particularly the gumshoe effort of tracking down these women—but it could be an interesting one.

On the basis of my interviews with apostate women, I could hazard a guess at what a more thorough investigation might unearth. My guess is that these apostates retain the more tenacious patterns of learned behavior—*sexual and dietary taboos.* An exUnificationist I talked to, who had been kidnapped and deprogrammed by her family and continued to live gratefully at home, confessed she *still* (seven years later) felt the compulsion to blow on her food (to ward off evil spirits); while her parents are saying grace, she glances around and furtively blows "hoo, hoo, hoo!" on her plate (!). Another ex-Unificationist has resolved to remain celibate until she is at least engaged to be married, and checks under her bed at night, sometimes strewing the floor with salt, in case there are rapist spirits at large. A former follower of Elizabeth Clare Prophet has retained a horror of oral sex, for her leader prophesied that such an indulgence would "propel the soul into outer darkness for twenty thousand eons."

My second guess is that *sexual etiquette* learned in spiritual communities is not easily shrugged off. One loosely affiliated Rajneesh disciple, who had just returned to Montreal from a "tantra sex" workshop in Poona, related the story of how he had gone to a party and met and talked to a woman there whom he found very attractive and, in his most sincere Rajneeshee manner, had established "deep eye contact" and spoken "from the heart," saying, "Look, I feel a lot of sex energy for you. It would be very beautiful if we could spend the night together." He was shocked and devastated when she slapped his face and stormed off, and concluded, "I don't see how I can go back to living in this society where everyone is hypocritical and repressed and if you let yourself be open and vulnerable, people get mad at you."

Models of sexual-spiritual identity also show a durability. A Black Muslim (Ansaarullah) apostate accepts her husband's superordinate position in the home, and although she is a student and holds a part-time job, she continues to pay lip service to the ideal of woman as wife, mother, and homemaker—and to look on whites as Satanic lepers! An ex-Gold student described how she instigated a love affair with a colleague in her office by saying to him, "When I first looked into your eyes I had the strangest feeling that we were once lovers in a previous life." A former resident of Rajneeshpuram continues to ignore her children who reside with their Papa as she travels around the world and takes pleasure in going to restaurants (by herself), skiing (by herself), and theater (by herself), and she acknowledges, "One thing I learned from Osho was *how to take care of myself!*" A couple who were together in the Montreal Rajneesh commune have settled down in a relationship that is not so unlike a conventional marriage. Nevertheless, they retain elements of the commune's ethic of sexual communism in sharing their apartment with another Rajneesh disciple and in overtly expressing their ongoing sexual interest in members of the opposite sex. They do not act upon these impulses, however, but vigorously deny that their fidelity has required any repressive effort. "We still have a lot of *energy* for each other," they explained, "but the fact that we feel attracted to others keeps our relationship alive."

In emulating these New Eves and New Adams, if only for a few months or years, new religious participants are finding an arena for the symbolic and ritual expression of their own half-formulated and conflicting notions of sexuality and its place in the divine cosmos. For the researcher, investigating these alternative and sacred patterns of sexuality tends to confirm

Durkheim's theory on religion's representational and interpretive function (Durkheim 1913). By replicating, resolving, and even parodying the pluralistic approaches toward sexuality prevailing in our transitional age, new religious Eves and Adams hold up fragments of a mirror, inviting society to see itself and to become self-conscious.

Notes
Bibliography
Index

Notes

2. Mothers and Widows in Krishna Consciousness

1. For accounts of the history of ISKCON, see Rochford (1985), Johnson (1976), and Shinn (1987).

2. This account of women's behavior during the *kirtan* is based on field research with Dawson students at the Montreal temple.

3. The information on changing policies toward feminine leadership in ISKCON was supplied by three senior devotees, "widows" Mother Yadhurani and Mother Parvati and a brahmin, Gaura Das.

4. The interviews with ISKCON "mothers" were conducted by me and by researcher Adele Banarjea working at Concordia University under Fred Bird (1974–76), and my students at Dawson College: Gemlyn Lewis, Christine Garcia, and Eunice Greer.

3. Lovers and Leaders in the Rajneesh Movement

1. This version of the history of the Rajneesh movement is based primarily on reading the 1984–86 editions of the *Rajneesh Times*. Gordon (1986), Braun (1984), and Fitzgerald (1986) were also consulted.

2. I observed the social interactions between *sannyasins,* spending many hours drinking café au lait at the Grada Rajneesh Café Restaurant and Meditation Center on Park Avenue, between 1985 and 1986.

3. The Rajneesh communal way of life was explained to me by the Montreal director, Ma Anurag Paras, and Swami Prem Shraddan, over several visits and dinner at the commune on Côte St. Catherine in September 1985.

4. The observations on the role of therapy in educating members in the alternative sexual ethics of the Rajneesh communes are based on my participation in five Rajneesh therapy groups between 1985 and 1987 (see Palmer and Bird 1992).

4. Sisters in the Unification Church

1. This account of the different stages of marriage in the Unification Church is based on a series of interviews with three "sisters" at the

Montreal Unification Center in July 1985, and on the videocassette, "Holy Wedding" (1982).

2. This information about recent developments in the movement was communicated by Robert Duffy, former president of the HSAUWC in Canada. The activities of WWP were observed during field research on March 22, 1992, when I attended the first WWP rally in Canada.

3. The information on the Unification Church's Canadian membership is based on an interview with Robert Duffy, which took place in the Unification Center on Bellevue Avenue in Toronto in July 1990.

4. The interviews with "Hortense," "Anthea," and "Ayesha" were conducted in July 1985 at the Montreal Unification Center by me. The "sisters" cooperated enthusiastically because they had been putting off writing their "testimonies" and saw the interview as an opportunity to get someone else to do it for them.

5. The interview with "Gudren" was conducted by Karen Birch, student at Dawson College.

5. Actualizers in the Institute of Applied Metaphysics

1. There are no published studies of this obscure commune and I have relied upon three sources of data: interviews with three former citizens who were leaders (three out of the "Four Beasts") were collected; literature issued by the institute in the 1960s and 1970s (five books written by Winifred Barton and two illustrated magazines put out by the institute, which portray in rich detail many aspects of their utopian ideals and daily life); and Madeline Morris's excellent senior essay (1986) written under Rosabeth Moss Kanter at Yale University has proved a valuable source of information.

This study betrays some methodological limitations. The sample size is small. Morris collected twenty interviews in 1986 of ex-members, and I have only collected three; this limits the reliability of the findings. This research relies on retrospective survey data and is therefore dependent upon the psychological mechanisms involved in reconstructing the past, which limits the scope of the ethnographer. Nevertheless, this NRM warrants this attempt to reconstruct its history and family patterns despite these methodological obstacles, if only because it is rare to find a female founder of a communal movement in Canada (or any other country). Moreover, IAM patterns of sexuality are sufficiently alternative, experimental, and religiously validated to be of interest to future historians of communal societies.

2. This account of IAM's history is based on two interviews with former "beasts" and on Morris's senior essay (1986).

3. These stories about Barton's "end of the world" were related by three eyewitnesses at the event.

4. There was an unsuccessful effort made by ex-Citizens to prevent this marriage through consulting a lawyer and putting pressure on relatives of the girl (personal communication).

5. Barton's confinement to the psychiatric ward of the Royal Ottawa Hospital for several years lends credence to the "self-destruct" theory. Since being released from the hospital in the late 1980s, she has sent out memos announcing the end of the world to former Citizens several times, and has gathered a small group of former disciples around her (personal communication).

6. Helpmeets in the Messianic Community

1. This historical account of the movement is based on interviews with Kharash, a Teacher in the Island Pond Community, and with Yonah, an Elder now living in the Boston Community.

2. This account of sex roles in the community is based on five visits to the Community in Island Pond, in the company of my friend, Stephen, and my two children, who proved to be of valuable (if unintentional) assistance in my research endeavors. My kids were befriended by some community children, who took them off to play in the garden while I was talking to the Elders. After listening to the Elders' ideas on how to raise children—not to give them (among other things) "fantasy toys," pocket money, or candy—I collected my children and during the drive home they excitedly reported helping the Messianic kids dig up a "treasure chest" behind the clump of trees in the garden—which was filled with candy, coins, and toy cars.

I found the experience of data collection at once exciting and frustrating. I was impressed by the warm hospitality extended to all visitors and the openness and honesty of the brothers and sisters. However, although three women and two men agreed to an interview, the Elders, after a conference, rejected my request to undertake an extensive and ongoing research project on their community. At the same time, they extended an open invitation to visit or move in with them. Because they refused to accept money for delicious home-cooked food and delightful Victorian-style lodging, I began to feel uncomfortable, for I did not believe it was very likely I would join. Part of me, however, (the Lapsed Mormon) was falling in love with the community and secretly hoping I *would* end up joining. Another "self" (the intrepid researcher) was horrified at this possibility. Internal dialogues waged between them, which would last days after my visits. I kept meeting women who had been in my position—single mothers with unruly children and uncooperative or abusive ex-husbands—and began to understand the strong appeal of a religious community that offers to help such women raise their kids. It was ironic that of all the NRMs I had researched, the "patriarchal" Northeast Kingdom, infamous in 1983 for child beating, was the one I was tempted to join, and mainly because I felt it would be good for my children.

Another problem emerged when, after several visits, it became evident I was more interested in writing about the community than in accepting their love, and its members became less inclined to be interviewed. I then hung around as a "friend" of two of the Elders, but could not stop asking questions or jotting down notes relevant to my research, so I began to feel furtive and sneaky. Sensing my discomfort, at one point all the members of the Household sat me down and declared that because they had allowed me to interview them, it was only fair that I should reciprocate, and that they were now going to interview me on *my* religious experiences(!). I accepted the challenge, but found the process intensely embarrassing as my syncretism and wishy-washiness were unveiled, and sought refuge in a fit of laughing. After that it was difficult to maintain the role of a researcher, for the members would tease me whenever I became inquisitive. I resolved the conflict by bringing them honey, fruit, and nuts when I arrived, and only staying for the Friday or Saturday night Gatherings, not for extended periods.

Thus, the research data are incomplete, for no questionnaires or surveys were done. It would be useful to have statistics on the ages and religious and social backgrounds of Messianic women. Nevertheless, I am convinced that my portrait of woman's role in the movement does not lack the depth and clarity that make it worth including in this study.

3. This article was found in the Centre de l'Information des Nouvelles Religions (CINR) in Montreal, and, unfortunately, it lacked the front page with the reference.

4. The poster was collected and passed on to me by Lewis Poteet.

5. This account of courtship and marriage in the community was given to me by Hannah, an older woman in Island Pond.

6. This information was collected by Prof. Lewis Poteet during his interview with Eddie Wiseman.

7. Playmates in the Raelian Movement

1. This account of the history, aims, and activities of the Raelians is based on interviews with two assistant guides, Michel Beluet and Gabriel, and on conversations with Alain Bouchard, professor at CEGEP St. Foy, who is writing his Ph.D. thesis on the Raelian Movement.

2. My friends and students of Dawson College and I have attended these meetings regularly between 1988 and 1993.

3. My students, Donald Hermann, Jerry Evangelista, Thi Phuong Thau Nguyen, and Tosca Rulli, and I conducted the interviews in these four portraits.

8. Secret Shamans in the Institute for the Development of the Harmonious Human Being

1. This description of the IDHHB is a précis of the history of "Shakti, the Spiritual Science of DNA," written for my unpublished M.A. thesis (Concordia University, 1976).

2. This analysis of Gold's modus operandi was made by "Adrianna," an older disciple, who hosted E. J. and his five "wives" when they visited Montreal in the spring of 1983.

3. This material was gleaned from an interview with "Ilona," member of Core Group, in 1974.

4. This information was shared by my fellow Shakti students, Rae and Jack, who had just returned from their Christmas visit to the Crestline Center in January 1974.

Bibliography

Aidala, Angela. 1985. "Social Change, Gender Roles, and New Religious Movements." *Sociological Analysis* 46, no. 3:287–314.

Albrecht, Mark. 1981. "New Religious Movements." *Update* 5, no. 1:15–18.

Allen, Prudence. 1987. "Two Mediaeval Views on Woman's Identity: Hildegarde of Bingen and Thomas Aquinas." *Studies in Religion/ Sciences Religeuses* 16, no. 1:21–36.

Anderson, Michael. 1980. *Approaches to the History of the Western Family.* London: Macmillan.

Apocalypse. Bulletin de Liaison du Mouvement Raelien International. Tokyo.

Babb, Lawrence. 1986. "The Brahmakumaris: Otherworldy Feminism." In *Redemptive Encounters:Three Modern Styles in the Hindu Tradition,* edited by Lawrence Babb, 110–55, Berkeley: Univ. of California Press.

Baker, Maureen, ed. 1984. *Families: Changing Trends in Canada.* Toronto: McGraw-Hill Ryerson.

Balch, Robert. 1982. "Bo and Peep: A Case Study of the Origins of Messianic Leadership." In *Millennialism and Charisma,* edited by Roy Wallis, 13–22. Belfast: Queen's Univ.

Barker, Eileen. 1984. *The Making of a Moonie: Choice or Brainwashing?* New York: Blackwell.

———. 1991. *New Religious Movements: A Practical Introduction.* London: HMSO.

Barton, Winifred G. 1963. *The Inner Power.* Ottawa: Bartonian Metaphysical Society.

———. 1968. *Loliad R. Kahn.* Ottawa: PSI Science.

———. 1968. *Canada's PSI Century.* Ottawa: Bartonian Metaphysical Society.

———. 1973. *The Human Aura.* Ottawa: PSI Science.

———. 1973. *Metaphysics, What Is It?* Ottawa: PSI Science.

Bednarowski, Mary Farrell. 1980. "Outside the Mainstream: Women's Religion and Women Religious Leaders in Nineteenth Century America." *Journal of the American Academy of Religion* 48:207–31.

Belfrage, Sally. 1981. *Flowers of Emptiness.* New York: Dial.

Berger, Peter L., and Hansfried Kellner. 1970. "Marriage and the Construction of Reality: An Exercise in the Microsociology of Knowledge." *Recent Sociology No.2*, 52–72.

Berger, Peter. 1974. "Some Second Thoughts on Substantive versus Functional Definition of Religion." *Journal for the Scientific Study of Religion* 13, no. 2:125–35.

Bibby, Reginald W. 1987. *Fragmented Gods: The Poverty and Potential of Religion in Canada*. Richmond Hill, Ont.: Irwin.

Biermans, John T. 1988. *The Odyssey of New Religions Today: A Case Study of the Unification Church*. Lewiston, N.Y.: Edwin Mellen.

Bird, Frederick. 1978. "Charisma and Ritual in New Religious Movements." In *Understanding the New Religions*, edited by Jacob Needleman and G. Baker, 173–89. New York: Seabury.

———. 1979. "The Pursuit of Innocence: New Religious Movements and Moral Accountability." *Sociological Analysis* 40, no. 4:335–46.

Bird, Fred, and William Reimer. 1982. "Participation Rates in New Religious Movements and Parareligious Movements." *Journal for the Scientific Study of Religion* 21, no. 1:1–14.

Bouchard, Alain. 1989. "Mouvement Raelien." In *Nouvel Age . . . Nouvelles Croyances*. (Sous la direction du Centre de l'Information sur les Nouvelles Religions). Montreal: Editions Paulines & Mediaspaul.

Bozeman, Jon M. 1992. "A Preliminary Examination of the Role of Women Within the New Vrindaban Community." Paper presented at the Communal Societies meeting, Nauvoo, Ill. October 15, 1992.

Braun, Kirk. 1984. *Rajneeshpuram: The Unwelcome Society*. West Linn, Ore.: Scouts Creek.

Bromley, David G., and Anson D. Shupe. 1979. *The Moonies in America*. Beverley Hills, Calif.: Sage.

———. 1981. *Strange Gods: The Great American Cult Hoax*. Boston: Beacon Press.

Bromley, David G., and Bruce C. Busching. 1988. "Understanding the Structure of Contractual and Covenantal Social Relations: Implications for the Sociology of Religion." *Sociological Analysis* 49S:15–32.

Bryant, Darrol M. 1978. *A Time for Consideration*. Lewiston, N.Y.: Edwin Mellen.

Carter, Lewis. 1987. "The New Renunciates of Bhagwan Shree Rajneesh." *Journal for the Scientific Study of Religion* 26, no. 2:148–72.

Clark, Elizabeth, and Herbert Richardson. 1977. *Women and Religion*. New York: Harper and Row.

Coast Guard. January 1, 1989. "The Cult" in '88: Tension Runs High, Restaurant Opened." Sherbourne, Nova Scotia.

Cohn, Norman. 1970. *Pursuit of the Millennium: Revolutionary Millenarians and Mystical Anarchists of the Middle Ages*. New York: Oxford Univ. Press.

"Conference on Eve" notes. April 10, 1983.

Cox, Harvey. 1977. *Turning East: The Promise and Peril of the New Orientalism.* New York: Simon and Schuster.

Davidman, Lynn. 1988. "Women's Search for Family, Community and Roots: A Traditional Solution to a Contemporary Dilemma." In *In God's We Trust,* edited by Tom Robbins and Dick Anthony, 385–408. Beverley Hills, Calif: Sage.

————. 1991. *Tradition in a Rootless World: Women Turn to Orthodox Judaism.* Berkeley: Univ. of California Press.

Don Nori. 1984. "Persecution at Island Pond." *Charisma* 10, no. 4: 12–15.

Durkheim, Emile. 1915. *The Elementary Forms of Religious Life.* Reprint 1965. New York: Free Press.

Ellwood, Robert S. 1977. *Alternative Altars: Unconventional and Eastern Spirituality in America.* Chicago: Univ. of Chicago Press.

Ewald, Richard. 1991. "Building Bridges at Island Pond." *Vermont,* no. 2:44–51.

Feuerstein, George. 1991. *Holy Madness.* New York: Paragon House.

Fitzgerald, Frances. 1986. "A Reporter at Large: Rajneeshpuram I." *New Yorker,* Sept. 22.

Foster, Lawrence. 1981. *Religion and Sexuality: Three American Communal Experiments of the Nineteenth Century.* New York: Oxford Univ. Press.

Freed, Josh. 1980. *Moonwebs.* Toronto: Virgo.

Gelberg, Steven J., ed. 1983. *Hare Krishna, Hare Krishna: Five Distinguished Scholars on the Krishna Movement in the West.* New York: Grove Press.

Glendon, Mary Ann. 1985. *The New Family and the New Property.* Toronto: Butterworth.

Gold, Cybele and E. J. Gold. 1977. *Joyous Childbirth.* Crestline, Calif.: And/Or Press.

————. 1978. *Beyond Sex.* Crestline, Calif.: IDHHB and Holm Press.

Gold, E. J. 1973. *The Creation Story Verbatim: The Autobiography of God As Told by Archangel Gabriel.* Published by the IDHHB. No. 64 of 200 copies bound by Djinn and Eddin.

————. 1975. *The American Book of the Dead.* San Francisco: And/Or Press.

————. 1977. *Autobiography of a Sufi.* Crestline, Calif.: IDHHB, Inc.

————. 1990. *Pure Gesture: Macrodimensional Glimpses of Other Realities.* Nevada City, Calif.: Gateways Fine Art Series.

Gordon, James. 1986. *The Golden Guru.* Lexington, Mass.: Stephen Greene Press.

Gross, Rita. 1987. "Tribal Religions: Aboriginal Australia." In *Women in World Religions,* edited by Arvind Sharma, 37–58. New York: State Univ. of New York Press.

Haywood, Carol L. 1983. "The Authority and Empowerment of Women among Spiritualist Groups." In *Journal for the Scientific Study of Religion* 22, no. 2 : 156–66.

Heelas, Paul. 1982. "California Self Religions and Socializing the Subjective." Pp. 69–85 In *New Religious Movements: A Perspective for Understanding Society,* edited by Eileen Barker, 69–85. Lewiston, N.Y.: Edwin Mellen.

The Holy Wedding of 2075 Couples in Madison Square Garden. July 1, 1982. (videocassette)

I AM THE MILLENNIUM. 1980. Nominingue, Que.: Quadrant Press (Bartonian Institute).

Jacobs, Janet. 1984. "The Economy of Love in Religious Commitment: The Deconversion of Women from Non-Traditional Movements." *Journal for the Scientific Study of Religion* 23, no. 2:155–71.

Johnson, Gregory. 1976. "The Hare Krishna in San Francisco." In *The New Religious Consciousness,* edited by Charles Glock and Robert Bellah, 31–51. Berkeley: Univ. of California Press.

Joshi, Vasant. 1982. *The Awakened One: The Life and Work of Bhagwan Shree Rajneesh.* San Francisco: Harper and Row.

Judah, Stillson J. 1974. "The Hare Krishna Movement." In *Religious Movements in Contemporary America,* edited by Irving I. Zaresky and Mark P. Leone, 463–78. Princeton, N.J.: Princeton Univ. Press.

Kanter, Rosabeth Moss. 1972. *Commitment and Community; Communes and Utopias in a Sociological Perspective.* Cambridge, Mass.: Harvard Univ. Press.

Kern, Louis. 1981. *An Ordered Love.* Chapel Hill: Univ. of North Carolina Press.

Kim, Won Pil. 1982. *Father's Course and Our Life of Faith.* London: HSA-UWC.

Knott, Kim. 1986. *My Sweet Lord: The Hare Krishna Movement.* Wellingborough, U.K.: Aquarian.

———. 1987. "Men and Women or Devotees?" In *Women in the World's Religions, Past and Present,* edited by Ursula King, 112–16. New York: Paragon House.

Kolmerten, Carol A. 1993. "Women's Experiences in the American Owenite Communities." In *Women in Spiritual and Communitarian Societies in the United States,* edited by Wendy Chmielewski et al., 38–51. Syracuse: Syracuse Univ. Press.

Larose, André. 1977. *Histoire Sociale/Social History* (annual bibliographies on historical demography).

Latkin, Carl A. 1987. "Rajneeshpuram, Oregon—An Exploration of Gender and Work Roles, Self Concept, and Psychological Well-Being in an Experimental Community." Ph.D. diss., Univ. of Oregon, Eugene.

Levine, Saul. 1984. *Radical Departures: Desperate Detours to Growing Up*. Toronto: Harcourt, Brace Jovanovich.

————. 1984. "Radical Departures." *Psychology Today*, Aug.:21–27.

Lewis, Warren. 1982 "Coming Again: How Society Functions Through Its New Religions." Pp. 191–215 In *New Religious Movements: A Perspective for Understanding Society*, edited by Eileen Barker, 191–215. Lewiston, N. Y.: Edwin Mellen.

Lewis, I. M. 1971. *Ecstatic Religion: An Anthropological Study of Spirit Possession and Shamanism*. Harmondsworth, Eng.: Penguin.

Lincoln, Bruce. 1991. *Emerging from the Chrysalis: Rituals of Women's Initiation*. New York: Oxford Univ. Press.

Lofland, John. 1977. *Doomsday Cult: A Study of Conversion, Proselytization, and Maintenance*. New York: Irvington.

Mann, Edward. "The Quest for Total Bliss" (unpublished manuscript).

McLoughlin, William G. 1978. *Revivals, Awakenings, and Reform*. Chicago: Univ. of Chicago Press.

Melton, Gordon J., and Robert L. Moore. 1982. *The Cult Experience: Responding to the New Religious Pluralism*. New York: Pilgrim.

Melton, Gordon. 1986. *The Encyclopedic Handbook of Cults in America*. New York: Garland.

————. 1992. "European Receptivity to the New Religions." In *Syzygy*, 3–13. Stanford, Calif.: Center for Academic Publishing.

Meredith, George. 1987. *Bhagwan the Godless and Yet the Most Godly Man*. Poona, India: Rebel.

Milne, Hugh. 1986. *Bhagwan the God That Failed*. London: Caliban.

Moon, Rev. Sun Myung. 1985. *God's Will and the World*. New York: HSAUWC.

Moore, Laurence R. 1977. *In Search of White Crows: Spiritualism, Parapsychology, and American Culture*. New York: Oxford Univ. Press.

Morris, Madeline. 1986. "IAM: A Group Portrait." Unpublished senior essay, Yale Univ.

Mullan, Robert. 1983. *Life as Laughter: Following Bhagwan Shree Rajneesh*. London: Routledge and Kegan Paul.

Mumford, Lewis. 1922. *The Story of Utopias*. New York: Boni and Liveright.

Muncy, Raymond Lee. 1973. *Sex and Marriage in Utopian Communities: Nineteenth Century America*. Bloomington: Indiana Univ. Press.

Myerkoff, Barbara. 1982. "Rites of Passage: Process and Paradox." In Victor Turner (ed.), *Celebration: Studies in Festivity and Ritual*, edited by Victor Turner. Washington, D.C.: Smithsonian Institute Press.

Neitz, Mary Jo. 1988. "Sacramental Sex in Modern Witchcraft Groups." (Presented at the Midwest Sociological Society, Minneapolis)

Nordhoff, Charles. 1965. *The Communistic Societies of the United States*. New York: Schocken.

Oregonian. 1985. "For Love and for Money." Twenty-part series, June 30–July 19, Portland, Ore.

Ottawa Citizen. 1988. "Impact of Commune Worries Small Town," October 8.

Palmer, Susan. 1976. "Shakti! The Spiritual Science of DNA." Master's thesis, Department of Religion, Concordia Univ., Montreal.

———. 1988. "Charisma and Abdication: A Study of the Leadership of Bhagwan Shree Rajneesh." *Sociological Analysis* 49:119–35.

Palmer, Susan J., and Frederick Bird. 1992. "Therapy, Charisma, and Social Control in the Rajneesh Movement." *Sociological Analysis* 53:S71–S85.

Parr, Joy (ed.). 1982. *Childhood and Family in Canadian History.* Toronto: McClelland and Stewart.

People Serving People. 1985. New York: HSA-UWC.

Poling, Tommy H., and Frank J. Kenney. 1986. *The Hare Krishna Character Type: A Study of the Sensate Personality.* Lewiston, N.Y.: Edwin Mellen.

Poteet, Lewis. 1988. "Talk in and about the Twelfth Tribe: Kingdom Church and Other Communities on Nova Scotia's South Shore" (unpublished manuscript).

Prince, Raymond. 1974. "Cocoon Work: An Interpretation of the Concern of Contemporary Youth with the Mystical." In *Religious Movements in Contemporary America,* edited by Irving I. Zaretsky and Mark P. Leone, 255–74. Princeton, N.J.: Princeton Univ. Press.

Rajneesh, Bhagwan Shree. 1987. *A New Vision of Women's Liberation.* Poona, India: Rebel.

Reuther, Rosemary Radford. 1983. *Sexism and God Talk.* Boston: Beacon Press.

Rhinehart, Luke. 1976. *The Book of est.* New York: Holt, Rinehart, and Winston.

Richardson, James T., Mary W. Stewart, and Robert B. Simmonds. 1979. *Organized Miracles: A Study of a Contemporary Youth, Communal, Fundamentalist Organization.* New Brunswick, N.J.: Transaction.

Robbins, Tom, and David Bromley. 1992. "Social Experimentation and the Significance of American New Religions: A Focused Review Essay." *Research in the Social Scientific Study of Religion* 4:1–28.

Robbins, Tom. 1988. *Cults, Charisma, and Converts.* Beverly Hills, Calif.: Sage.

Rochford, Burke, Jr. 1985. *Hare Krishna in America.* New Brunswick, N.J.: Rutgers Univ. Press.

Rodman, Hyman. 1970. "The Black Family: Myth or Reality." *Psychiatry* 33, no. 2:145–55.

———. 1981. "Lower-Class Family Behaviour." In *Families in Transition,* edited by Arlene Skolnick and Jerome Skolnick. Boston: Little, Brown.

Rose, Susan. 1987. "Women Warriors: The Negotiation of Gender in a Charismatic Community." *Sociological Analysis* 48, no. 3:245–58.

Satsvarupa dasa Goswami. 1981. *Only He Could Lead Them.* Vol. 3. Los Angeles: Bhaktivedanta Book Trust.

Sharma, Arvind. 1985. "The Rajneesh Movement." In *Religious Movements: Genesis, Exodus, and Numbers,* edited by Rodney Stark. New York: Paragon House.

Shinn, Larry. 1987. *The Dark Lord: Cult Images and the Hare Krishnas in America.* Philadelphia: Westminster Press.

Soliday, Gerald L., ed. 1980. *History of the Family and Kinship: A Select International Bibliography.* Millwood, N.Y.: Kraus.

Sontag, Frederick. 1977. *Sun Myung Moon and the Unification Church.* Nashville: Abingdon.

Spurgin, Nora. 1978. "On Being a Woman in the Unification Church." *Blessing Quarterly* 2, no. 2:41.

Stone, Donald. 1976. "The Human Potential Movement." In *The New Religious Consciousness,* edited by Charles Glock and Robert Bellah, 93–115. Berkeley: Univ. of California Press.

Stone, Lawrence. 1977. *Family, Sex, and Marriage in England, 1500–1800.* New York: Harper and Row.

Strelley, Kate, with Robert Sans Souci. 1987. *The Ultimate Game: The Rise and Fall of Bhagwan Shree Rajneesh.* San Francisco: Harper and Row.

Tipton, Stephen. 1982. *Getting Saved from the Sixties: Moral Meaning in Conversion and Cultural Change.* Berkeley: Univ. of California Press.

Toffler, Alvin, ed. 1972. *The Futurists.* New York: Random House.

Turner, Victor. 1968. *The Ritual Process.* Chicago: Aldine.

Unification News. July 1, 1982.

Van Leen, W. A. 1980. *O Is for Orange.* Perth, Western Australia: Concerned Christians Growth Ministries.

Vorilhon, Claude. 1986. *Extraterrestrials Took Me to Their Planet.* Brantome: l'Edition du Message.

———. 1977. *La Geniocratie.* Brantome: l'Edition du Message.

———. 1986. *Sensual Meditation.* Tokyo: AOM.

———. 1986. *Let's Welcome Our Fathers from Space: They Created Humanity in Their Laboratories.* Tokyo: AOM.

Wagner, Jon, ed. 1982. *Sex Roles in Contemporary Communes.* Bloomington: Indiana Univ. Press.

Wagner, Jon. 1986. "Sexuality and Gender Roles in Utopian Communities: A Critical Survey of Scholarly Work." In *Communal Societies* 6:172–88. Evanston, Ind.: Nat. Historic Communal Societies Assoc.

Waldman, Stephen. 1992. "Freedom's Just Another Word for Much Too Much to Choose." In *The Globe and Mail.* Toronto.

Wallis, Roy. 1979. *Salvation and Protest.* London: Francis Pinter.

———. 1982. *Millenialism and Charisma.* Dublin: Queens Press.

———. 1984. *The Elementary Forms of the New Religious Life.* London: Routledge and Kegan Paul.

———. 1986. "Religion as Fun: The Rajneesh Movement." In *Sociological Theory and Collective Action,* edited by Roy Wallis and Steve Bruce. Belfast: Queens Univ. Press.

Werner, Paul. 1986. *Love, Blessed Marriage, and Family Life.* HSAUWC.

Wessinger, Catherine, ed. Forthcoming. *Women Outside the Mainstream: Female Leaders in Marginal Religions in 19th and 20th Century America.* Urbana: Univ. of Illinois Press.

Westley, Frances. 1983. *The Complex Forms of Religious Life: A Durkheimian View of New Religious Movements.* Chico, Calif.: Scholars Press.

Wood, Allen Tate, with Jack Vitek. 1979. *Moonstruck: A Memoir of My Life in a Cult.* New York: William Morrow.

Woodruff, Michael J. 1984. "Cultism and Child Abuse: Cases of Convergence." *The Cult Observer* 1 (Sept.):13–14.

Worseley, Peter. 1968. *The Trumpet Shall Sound.* New York: Schocken.

Wright, Stuart, and Elizabeth S. Piper. 1986. "Families and Cults: Familial Factors Related to Youth Leaving or Remaining in Deviant Religious Groups." *Journal of Marriage and Family* 48:15–25.

Wuthnow, Robert. 1976. *The Consciousness Reformation.* Berkeley: Univ. of California Press.

———. 1988. *The Restructuring of American Religion and Faith Since World War II.* Princeton, N.J.: Princeton Univ. Press.

Yankelovitch, D. 1981. "New Rules in American Life: Searching for Self Fulfillment in a World Turned Upside Down." *Psychology Today* 15, no. 4:35–91.

Young, Katherine. 1987. "Hinduism," In *Women in World Religions,* edited by Arvind Sharma, 59–105. Albany: State Univ. of New York Press.

Zia, Helen. 1991. "Women in Hate Groups" *Ms* magazine, March/April.

Index